WHAT TO DO
WHEN YOU
DON'T KNOW
WHAT TO DO

THE BOOK OF JAMES

DR. DAVID JEREMIAH

WHAT TO DO
WHEN YOU
DON'T KNOW
THE BOOK OF JAMES **WHAT TO DO**

WHAT TO DO WHEN YOU DON'T KNOW WHAT TO DO
Published by David C Cook
4050 Lee Vance View
Colorado Springs, CO 80918 U.S.A.

David C Cook Distribution Canada
55 Woodslee Avenue, Paris, Ontario, Canada N3L 3E5

David C Cook U.K., Kingsway Communications
Eastbourne, East Sussex BN23 6NT, England

The graphic circle C logo is a registered trademark of David C Cook..

LCCN 2006926161
ISBN 978-1-4347-6451-5

© 2009 David Jeremiah, third edition,
previous ISBN: 1-56476-070-7
First edition published by Victor Books/SP Publications, Inc. © in 1993.

Readers' Guide prepared by Patricia Picardi.
Cover Design: Nathan Johnson

While this book is intended for the reader's personal enjoyment and profit, it is also designed
for group study. A personal and group study guide is located at the end of this text.

Printed in the United States of America
Third Edition 2009

5 6 7 8 9 10 11 12 13

021714

To my sister,
Dr. Maryalyce Jeremiah,
who has demonstrated the integrity of her
faith as a coach and administrator in the
challenging world of major college athletics

CONTENTS

Introduction 9

1. What to Do When the Heat's Turned Up 13
   (James 1:1–12)

2. What to Do When Wrong Seems Right 29
   (James 1:13–18)

3. What to Do When the Mirror Doesn't Lie 47
   (James 1:19–27)

4. What to Do When Justice Isn't Blind 64
   (James 2:1–13)

5. What to Do When Faith Doesn't Work 82
   (James 2:14–26)

6. What to Do When Your Tongue Isn't Tied 98
   (James 3:1–12)

7. What to Do When Wisdom Is Foolish 114
   (James 3:13–18)

8. What to Do When Worship Turns to War 133
   (James 4:1–12)

9. What to Do When Your Goals Are Not God's 152
   (James 4:13–17)

10. What to Do When Your Net Worth Is Worthless 167
    (James 5:1–6)

11. What to Do When You're in a Hurry and God Isn't 182
    (James 5:7–12)

12. What to Do When Pain Leads to Prayer 199
    (James 5:13–20)

Readers' Guide 219

Notes 242

Commentaries 251

Additional Books 252

Stay Connected 254

INTRODUCTION

In life, we often find ourselves not knowing what to do when faced with trials and temptations. This book is the perfect guide for those uncertain situations. *What to Do When You Don't Know What to Do* explains how to have the kind of faith that perseveres in persecution, resists temptation, responds obediently to God's Word, overcomes prejudice, produces good works, controls the tongue, follows God's wisdom, considers God in all its plans, depends on God rather than wealth, waits patiently for the return of the Lord, and makes prayer, not personal effort, its spiritual resource.

According to James, genuine faith should make a genuine difference in the way a person lives. One's creed should determine his conduct! And those who knew James considered him qualified to address this subject. Because of his righteous life, they called him "James the Just." The words of this letter reflect his righteous standards and echo the high and lofty principles of his Brother. In the book of James, there are at least fifteen allusions to Jesus' Sermon on the Mount.

Three prominent men in the New Testament are called James. James, the son of Zebedee, was one of the twelve disciples and the brother of John (Matthew 4:21; Mark 1:19; Luke 5:10). He became the first apostolic martyr when Herod "stretched out his hand to harass some from the church ... and killed James the brother of John with the sword" (Acts 12:1–2).

James, the son of Alphaeus, was also one of the Twelve (Matthew 10:3; Mark 3:18; Luke 6:15; Acts 1:13). Because he was shorter than James, the son of Zebedee, he is sometimes referred to as "James the Less."

The third man who bore the name "James" was the half brother of the Lord, the son of Mary and Joseph (Galatians 1:19), and the human writer of this epistle. Because he is always mentioned first whenever the Lord's brothers are listed, it is usually concluded that he was next in age after Jesus (Matthew 13:55; Mark 6:3).

It is intriguing to read the epistle of James knowing that the one who penned it grew up with the Lord Jesus Christ:

> For thirty years eating every meal at the same table with Him; working six days of the week in the same workshop with Him; going up on the seventh day to the same synagogue with Him; and once every year going up to Jerusalem to the same Passover with Him. For James was, actually, the Lord's brother.... And the child James would be the daily delight of his elder Brother; he would be His continual charge and joy; just as you see two such brothers in your own family life at home....
>
> I wish I had the learning and the genius to let you see and hear all that must have gone on in Joseph's house.... The family perplexities about Jesus; the family reasonings about Him; the family divisions and disputes about Him; their intoxicating hopes at one time over Him, and their fears and sinkings of heart because of Him at another time. Think out for yourselves those ... years, the like of which never came to any other family on the face of the earth.[3]

And here is a fact yet more intriguing. James lived with Jesus for those thirty years and, until seven months before the crucifixion, remained an unbeliever. "For even His brothers did not believe in Him" (John 7:5).

After Jesus rose from the dead, He made a special appearance to James (1 Corinthians 15:7). When Jesus showed Himself to those gathered in the upper room in Jerusalem, James was there (Acts 1:14). When Peter was miraculously released from prison, he told those at the prayer meeting to go tell James (12:17).

Paul refers to James as one of the "pillars" of the church (Galatians 2:9), and by the time the first Jerusalem convention was convened (about AD 51), James had become the authoritative leader. In that first church counsel after Peter, Paul, and Barnabas had spoken, James summed up their discussion; and his statement was adopted by the whole assembly, formulated in a letter, and sent to the church in Antioch (Acts 15:13–21).

Several years later (AD 58), when Paul reported to the church about his third missionary journey, James was apparently still the recognized leader (21:17–25).

First-century historian Josephus records that James' life ended when he was stoned to death on orders of the Sadducean high priest Annas.[4]

The epistle of James was written to Jews who were scattered abroad throughout the ancient world (James 1:1). From Babylon to Rome, wherever any community of Hebrews might be gathered for commercial or social reasons, these exhortations of James were likely to be read.

Generally considered the earliest book in the New Testament era, James is also one of the most practical. James writes with the passion of Elijah; and because of his fiery eloquence and prophetic fervor, he has often been called the Amos of the New Testament. In the 108 verses of this short letter, there are 54 imperatives!

Outside of our Lord, James is the best illustrator among the New Testament writers. His knowledge of nature is the source of many stories that find their meaning in the creative work of God. In fact, there is more of an appreciation of nature in the epistle of James than in all of Paul's letters put together.

In spite of James' unvarnished style as a writer, there is a genuine warmth in this epistle. Eleven times he refers to his readers as "my brethren." Three times he calls them "my beloved brethren." His words may at times seem harsh, but they are meant to help, not harm! There has never been a more important time to study the book of James. Its strong message of "genuine faith" cries out against the emptiness of so many modern claims:

> The overwhelming majority of Americans—more than 85 percent—still identify themselves as Christians. But if the statistical indicators of faith are up, the social influence is down and the reasons are becoming plain. There has been a carelessness about Christian orthodoxy, a corruption of Christian obedience, a vacuum of Christian leadership, and

a disarray among many of the public initiatives in which Christians have recently placed their confidence. Much of the public face of "American Christianity" is a stunning testament to the power of religion without God.[5]

We can know what to do if we will earnestly study James' words and become not just hearers, but doers of all he says.

WHAT TO DO WHEN THE HEAT'S TURNED UP
(JAMES 1:1–12)

My brethren, count it all joy when you fall into various trials.

They came up to this ensign and poured a glass of ice water down his back and threw another in his face. The ensign, who had fallen asleep in the chow hall after five sleepless nights, opened his eyes for a second, just long enough to utter a dull "Thank you, sir." A moment later his eyes rolled upward and then closed. His head went down again. He didn't touch his meal.

It's called Hell Week and is part of the navy's Basic Underwater Demolition School where sailors are turned into SEALs—Sea-Air-Land commandos. By undergoing a grueling regimen of sleepless days and nights, sensory overload, and physical testing, these men are transformed into some of the toughest human beings in the world.

The effort to change average men into commandos starts at the Coronado Naval Amphibious Base in San Diego, California. The class commences in October with a three-hundred-yard swim, and the physical regimen becomes increasingly difficult as it builds to the ultimate challenge known as Hell Week.

This final period of torturous physical and psychological training begins on Sunday night. Lights flash on as the recruits are awakened by an instructor. Next to one ear, a machine gun with blanks is fired. A jet from a garden hose is digging into the other ear. An instructor shouts out instructions, "We have a mission to perform this evening. I want you to listen to every detail I have for you." The mission turns out to be exercising and lying wet and almost naked on cold steel plates, installed on a nearby pier.

On Monday the six-man teams are ordered to run races with a 250-pound Zodiac rubber assault boat on their heads. On Tuesday, with less than an hour of sleep the night before, they have to row those Zodiac boats to Mexican waters and back, a trip of eighteen miles.

Because of sleep deprivation, many of the trainees confess to drifting in and out of consciousness throughout the trip. Back at the base, most students learn to sleep while eating.

On Wednesday the men continue the races with boats bouncing on their heads, their combat boots sinking in the soft sand. That evening they run again. At midnight, they are ordered to lie naked in the cold, pounding surf. Every ten minutes during the night they are made to stand up to get the full effect of the wind.

After the surf torture, the chance to disenroll awaits each student. All he has to do is to ring a certain bell three times and say, "I quit."

By Thursday everyone is hallucinating. By Friday afternoon, the week is over, and the new SEALs are lined up to be checked by a doctor.[1]

Only in terms of the ugliness of war can punishment like this make any sense. By pushing these men to the very brink of insanity during times of peace, the navy is giving them the best chance to be ready to face the cruelty of real war if it comes.

With his first words in this letter, James reminds his suffering brothers and sisters that they should not be surprised when they experience intense periods of testing. He knows that they face a spiritual conflict that will require a toughness learned only through proper instruction and monitored experience. James calls God's training regimen "various [kinds of] trials" (1:2). As he prepares his friends for the inevitable test, he outlines for them and for us the following five strategies to employ when times of testing invade.

CELEBRATE THE REASON BEHIND YOUR TRIALS

When James addresses his letter to the twelve tribes, he is employing a common designation of the Jewish nation (Acts 26:7). When he speaks of them as "scattered abroad," the word he chooses is *Diaspora*, a technical term employed after the Babylonian captivity for Jews who lived outside of Palestine among the Gentiles.

The Diaspora began in 722 BC when the Assyrians captured the ten tribes of the northern kingdom (2 Kings 17:6). When Nebuchadnezzar carried away the southern kingdom to Babylon in 586 BC (2 Kings 25:11), the process continued. In the early days of the church as great waves of persecution swept over Jerusalem, the dispersion persisted: "Now those who were scattered after the persecution that arose over Stephen traveled as far as Phoenicia, Cyprus, and Antioch, preaching the word" (Acts 11:19; see also Acts 8:1, 4).

Peter wrote his first letter to "the pilgrims of the Dispersion in Pontus, Galatia, Cappadocia, Asia, and Bithynia" (1:1).

In some of the major cities of the world, like Alexandria, large populations of expatriate Jews were persecuted by their own countrymen, abused by the Gentiles, and in many places had less standing than slaves.

This is the context of the trials mentioned in this first section. James pictures these disenfranchised Israelites as "falling into" trials. It is a description that is similar to the way Paul portrayed his Roman imprisonment. He referred to it as "the things which happened to me" (Phil. 1:12).

The phrase "falling into" might be better translated "encountering." It is the same term used in the story of the good Samaritan of the man who "fell among thieves" (Luke 10:30).

By the use of this word it is obvious that the suffering believers were not overtaken by some sinful activity or temptation. Rather, they were being exploited and slandered and litigated by the rich. God was allowing these experiences to strengthen and mature their faith.

For the Jews, the trials were packaged as persecution. For us today, they could be any number of things: the loss of a job, a divorce, trouble with our children, severe financial strain, illness or death in the family, or relational problems over which we have little control. One writer has observed that this emphasis by James stands in stark contrast to much modern Christian thinking:

> A matter worth pondering is the fact that the very first topic James discussed involved the difficulties encountered in the Christian life. Totally foreign to him was the curious modern notion that becoming a Christian will make life easier, that all problems will disappear, and that the prospect in this life for each believer is that he will live "happily ever after."[2]

It would be easy for us to reason that since we are not experiencing any difficulty at this time, such teaching on trials is not applicable to us. But please note that James does not say *if* you encounter trials, but *when* you encounter trials.

And when these inevitable trials come, our first strategy, according to James, is to consider it all joy. What could he possibly mean?

In his book *Where Is God When It Hurts?* Philip Yancey tells about Claudia, a beautiful newlywed, who discovered that she had Hodgkin's disease. One of her greatest challenges in coping with her trial was presented by her host of well-meaning friends who came to the hospital to see her. One woman, whom Claudia described as the most spiritual in her church, came often to read aloud from books about praising God. Her speeches to Claudia routinely sounded like this:

> Claudia, you need to come to the place where you can say, "God, I love You for making me suffer like this. It is Your will. You know the best for me. And I just praise You for loving me enough to allow me to experience this. In all things, including this, I give thanks."

Claudia said that as she would ponder these words, her mind would be filled with gruesome visions of God:

> She imagined a figure in the shape of a troll, big as the

universe, who delighted in squeezing helpless humans between his fingernails, pulverizing them with his fists, dashing them against sharp stones. The figure would keep torturing these humans until they cried out, "God, I love You for doing this to me!"

The whole idea repulsed her, and Claudia knew that she could never worship or love a God like that.[3]

When James tells us to consider it all joy when we fall into various kinds of trials, he is not counseling us as Claudia's friend did. To consider it all joy in the midst of our trials is to respond with a deliberate, intelligent appraisal of our situation. Navy Captain Larry Bailey, commanding officer of the Coronado School for the training of SEALs, said, "Completing Hell Week is 90 percent mental. The men don't believe it at first, but it is."[4]

The same is true for Christians going through trials—90 percent of their success is mental and spiritual. They must learn to look at the experience from God's perspective and recognize the trial not as a happy experience in itself, but as the means of producing something very valuable in life.

Dr. Spiros Zodhiates explains that the word *consider* "should rather be translated, 'think forward, consider, regard.' As you live in the present consider the future, think forward to the future. Gloom now, but glory in the days to come."[5]

Jesus taught this kind of joy when He delivered His Sermon on the Mount:

> Blessed are those who are persecuted for righteousness' sake, for theirs is the kingdom of heaven. Blessed are you when they revile and persecute you, and say all kinds of evil against you falsely for My sake. *Rejoice and be exceeding glad*, for great is your reward in heaven, for so they persecuted the prophets who were before you. (Matt. 5:10–12)

Paul experienced this strange joy. He wrote, "I am exceedingly *joyful* in all our tribulation" (2 Cor. 7:4). When the apostles were beaten because of their bold testimony for Christ, they went out "*rejoicing* that they were counted worthy to suffer shame for His name" (Acts 5:41).

Peter also believed that this unique joy was possible. In his first letter he wrote:

> In this you greatly rejoice, though now for a little while, if need be, you have been grieved by various trials, that the genuineness of your faith, being much more precious than gold that perishes, though it is tested by fire, may be found to praise, honor, and glory at the revelation of Jesus Christ (1:6–7).

> Beloved, do not think it strange concerning the fiery trial which is to try you, as though some strange thing happened to you; but rejoice to the extent that you partake of Christ's sufferings, that when His glory is revealed, you may also be glad with exceeding joy. (4:12–13)

Once again Philip Yancey helps us to understand this often misunderstood concept:

> By those words [*rejoice* and *be glad*], the apostles did not intend a grin-and-bear-it or act-tough-like-nothing-happened attitude. No trace of those attitudes can be found in Christ's response to suffering or in Paul's…. Nor is there any masochistic hint of enjoying the pain. "Rejoicing in suffering" does not mean Christians should act happy about tragedy and pain when they feel like crying. Such a view distorts honesty and true expression of feelings. Christianity is not phony. The Bible's spotlight is on the end result, the use God can make of suffering in our lives. Before He can produce that result, however, He first needs

our commitment of trust in Him, and the process of giving
Him that commitment can be described as rejoicing.[6]

Dr. R. A. Torrey was one of the great Bible teachers of a past generation and founder of the Bible Institute of Los Angeles (BIOLA). He
and Mrs. Torrey went through a time of great heartache when their
twelve-year-old daughter was accidentally killed. The funeral was held
on a miserable, rainy day. They stood around the grave and watched
as the body of their little girl was put away. As they turned away, Mrs.
Torrey said, "I'm so glad that Elizabeth is with the Lord and not in
that box."

But even knowing that to be true, their hearts were broken. Dr.
Torrey said that the next day, as he was walking down the street, the
whole thing broke anew—the loneliness, the years ahead without her
presence, the heartbreak of an empty house, and all the other implica-
tions of her death. As he reflected back on that moment, he wrote:

> And just then, this fountain, the Holy Spirit I had in my
> heart, broke forth with such power as I think I had never
> experienced before, and it was the most joyful moment I
> had ever known in my life! Oh, how wonderful is the joy of
> the Holy Ghost! It is an unspeakable, glorious thing to have
> your joy not in things about you, not even in your most
> dearly loved friends, but to have within you a fountain ever
> springing up ... 365 days in every year, springing up under
> all circumstances unto everlasting life.[7]

CALCULATE THE RESULTS OF YOUR TRIALS

The believer has to look above the immediate unpleasantness of the
trial and find joy in what God will accomplish by it. Paul said something
to the Roman Christians that is very helpful here:

> And not only that, but we also glory in tribulations,
> knowing that tribulation produces perseverance; and

perseverance, character; and character, hope. Now hope
does not disappoint, because the love of God has been
poured out in our hearts by the Holy Spirit who was given
to us. (Rom. 5:3–5)

In his book *The Fight*, John White writes, "Tough times … either
make you or break you. If you are not utterly crushed by them … you
will be enlarged by them. The pain will make you live more deeply and
expand your consciousness."[8]

Trials Produce Durability

James says that the testing of our faith produces patience. Patience
is not a passive term but an active one. It is not a resignation to whatever happens, but a strong and tough resolution in the midst of very
adverse circumstances. It would be better translated as "steadfastness,"
"perseverance," or "brave endurance."

This word is used of Job in James 5:11: "Indeed we count them
blessed who endure. You have heard of the perseverance of Job and
seen the end intended by the Lord—that the Lord is very compassionate and merciful." Trials in the lives of believers refine their faith so that
the false is stripped away and the genuine faith that continues to trust
God can develop victorious positive endurance.

William Barclay points out that the endurance of the early
Christians was not a passive quality: "It is not simply the ability to bear
things; it is the ability to turn them to greatness and glory. The thing
which amazed the heathen in the centuries of persecution was that the
martyrs did not die grimly; they died singing."[9]

Trials Produce Maturity

James uses two expressions here to define maturity in the life of
the believer. When durability has done its perfect work, it causes the
Christian to be *perfect* and *complete*.

First of all, mature believers are *perfect*. This word means "to be
fully developed." Without durability in trials, believers have not yet

fully matured. They must learn to persevere in trials so that the work that God has begun in them will be brought to completion.

Three times Paul asked the Lord to remove the thorn in his flesh. While that request was not answered as Paul desired, God did answer him: "My grace is sufficient for you, for My strength is made *perfect* in weakness" (2 Cor. 12:9). The term *perfect* is the same word that James uses here. We are to persevere in our trials so that the work that God has begun in us may be brought to completion.

On one occasion, David prayed about this aspect of the Lord's work: "The Lord will *perfect* that which concerns me; Your mercy, O Lord, endures forever; do not forsake the works of Your hands" (Ps. 138:8).

Second, mature believers are *complete*. This word refers to something that has all its parts and therefore is whole. It is possible for Christians to be fully grown or mature in most areas of life but be missing this ingredient of steadfastness in trials. Until this has been experienced, they are not yet complete.

The great theologian John Calvin was weak and sickly and hounded by persecution, and yet he brilliantly guided thousands of believers during the Reformation. Suffering from rheumatism and migraine headaches, he continued to write proliferously and preach powerfully, as well as govern the city of Geneva for twenty-five years. Said Calvin, "You must submit to supreme suffering in order to discover the completion of joy."[10]

CALL UPON GOD'S RESOURCES IN YOUR TRIALS

A poster from a few years ago read like this:

> A prayer to be said
> When the world has gotten you down
> And you feel rotten,
> And you're too doggone tired to pray,
> And you're in a big hurry,
> And besides, you're mad at everybody...
> "Help!"

Most of us have found ourselves at the point of crying out for help at one time or another, but it's usually our last resort. We commonly try every device known to man to escape admitting that we need help! James takes the word "lacking" from verse 4 and ties it to verse 5, reminding us that the prerequisite to obtaining help with our troubles is to realize that we lack sufficient wisdom to sort them out! The argument is this: "When facing trials, it is important to know how to cope with them. The only way that we will be able to understand these trials and respond to them properly is to ask for the wisdom God alone can give."

In a book entitled *The Wisdom of God*, the following ideas about wisdom were brought together:

> What is wisdom? Coleridge says, "Wisdom is common sense in an uncommon degree." C. H. Spurgeon defines wisdom as "The right use of knowledge." Francis Hutchison says it is "Pursuing the best ends by the best means." Cicero says, "Wisdom is the knowledge of things human and divine and the causes by which they are controlled." Someone, unknown to me, has simply added this definition, "Wisdom is knowledge using its head." If I had to choose my favorite secular definition, I think it would be this one, "Wisdom is doing the right thing without precedent."[11]

When our friends and loved ones are going through trials, we may think we see what God is doing through the ordeal. But when we are the sufferers, when we are going through the fire, it is very difficult to be as wise. This is why we are to ask God for wisdom. Nine Hebrew words and five Greek words are translated *pray*, but the Holy Spirit passes by all of them and chooses the more common word *ask*. All we have to do is ask, and He will give us the wisdom that we need to get through the storm.

I came across a motto several years ago that has helped me more than once to understand the need to seek God's help. It goes like this:

> Unless there is within us
> that which is above us,
> we will soon yield
> to that which is around us.

As James motivates troubled believers to seek wisdom, he describes God in such a way as to make us wonder why we wait so long to reach out for His help.

God Is Good

The Scriptures affirm that God is the source of true wisdom:

> Every good gift and every perfect gift is from above, and comes down from the Father of lights, with whom there is no variation or shadow of turning. (James 1:17)

> With Him are wisdom and strength, He has counsel and understanding. (Job 12:13)

> From where then does wisdom come? And where is the place of understanding? ... God understands its way, and He knows its place. (Job 28:20, 23)

> For the Lord gives wisdom; from His mouth come knowledge and understanding. (Prov. 2:6)

Paul prayed "that the God of our Lord Jesus Christ, the Father of glory, may give to you the spirit of wisdom" (Eph. 1:17). This God who is the source of wisdom gives to all men. He is good and is not partial to any. He will always answer the prayer for wisdom. He never turns away a request. He may not always answer on our time schedule ... but He always answers!

God Is Generous

James says that God gives to all men liberally. The word *liberal* has two meanings associated with it. The first means "to stretch out" and pictures God stretching or spreading out His table of wisdom. The way God dispenses His wisdom to those who ask is by lavishly pouring out to them the full supply of that which they need.

The second meaning teaches the *method* of His giving. *Liberally* is also translated "singly." God is the opposite of the double-minded man mentioned in verse 8. God gives His wisdom simply, plainly, straight-forwardly, and individually to all who will ask of Him.

God Is Gracious

James says that God gives His wisdom without reproach. The word *reproach* means "to insult," "to hurl an invective," "to harm." When we come to God for wisdom, He never scolds us for coming, no matter how often we approach Him.

Because God is good and generous and gracious, no seeker should approach Him with doubt. He can be trusted! But if we fail to trust Him, we should not expect Him to answer us:

> But let him ask in faith, with no doubting, for he who
> doubts is like a wave of the sea driven and tossed by the
> wind. For let not that man suppose that he will receive
> anything from the Lord; he is a double-minded man,
> unstable in all his ways. (James 1:6–8)

The word *faith* is found only twice in the Old Testament (Deut. 32:20, Hab. 2:4), but it is found sixteen times in the book of James alone. The book of Hebrews reminds us that "without faith it is impossible to please Him, for he who comes to God must believe that He is, and that He is a rewarder of those who diligently seek Him" (11:6). If we approach God without faith, we have decided to live life our own way, to make our own decisions, to separate ourselves from Him. Then the cause of God not answering us belongs to us and not to Him.

When James likens the double-minded man to the billowing sea, it is the first of many references to nature in his letter. He also refers to the wind (1:6; 3:4); the sun (1:11, 17); the grass and flowers (1:11); horses (3:3); other animals, birds, and sea creatures (3:7); springs (3:11); figs, olives, and grapevines (3:12); agriculture (5:7); and rain (5:17–18).

James says that a person who prays doubting is like the sea that is blown and tossed about by the wind. He no doubt had in mind the Sea of Galilee, which is only fifteen miles long and seven miles wide but often very violent. The strong winds sweep down from the surrounding mountains like a cyclone, whipping up the waters in a fury. To James, the constant churning of the water suggested the agitation of a doubter's heart. Such persons are encouraged one moment, discouraged the next. Paul uses the same figure to portray immature believers. He speaks of them as "tossed to and fro and carried about with every wind of doctrine, by the trickery of men, in the cunning craftiness of deceitful plotting" (Eph. 4:14).

The man of faith is a stable man looking in only one direction for the wisdom he needs. He knows that the God to whom he prays is able and willing to respond to his need. As Dorothy Sayers reminds us, God is able to help us in our trials because He Himself has chosen the way of suffering:

> For whatever reason God chose to make man as he is—limited and suffering and subject to sorrows and death—He had the honesty and courage to take His own medicine. Whatever game He is playing with His creation, He has kept His own rules and played fair. He can exact nothing from man that He has not exacted from Himself. He has Himself gone through the whole of human experience, from the trivial irritations of family life and the cramping restrictions of hard work and lack of money to the worse horrors of pain and humiliation, defeat, despair, and death. When He was a man, He played the man. He was born in poverty and died in disgrace and thought it well worthwhile.[12]

Consider Your Reactions to Your Trials

When you experience trials, you often catch yourself reevaluating life. If you happen to be rich, you realize that trials can bring you down to poverty. Most of James' readers were poor and had become even poorer through the persecution leveled against them. But James would not let them be discouraged. He told them that they should rejoice in the fact that they were being exalted. They had been low and were made high! Through poverty, they had developed a humble spirit that would keep their hearts open toward God. "Blessed are the poor in spirit, for theirs is the kingdom of heaven" (Matt. 5:3). R. W. Dale reminds the poor man of his true position in Christ:

> Let him remember that he is a prince, and glory in it. He is a prince on his way to his kingdom, traveling by rough roads, enduring many hardships, suffering from hunger, cold, and weariness, and the people among whom he is traveling do not know anything about his greatness; but he knows; let him glory in his high estate![13]

God's testings have a way of bringing about equality in His family. When testing comes to the poor man, he lets God have His way and rejoices that he possesses spiritual riches that cannot be taken from him. When testing comes to the rich man, he also lets God have His way and rejoices that his riches in Christ cannot wither or fade away.

James' reference to the wealthy man and the comparative shortness of human life reminds him of the wildflowers that carpeted the hillsides of his native land. They were dazzlingly beautiful for a few weeks in the spring after the rains had come, but their beauty was always short lived. Using poetic language that should have been familiar to his Jewish readers (Job 14:2; Ps. 102:11; 103:15–16; Isa. 40:6–8; 1 Peter 1:24–25), James describes the blistering heat that followed the rainy season and withered the flowers. The short life of blossoms in Palestine provided a good illustration of the rich man. When the heat of trials separated the wealthy from his wealth, the Christian rich man calculated that he would have had it for only a short time anyway. He knew that he had really lost nothing since Christ was everything to him.

Hudson Taylor, founder of the China Inland Mission, was talking to a young missionary who was about to start work in China. "Look at this," Taylor said, and then proceeded to pound his fist on the table. The teacups jumped, and the tea was spilled all over the table. While the startled young man was wondering what was going on, Taylor said, "When you begin your work, you will be buffeted in numerous ways. The trials will be like blows. Remember, these blows will bring out only what is in you."[14]

CONTEMPLATE THE REWARD OF YOUR TRIALS

James has made us aware that our trials produce patience and maturity and cause us to seek and follow God's wisdom. But adversity is also riveted to the future, for trials guarantee future blessing as well: "Blessed is the man who endures temptation; for when he has been approved, he will receive the crown of life which the Lord has promised to those who love Him" (James 1:12).

Jesus also promised a reward for those who are faithful under persecution: "Blessed are those who are persecuted for righteousness' sake…. Rejoice and be exceedingly glad, for great is your reward in heaven" (Matt. 5:10, 12).

The reward that James promised is a "crown," from the Greek word *stephanos*. This word was used to identify the woven thorns that were placed upon the head of our Lord as He was prepared for crucifixion (Matt. 27:29; Mark 15:17; John 19:5). Paul referred metaphorically both to the Philippians and the Thessalonians as his "crown" (Phil. 4:1; 1 Thess. 2:19). Writing to Timothy, Paul described his future reward as "the crown of righteousness" (2 Tim. 4:8). Peter called it "the crown of glory that does not fade away," which will be given by the Chief Shepherd when He appears (1 Peter 5:4). The apostle John called it "the crown of life" (Rev. 2:10) and indicated that it would be among the crowns cast at the feet of Jesus in heaven (4:10). We are saved by trusting in Christ, but we are crowned when we are tested by fire and continue to love Him.

Andrew Murray was suffering from a terribly painful back, the result of an injury he had incurred years before. One morning while he was eating breakfast in his room, his hostess told him of a woman downstairs who was in great trouble, and wanted to know if he had any advice for her. Andrew Murray handed her a paper he had been writing on and said, "Give her this advice I'm writing down for myself. It may be that she'll find it helpful." This is what was written:

> In time of trouble, say, "First, He brought me here. It is by His will I am in this strait place; in that I will rest." Next, "He will keep me here in His love, and give me grace in this trial to behave as His child." Then say, "He will make the trial a blessing, teaching me lessons He intends me to learn, and working in me the grace He means to bestow." And last, say, "In His good time He can bring me out again. How and when, He knows." Therefore, say, "I am here (1) by God's appointment, (2) in His keeping, (3) under His training, (4) for His time."[15]

While the average number of sailors in each SEALs basic training class is seventy-five, an average of only thirty-eight graduate and go on to success as Sea-Air-Land commandos. Almost half of the class quit during the process.[16] When Christians face their basic training in trials, there are also many casualties. But James teaches us that we can be victors instead of victims, if we will mentally prepare ourselves by

1. celebrating the reason behind our trials;
2. calculating the results of our trials;
3. calling upon God's resources in our trials;
4. considering our reactions to our trials;
5. contemplating the reward of our trials.

WHAT TO DO WHEN WRONG SEEMS RIGHT
(JAMES 1:13–18)

When desire has conceived, it gives birth to sin; and sin,
when it is full-grown, brings forth death.

John Fischer is one of my favorite contemporary authors. In his book *Real Christians Don't Dance,* he tells this story:

> The two men walked down the street in the direction
> of the coffee shop. The old man was somewhere in his
> eighties and had been walking with the Lord longer than
> the younger one had been alive. Actually, "walking" is too
> passive a word … more like "fighting." He was a feisty
> old man and his fight had been one for truth and honesty
> from himself and from God. The resulting wisdom and
> lively charm made his companion look forward to these
> meetings.
>
> As the two men approached the coffee shop, they hap-
> pened to pass a young woman. She was dressed in such a
> way as to take fullest advantage of the warm weather and
> her physical attributes. The awkward silence that followed
> in her wake confused the young man. He had known this
> silence before with his peers. It was always full of uncom-
> fortable questions like, "Do I ignore this? Do I break the
> tension by making a joke? Do I say something spiritual?"
> With his peers, he could understand it, but with an old
> man whose eyesight was dim and whose glands were most

likely dried up, it didn't make sense. His curiosity finally
got the best of him and he blurted out, "Do you ever get
over that?"

"Not yet," replied the old man with a twinkle. The young
man was shocked. At his age, his maturity, his wisdom—
and he was still dealing with lust? Moments later, seated in
the coffee shop, the young man pursued the conversation.
"Do you mean to tell me that it doesn't get any better?"[1]

Most of us assume that as we get older, we will feel the tug of
temptation much less than in our younger years. In other words, if we
just hang on, we will overcome.

Well, I do believe we can overcome, but it is not because we outlive
temptation's pull. This oldest of man's problems will continue to dog us
until our last days. In fact, there are many who think that the intensity
of temptation has increased to an all-time high, even before we entered
the Internet age:

I think the struggle against sin and its power might be a
tougher fight for us now than at almost any other time in
recent history. From every direction, we are bombarded
with powerful temptations that can lead us away from
God. Men used to have to go out of their way to give
themselves to sin. Today the possibilities for sin are
present absolutely everywhere—in the shopping malls, on
TV, in school, at work, in the theaters, in the newspapers
and on every page of our magazines. We are exposed daily
to an incredible variety of opportunities for disobedience
in thought and action. The persuasive stimulation captures
our attention and feeds our fantasies. It seems like there
is no escape … the temptations we resist today come to us
charged with the raw power of advertising and couched in
the subtle and perverted genius of worldly persuasion. No
age has had to deal with things as we do. Everything from
soft drinks to tires is sold with sex.[2]

In chapter 1 of this book we learned that trials come from God to help us grow. In this chapter we will discover that temptation comes from Satan to cause us to sin. When we fall into trials, we are to count it all joy, but temptations are to be renounced and abandoned. Interpreting this passage is difficult, because the word for *trials* and *temptations* is the same in the original language. Outward troubles and inward enticements look alike, and only the context tells us which meaning is to be assigned. In verses 2 and 12 of James 1, the noun form of *peirasmos* is used to describe the outwardness of trials. In verses 13 and 14, the verb form of *peirasmos* is used to portray the inwardness of temptation.

When Satan tempts us, it is like Ralph Nader taking a General Motors car and running a group of tests on it. The purpose of his testing is to bring out the bad traits of the car. But when God tests us, it is like General Motors running the test on its own cars. The motivation is to bring out the good qualities.[3]

When a fiendish murderer takes a knife to slash the flesh of his victim, it is for the purpose of destroying the person. But when a skilled surgeon uses a blade to cut the flesh, it is for the purpose of healing. Satan is the murderous tempter. Our Lord is the skilled surgeon. In other words, Satan tempts us to bring out the bad (James 1:13–15). God tests us to bring out the good (vv. 2–12).

The Christian has the *external* world, the *internal* flesh, and the *infernal* Devil to deal with every day; however, it is the Devil who tempts to evil. He is actually called "the tempter" in Matthew 4:3 and 1 Thessalonians 3:5. If you have been a Christian for very long, the Tempter is no stranger to you. As he roars about like a lion seeking to devour, he has passed your way more than once.

While trials and temptations are different experiences, they do have this in common—without proper preparation, the believer can be victimized. Nothing tests the integrity of our faith like our response to temptation. Knowing the enticements his scattered Christian friends were facing, James offered five principles for overcoming temptation.

ACKNOWLEDGE THE REALITY OF TEMPTATION

A young priest was serving in the confessional booth for the first time and was being watched over by an older priest. At the end of the day, the older priest took the young man aside and said, "When a person finishes confession, you have got to say something other than 'Wow!'"

Most of us are not all that surprised when we hear of others falling prey to temptation, but we are often surprised when we face it. Yet temptation is inevitable! No one escapes it! The more we grow toward the Lord, the more we are tempted. John White reminds us of the inevitability of temptation:

> You will be tempted. The kinds of temptation may change.
> Candies for kids, sensuality for the young, riches for the
> middle-aged and power for the aging. The Evil One can
> ring the changes with greater skill than any advertising
> agency. He knows the Achilles' heel ... of every microbe.
> You will be tempted continuously. You will be tempted
> ferociously at times of crisis. Jesus Himself was tempted
> "in all points as we are" (that is, to commit adultery,
> to steal, to lie, to kill and on and on) "yet without sin."
> Therefore, temptation itself need not dismay you. It was
> your Saviour's lot and it will be yours. As long as you live,
> you will be tempted."[4]

Charles Ryrie catalogs a list of biblical people who were involved with temptation:

> Remember Noah's drunkenness? Or Abraham's cowardice
> and lying before a heathen ruler? Or Moses' self-exaltation
> which made him strike the rock and kept him out of the
> Promised Land? Or Jacob's stratagems? Or the Patriarchs'
> mistreatment of Joseph? Or Elijah's murmuring? Or
> David's double sin? Or Hezekiah's ostentations? Or Jonah's
> rebellious spirit? Or Peter's denial of his Lord? Or John

Mark's defection? Or Paul and Barnabas' strife? Some of the noblest men of the Bible have not only experienced temptation but have yielded to its power.[5]

Oswald Chambers rescues the concept of temptation from its totally negative environment with these words in his classic *My Utmost for His Highest*:

> The word temptation has come to mean something bad to us today, but we tend to use the word in the wrong way. Temptation itself is not sin; it is something we are bound to face simply by virtue of being human. Not to be tempted would mean that we were already so shameful that we would be beneath contempt.... Temptation is not something that we can escape; in fact it is essential to the well-rounded life of a person. Beware of thinking that you are tempted as no one else—what you go through is the common inheritance of the human race, not something that no one has ever before endured. God does not save us from temptations—He sustains us in the midst of them (Heb. 2:18; 4:15–16).[6]

All of these writers make the same point. Unless we acknowledge the reality of temptation, we have programmed our spiritual lives for failure. Paul concurs with James that temptation should not be considered unusual in the life of a Christian:

> No temptation has overtaken you except such as is common to man; but God is faithful, who will not allow you to be tempted beyond what you are able, but with the temptation will also make the way of escape, that you may be able to bear it. (1 Cor. 10:13)

The Living Bible paraphrases that verse, "But remember this—the wrong desires that come into your life aren't anything new and different. Many others have faced exactly the same problems before you."

ASSUME THE RESPONSIBILITY FOR TEMPTATION

Will Rogers said that there are two great movements in the history of America. The first is the passing of the buffalo, and the second is the passing of the buck. Nothing in life proves the truth of his words like temptation! Erwin Lutzer explains:

> We cannot exaggerate the harm that has come to individuals from the teachings of Sigmund Freud, that those who misbehave are sick. We do not hold people responsible for catching the flu, measles, or having cancer. We have hospitals, not prisons, for the physically sick, simply because they bear no moral blame for their illness. The reprehensible Freudian implication is clear: if we are not responsible for physical illness, why should we be blamed for crime, a symptom of mental illness?[7]

According to James we even blame God for our temptations, in spite of the fact that "God cannot be tempted by evil, nor does He Himself tempt anyone" (1:13).

The shifting of blame actually began in the garden of Eden. Adam excused himself for his disobedience to God by saying, "'The woman whom You gave to be with me, she gave me of the tree and I ate' ... [And] the woman said, 'The serpent deceived me, and I ate'" (Gen. 3:12–13).

Today we carry on the tradition of our first parents in a very subtle way. We say, "It must be God's will, or He would not let it happen," or, "God has allowed me to be in this situation ... He could have stopped it if He had wanted to!" But James will have none of our excuses. God does not condone or commend our sinful behavior.

The construction of James' statement is much stronger than the English translation conveys. He is saying, "Don't even remotely suggest that God has anything to do with your temptations." God may test you to strengthen your faith, but He never tempts you to subvert your faith! Sometimes we blame God by saying that "we are just human." Robert Burns poetically said it:

> Thou knowest Thou hast formed me
> With passions wild and strong;
> And listening to their witching voice
> Has often led me wrong.[8]

Some of the Jewish rabbis of James' day believed that God was at least indirectly responsible for evil's existence in the world. James' readers, then, had a built-in excuse for blaming God when they were overcome by temptation. Spiros Zodhiates explains their reasoning:

> God has ordained that I should yield to the temptation under which I have fallen. I have been driven to sin, not by God Himself since He hates sin, but by the very circumstances in which God has placed me. God is the ultimate cause and therefore I should absolve myself of the responsibility.[9]

Another author expresses this same idea in even more graphic terms:

> Some [Christians] resort to lying to get themselves out of a jam; they burst out with foul language in exasperation; they steal or cheat others to make up for hard times; they harbor festering resentments against others; they indulge in self-pity and bitter complaining; they cannot for a period have normal sexual relations with their married partners, and so satisfy their urges in immoral affairs with others. Then they blithely shift the blame for their sin to God and acquit themselves of any fault.[10]

Why is it impossible for God to tempt us to sin?

> A tempter to sin must be himself sinful, open to the
> seductions of evil. Now God cannot thus be tempted. His
> absolute blessedness, His infinite holiness, removed Him
> wholly from liability to temptation, and thus, from His
> very nature, He cannot be tempted to sin.[11]

One of the best illustrations of God's relationship to temptation is found in the life of Job. God *allowed* Satan to tempt Job, but God was not involved in the temptation. Satan was given permission to take away all of Job's possessions, but Job's response was one of worship: "Naked I came from my mother's womb, and naked shall I return there. The Lord gave, and the Lord has taken away; blessed be the name of the Lord" (Job 1:21).

When Job's wife told Job to curse God and die, he once again responded in faith: "'You speak as one of the foolish women speaks. Shall we indeed accept good from God, and shall we not accept adversity?' In all this Job did not sin with his lips" (2:10). This man who suffered so much loss and tragedy understood temptation and refused to implicate God.

ANTICIPATE THE ROUTINE OF TEMPTATION

If God is not responsible for temptation, then who is? James clearly answers that question in verses 14–16: "But each one is tempted when he is drawn away by his own desires and enticed. Then, when desire has conceived, it gives birth to sin; and sin, when it is full-grown, brings forth death. Do not be deceived, my beloved brethren." Besides declaring each person responsible for his own temptation, James is careful to point out that temptation is not an event, but a process:

> People don't lead moral lives one day and have an affair
> the next. It may appear that way, but it is a process. The
> process is often overlooked because some stages are not
> obvious to us, the viewer, and thus they are difficult to
> detect. That's why it seems to happen overnight. Any

of us could be in the process right now. None of us are immune. The earlier danger signals can be detected and responded to, the easier it is to change direction. If you love potato chips, and know that you can't stop eating them until the bag is empty, you are better off to never take the first bite. Some steps on the road to immorality are not wrong in and of themselves; yet those very steps may be the first potato chip for some people.[12]

If we don't want Satan to take advantage of us, it is vital that we understand the adversary's strategic process ... what Paul calls "his devices" (2 Cor. 2:11).

The Tempter has been using the same routine since the temptation of Adam and Eve in the garden. Here is his step-by-step scheme:

Step One—Enticement

Desires are all right if they are in proper place and in control. Satan wants to take routine desires and turn them into runaway desires. Obsessions with good things create bad things! We respond to temptation from within our own hearts. Jesus explained that in Mark 7:21–23:

> For from within, out of the heart of men, proceed evil thoughts, adulteries, fornications, murders, thefts, covetousness, wickedness, deceit, lewdness, an evil eye, blasphemy, pride, foolishness. All these evil things come from within and defile a man.

But the inward man is also responding to provocation from the outside:

> We engage temptation ... when something in us responds to stimulation from outside. If there was nothing in us that could feel the draw toward worldly powers and pleasures, there would be no temptation. James calls this inner responsiveness, "evil desire." ... All

of us seek the fulfillment of our desires. The desires or yearnings we experience are not in themselves wrong. God has created the earth and all that is in it for our enjoyment and pleasure. What is wrong is that we often try to satisfy our cravings in ways that are inappropriate, unhealthy, and contrary to God's will for our lives.[13]

John White explains how the inward desires respond to the outward temptations:

> Have you ever fooled around with a piano? Open the top. Press the loud pedal. Then sing a note into the piano as loudly as you can. Stop and listen. You will hear at least one chord vibrating in response to the note you sang. You sing and a string in the piano picks up your voice and plays it back.
>
> Here, then, is a picture of temptation. Satan calls and you vibrate. The vibration is the "lust" James speaks of. Your desire is to go on responding to his call. If pianos have feeling, I imagine they are "turned on" when the chord vibrates. There is nothing bad about vibrating. The cord was made to vibrate and to vibrate powerfully. But it was meant to vibrate in response to a hammer—not in response to a voice.
>
> The appropriate response, then, is not to vibrate rapturously to the voice of the devil but to release the loud pedal and close the top of the piano. As Luther put it quaintly, you cannot stop birds flying about your head, but you can prevent them from building a nest in your hair.[14]

Step Two—Entrapment

James says that the result of the enticement is entrapment. He pictures the tempted as one who is dragged away and enticed.

The two terms that James uses here come from the world of the outdoorsman. The term *dragged away* means "snared in a trap." The word *enticed* belongs to the world of the fisherman and means "lured by the bait."

The first word depicts the person as "carried away" or "drawn away" and appears only here in the New Testament. The second word comes from a root meaning "bait." It portrays something being lured and caught. Homer Kent summarizes the impact of the two words taken together to show how powerful this allurement really is: "Combining both concepts and viewing them as metaphors of a fisherman, one can visualize the fish being first aroused from its original place of safety and repose, and then being lured to the bait that hides the fatal hook."[15]

Satan knows how to use the right bait for each one of us. He knows our weaknesses and knows how to hide his hook with bait that will be enticing to us. Often we know that we are being enticed. We suspect that there is a hook in what Satan is doing, but we keep on playing with it, nibbling on it, until we get caught!

James describes this process as being deceived. This expression is found also in Galatians 6:7; 1 Corinthians 15:33; and Luke 21:8.

Step Three—Endorsement

The illustration that James uses in verse 15 is of a pregnant woman. "When desire has conceived," he says, "it gives birth to sin." Sin is the union of the will with lust. Just as at human conception a process is initiated that will result in the birth of a child in a prescribed period of time, so when temptation is coddled, it too has an inevitable outcome. James says that the child born to temptation is sin. Indulging temptation brings about an inevitable result.

Just as a child is a person before it is ever born, so sin is present in the heart before it ever gives evidence that it is there. The conception of the sin and the discovery of the sin may be many months apart, but the process has been set in motion. As the Scripture says, "Be sure your sin will find you out" (Num. 32:23).

Up to this point the overt sin has not been committed. Certainly there has been sin if the temptation has been fondled in the heart and fantasized in the mind. But the act has not been committed. However, now the deed is done! Sin has been born! And the discovery has been made that temptation looks better than it really is!

Step Four—Enslavement

When you overcome temptation, you receive the crown of life. When you give in to temptation, you receive death. The wages of sin is death.

You can choose how you want to live. You are free to choose the actions, but not the results. You are free to have your kicks, but not to avoid the kickbacks! You are free to make choices, but not to avoid the consequences.

William Shakespeare in his tragedy *Macbeth* illustrated the retrogressive steps of evil. Lady Macbeth had set her eyes upon becoming queen of Scotland. The one thing standing between her and the realization of her ambition was her husband's kinsman Duncan, the present king. So great was her desire to be queen that it motivated her to plot the murder of Duncan and then to persuade her husband to carry it out.

She arranged what appeared to be the perfect murder. There was just one problem—she had to live with herself. In the most tragic scene of the play, she comes on stage, walking in her sleep, crying, "Out, damned spot! Out I say!" And then she shrieks, "All the perfumes of Arabia will not sweeten this little hand."

ACTIVATE THE REPLACEMENT OF TEMPTATION

Verse 17 is pivotal in this whole discussion. Up to this point we have been concentrating on the evil of temptation. Now James turns the page to the goodness of God, reminding us that anything fulfilling, anything worthwhile, anything good or proper is found in the Lord. In contrast to the evil enticements that come from within us, all good gifts are from God who is over us, and come down to us in a steady stream from the Father of Lights. When James refers to God as the Father of Lights, he

encourages the reader to look up to the sky, where he will
see the brilliant light of the sun by day, the reflective light
of the moon by night, and the twinkling of the stars. God
is the creator of those heavenly lightbearers; He Himself
is nothing but light; ... Therefore darkness cannot exist in
the presence of God.[16]

James' reference to God as the Father of Lights reminds us of God's
unchanging nature. He is trustworthy! He is the giver, and ultimately
He is the gift. And according to James it is all good! Jesus Himself said:

If you then, being evil, know how to give good gifts to
your children, how much more will your Father who is in
heaven give good things to those who ask Him! (Matt. 7:11)

Now if God so clothes the grass of the field, which today
is, and tomorrow is thrown into the oven, will He not
much more clothe you, O you of little faith? (Matt. 6:30)

Paul told the Romans to "put on the Lord Jesus Christ, and make
no provision for the flesh, to fulfill its lusts" (13:14).

We should not only refrain from thinking about gratifying our
desires, but also avoid thinking about *not* gratifying our desires. The
way to deal with temptation is not to grit our teeth and make up our
minds that we will not do a certain thing. The key is to fill our minds
with other things.

Instead of resisting, refocus! The more you fight a feeling, the
more it grabs you! What you resist tends to persist! Since temptation
begins with your inner thoughts, changing your thoughts is the key
to victory. Mark McMinn, in his book *Dealing with Desires You Can't
Control*, writes:

The key is not *eliminating* temptation, but managing
temptation. For example, pretend you're on a diet. After
you finish your chef salad with low-cal Italian dressing,

the waiter returns with a tray of sumptuous desserts. You
have an impulse to eat dessert, but your well-reasoned
side insists on abstinence. How likely is it that any self-
management strategy will *eliminate* that conflict? ... Trying
to eliminate temptation makes it harder to manage.[17]

Anyone who has trained a dog to obey knows this scene. A bit of
meat or bread is placed on the floor near the dog and the master says,
"No!" which the dog knows means that he must not touch it. The
dog will usually take his eyes off the food, because the temptation to
disobey would be too great, and instead will fix his eyes on the master's
face. That is the lesson of the dog. Always look to the Master's face.
William Barclay summarizes this idea of replacement:

> The Christian can so hand himself over to Christ and to the
> Spirit of Christ that he is cleansed of evil desire. He can be
> so engaged in good things that there is no time or place
> left for wrong desires. It is idle hands for which Satan finds
> mischief to do. It is an unexercised mind which plays with
> desire and an uncommitted heart which is vulnerable to
> the appeal of lust.[18]

ACCEPT THE REASON FOR TEMPTATION

In verse 18, James reminds us that we experience temptation because
of who we are. In verse 15 he says that sin gave birth to death. In verse
18 he states that God gave us birth through the Word of Truth. James
is talking about spiritual birth here. We are members of God's family
because we have been born again by the Word of Truth. This is the
consistent pattern of all New Testament conversions:

> In Him you also trusted, after you heard the word of truth.
> (Eph. 1:13)

> Because of the hope which is laid up for you in heaven,

of which you heard before in the word of the truth of the gospel. (Col. 1:5)

Having been born again ... through the word of God. (1 Peter 1:23)

Faith comes by hearing, and hearing by the word of God. (Rom. 10:17)

When James uses the word "firstfruits" to describe his believing friends, he is reminding them that they belong exclusively to God. In the Old Testament, "firstfruits" described the firstborn of cattle and the early fruit of the ground, both of which belonged to God. (See Ex. 22:29; 23:16; 34:26; Lev. 23:10.) In the New Testament, the term is associated with new believers:

Likewise greet the church that is in their house. Greet my beloved Epaenetus, who is the firstfruits of Achaia to Christ. (Rom. 16:5)

I urge you, brethren—you know the household of Stephanas, that it is the firstfruits of Achaia, and that they have devoted themselves to the ministry of the saints. (1 Cor. 16:15)

It is because we are God's special people that we are targets of the Enemy. Satan does not concern himself with those who have not been born again by the Word of Truth. We must not be confused about this:

The danger lies in the possibility that we might be tricked into doubting the authenticity of our relationship with Christ on the basis of the fact that we struggle with sin. The truth is, the struggle itself is proof that God is very close to us. Our sensitivity to sin is a gift of God's Spirit. It is a sign of our salvation. There would be no inner battle if we were truly lost. Only when we can sin without remorse, with no experience of inner tension, only when sin has become easy for us are we in real danger.[19]

Looking back over James' teaching on temptation, here is what we have learned. To be victorious, we must
1. acknowledge the reality of temptation;
2. assume the responsibility for temptation;
3. anticipate the routine of temptation;
4. activate the replacement of temptation;
5. accept the reason for temptation.

In the front of my Bible I have written five simple words that seem to summarize all that we have learned so far from James and all that the New Testament writers seemed to be saying when they touched on the subject. These words and the Scriptures that accompany them should be written on the blackboard of our hearts and, along with James' reasoned argument, used in battle against the Enemy.

Fight

James 4:7—"Resist the devil and he will flee from you."

1 Peter 5:8–9—"Be sober, be vigilant; because your adversary the devil walks about like a roaring lion, seeking whom he may devour. Resist him, steadfast in the faith, knowing that the same sufferings are experienced by your brotherhood in the world."

Ephesians 6:11—"Put on the whole armor of God, that you may be able to stand against the wiles of the devil."

Follow

James 4:7–8—"Therefore submit to God.... Draw near to God and He will draw near to you."

1 Peter 2:21—"For to this you were called, because Christ also suffered for us, leaving us an example, that you should follow His steps."

Flee

1 Corinthians 10:14—"Therefore, my beloved, flee from idolatry."

2 Timothy 2:22—"Flee also youthful lusts."

Romans 13:14—"But put on the Lord Jesus Christ, and make no provision for the flesh, to fulfill its lusts."

Genesis 39:12—When tempted by Potiphar's wife, Joseph "left his garment in her hand, and fled and ran outside."

Fellowship

2 Timothy 2:22—"Pursue righteousness, faith, love, peace with those who call on the Lord."

Proverbs 13:20—"He who walks with wise men will be wise, but the companion of fools will be destroyed."

1 Corinthians 15:33—"Do not be deceived: 'Evil company corrupts good habits.'"

Feed

Psalm 119:11—"Your word I have hidden in my heart, that I might not sin against You."

Matthew 4:1–11—Christ defeated Satan by quoting

the Old Testament. His reply was introduced with, "It is written."

We began this chapter with a reminder that temptation cannot be *outgrown*. We end our discussion with an emphatic reminder that while it cannot be outgrown, it can be *overcome*.

Amy Carmichael was a missionary to Japan, China, Ceylon, and India. During her first assignment in Japan, she went through a time of severe temptation, as she began to contemplate the possibility of being single all her life. Her temptation was very personal and very private, and it was not until forty years later that she was able to share the details with a close friend:

> On this day many years ago, I went away alone to a cave in the mountain called Arima. I had feelings of fear about the future. That was why I went there—to be alone with God. The Devil kept on whispering, "It's all right now, but what about afterwards? You are going to be very lonely." And he painted pictures of loneliness—I can see them still. And I turned to God in a kind of desperation and said, "Lord, what can I do? How can I go on to the end?" And He said, "None of them that trust in Me shall be desolate." That word has been with me ever since. It has been fulfilled to me. It will be fulfilled to you.[20]

WHAT TO DO WHEN THE MIRROR DOESN'T LIE
(JAMES 1:19–27)

*But be doers of the word, and not hearers only,
deceiving yourselves.*

A New England teacher quizzed a group of college-bound high school juniors and seniors on the Bible. The quiz preceded a Bible as Literature class he planned to teach at what was generally considered one of the better public schools in the nation. Among the more unusual answers from these students were, "Sodom and Gomorrah were lovers," and "Jezebel was Ahab's donkey."

Other students thought that the four horsemen appeared on the Acropolis; that the New Testament Gospels were written by Matthew, Mark, Luther, and John; that Eve was created from an apple; and that Jesus was baptized by Moses.

The answer that took the misinformation prize was given by a fellow who was academically in the top 5 percent of his class. The question, "What was Golgotha?" The answer, "Golgotha was the name of the giant who slew the apostle David."

In case you think this is an isolated instance of biblical illiteracy, let me quote the findings of a recent Gallup Poll:

Eighty-two percent of Americans believe that the Bible is either the literal or "inspired" Word of God ... more than half said they read the Bible at least monthly. Yet half

couldn't name even one of the four Gospels.... And fewer
than half knew who delivered the Sermon on the Mount.[1]

USA Today reported a poll showing that only 11 percent of
Americans read the Bible every day. More than half read it less than
once a month or not at all.[2] The Barna Research Group conducted
a survey that focused only on "born-again" Christians and came up
with the following statistics: "Only 18 percent—less than two in every
ten—read the Bible every day. Worst of all, 23 percent—almost one in
four professing Christians—say they never read the Word of God."[3]

The Bible is available in more than 1,800 languages, and yet someone has observed that the worst dust storm in history would happen if
all church members who were neglecting their Bibles dusted them off
simultaneously.

I read about a very religious father whose son was studying for
the ministry. The boy had decided to go to Europe for an advanced
degree, and the father worried that his simple faith would be spoiled by
sophisticated, unbelieving professors. "Don't let them take Jonah away
from you," he admonished, figuring the swallowed-by-a-great-fish story
might be the first part of the Bible to go. Two years later when the son
returned, the father asked, "Do you still have Jonah in your Bible?"

The son laughed, "Jonah! That story isn't even in your Bible."

The father replied, "It certainly is! What do you mean?"

Again the son laughed and insisted, "It's not in your Bible. Go
ahead, show it to me."

The old man fumbled through his Bible, looking for the Book of
Jonah, but he couldn't find it. At last he checked the table of contents
for the proper page. When he turned there, he discovered the three
pages composing Jonah had been carefully cut from his Bible.

"I did it before I went away," said the son. "What's the difference
between my losing the Book of Jonah through studying under nonbelievers or your losing it through neglect?"

James has just written to his believing friends that their spiritual birth
was the product of God's Word (1:18). Now he is about to challenge
them to take this same Word seriously in their daily walk. The reality of

outward trials and inward temptations calls for something more than an initial experience with God. His wisdom is needed every day.

In this central passage on the importance and priority of God's Word, James takes us through a six-step process that begins with the necessary preparation for study and ends with a powerful illustration of the difference the Bible can make in one's life.

STEP ONE—PREPARATION

Here are four clear directives to help you get started in this important endeavor.

Concentrate Your Attention

James begins his instructions with the encouragement to be "swift to hear." In James' day, this was very important, because most learning was done through listening. Since few believers had copies of the Scriptures in their possession, they depended on hearing it read and preached in public services. If they were not "swift to hear," they were left behind! Paul reminded the Romans that "faith comes by hearing, and hearing by the word of God" (10:17). The members of the church in Thessalonica captured the meaning of James' words in their approach to the Word of God:

> For this reason we also thank God without ceasing,
> because when you received the word of God which you
> heard from us, you welcomed it not as the word of men,
> but as it is in truth, the word of God, which also effectively
> works in you who believe. (1 Thess. 2:13)

In our culture today, many believers are indifferent to the Word of God. We may be living in the period Paul warned Timothy about when he challenged him to be a courageous preacher:

> For the time will come when they will not endure
> sound doctrine, but according to their own desires,

> because they have itching ears, they will heap up for
> themselves teachers; and they will turn their ears
> away from the truth, and be turned aside to fables.
> (2 Tim. 4:3–4)

If, as believers, we have no interaction with non-Christians, no vital ministry to growing believers, and no personal struggle for godliness, it will not be long before the Bible will seem irrelevant to us.

A U.S. Army officer told of the contrast in his pupils during two different eras of teaching at the artillery training school at Fort Sill, Oklahoma. In 1958–60 the attitude was so lax that the instructors had a problem getting the men to stay awake to listen. During the 1965–67 classes, however, the men, hearing the same basic lectures, were alert and took copious notes. The reason: They knew that in less than six weeks they would be facing the enemy in Vietnam.

Control Your Tongue

When James urged his readers to be "slow to speak," he may have had in mind the open interaction that often took place in the unstructured churches to which he was writing. Sometimes, the assembly would be taken over by those who wished to demonstrate their knowledge by their prolonged speaking.

There is nothing wrong with questions and responses, but it does not take an experienced teacher long to determine whether questions are being asked because answers are being sought or because the questioner thinks he has all the answers already! James' reminder is an echo of these words of our Lord:

> But I say to you that for every idle word men may speak,
> they will give account of it in the day of judgment. For by
> your words you will be justified, and by your words you
> will be condemned. (Matt. 12:36–37)

If you have studied the Wisdom Literature of the Old Testament, you have seen this counsel over and over again:

In the multitude of words sin is not lacking, but he who
restrains his lips is wise. (Prov. 10:19)

He who has knowledge spares his words, and a man of
understanding is of a calm spirit. Even a fool is counted
wise when he holds his peace; when he shuts his lips, he is
considered perceptive. (Prov. 17:27–28)

Do not be rash with your mouth, and let not your heart
utter anything hastily before God. For God is in heaven,
and you on earth; therefore let your words be few. For a
dream comes through much activity, and a fool's voice is
known by his many words. (Eccl. 5:2–3)

It is said that on one occasion, a young man came to the great philosopher Socrates to be trained as an orator. In his first meeting with his
teacher, he began to talk without stopping. When Socrates could get a
word in, he said, "Young man, I will have to charge you a double fee."

"A double fee? Why is that?"

"I will have to teach you two sciences. First, how to hold your
tongue, and then how to use it."

Contain Your Anger

Often in the early church assemblies, the anger of the participants
would explode as different ones expounded their own personal opinions about various issues. When James commanded them to be "slow
to wrath," the term *wrath* meant "an ongoing attitude of bitterness
and dislike." Such an attitude was in opposition to the righteousness of
God. Look at these warnings:

He who is impulsive exalts folly. (Prov. 14:29)

He who is slow to anger is better than the mighty, and
he who rules his spirit than he who takes a city.
(Prov. 16:32)

A fool vents all his feelings, but a wise man holds them back. (Prov. 29:11)

An angry man stirs up strife, and a furious man abounds in transgression. (Prov. 29:22)

When Paul wrote to the Ephesians, he told them, "Let all bitterness, wrath, anger, clamor, and evil speaking be put away from you, with all malice" (4:31).

Clean Up Your Life

The fourth guideline is to lay aside all filthiness and overflow of wickedness. If a person's moral life is out of control (which may include the tongue and temper), the result can be devastating to any hearing or understanding of God's Word. James' instruction is clear. There must be a spiritual housecleaning. It is not enough to clean up the outside of the house; the inside must be swept clean of all filth and evil. The use of the word *filthiness* in this regard is most instructive:

> The word … strictly speaking is used of wax in the ear.…
> Sin in our lives is like having wax in our ears; it prevents
> the Word of truth from reaching our hearts; for if it cannot
> penetrate through the ear, it will not come down to the
> heart.… We as Christians must take the wax out of our
> ears, so that the Word may influence our lives. I believe
> definitely that James here speaks of the born-again
> Christian whose sin may be like wax in his ear preventing
> him from hearing and doing the Word of God.[4]

STEP TWO—EXAMINATION

By concentrating their attention, controlling their tongue, containing their anger, and cleaning up their lives, the believers are now ready to receive the Word that had already been planted in them. This is not the Word of salvation—they have already received that (1:18)! This is rather the Word of instruction that is so crucial to growth. Humbly, each believer is to prepare to hear that Word which is able to bring him to maturity in Christ. Simon J. Kistemaker comments:

> Once again, the writer resorts to an illustration from
> nature. A plant needs constant care. If a plant is deprived
> of water and nurture, it will die. Thus if the readers
> who have heard the Word fail to pay attention, they will
> die a spiritual death. The Word needs diligent care and
> application, so that the readers may grow and increase
> spiritually.[5]

The word *receive* is translated several times in the New Testament as "welcome" (Matt. 10:40; Gal. 4:14; Heb. 11:31). We are not to passively examine the Word that is spoken but are to welcome it into our hearts with anticipation and excitement. We are to come to the reading and the preaching of the Word of God with a sense of anticipation! This should be our attitude each time we approach God's truth.

Mortimer J. Adler in his classic *How to Read a Book* makes this intriguing observation:

> The one time people read for all they are worth is when
> they are in love and are reading a love letter. They read
> every word three ways. They read between the lines
> and the margins. They read the whole in terms of the
> parts, and each part in terms of the whole. They grow
> sensitive to context and ambiguity, to insinuation and
> implication. They perceive the color of words, the order
> of phrases, and the weight of sentences. They may
> even take the punctuation into account. Then, if never
> before, or after, they read carefully and in depth.[6]

When Adler's book first came out, it was advertised in the *New York Times* under the slogan "How to Read a Love Letter." A picture showed a puzzled adolescent perusing a letter, with the following copy underneath:

> This young man has just received his first love letter.
> He may have read it three or four times, but he is just
> beginning. To read it as accurately as he would like, would
> require several dictionaries and a good deal of close work
> with a few experts of etymology and philology. However,
> he will do all right without them. He will ponder over the
> exact shade of meaning of every word, every comma. She
> has headed the letter, "Dear John."
>
> "What," he asks himself is the exact significance of
> those words? Did she refrain from saying "Dearest"
> because she was bashful? Would "My Dear" have
> sounded too formal? Jeepers, maybe she would have
> said "Dear So-and-So" to anybody! A worried frown will
> now appear on his face. But it disappears as soon as
> he really gets to thinking about the first sentence. She
> certainly wouldn't have written that to anybody! And
> so he works his way through the letter, one moment
> perched blissfully on a cloud, the next moment huddled
> miserably behind an eight-ball. It has started a hundred
> questions in his mind. He could quote it by heart. In
> fact, he will—to himself—for weeks to come....
>
> If people read books with anything like the same
> concentration, we'd be a race of mental giants.[7]

I cannot help but wonder what "spiritual giants" we might become if we learned to read the Word of God like this!

Step Three—Application

Jesus concluded the Sermon on the Mount with the story of the wise and foolish builders. When He had finished with the story, He said,

"Therefore whoever hears these sayings of Mine, and does them, I will liken him to a wise man who built his house on the rock" (Matt. 7:24). On another occasion the Savior said, "Blessed are those who hear the word of God and keep it" (Luke 11:28).

It is important to become a good listener to the Word of God, but that in itself is of no lasting value. Having heard what the Word says, we must develop the discipline to put it into practice. We must learn to be more than just hearers; we must learn to be doers. The apostle John understood this truth when he wrote, "My little children, let us not love in word or in tongue, but in deed and in truth" (1 John 3:18).

In James' day, the word *hearer* was used as *auditor* is today. In our college, if a person is auditing a course we offer, he does not take tests, does not get grades, is not working for a degree, and is ineligible for any awards. He is just listening in on the teaching. We cannot allow ourselves to become auditors of the Word of God. Our primary purpose in hearing or reading the Bible must be to do what it says.

The Casual Approach

In order to illustrate his words, James once again reaches into the everyday life of his readers, as he asks them to consider the mirror. The mirrors of the first century were made out of highly polished metal. They were not mounted on walls but rather were placed flat on tables so that the person who wished to see his reflection had to bend over and look down. Even then he would see a very poor reflection of himself.

If we hear the Word of God and fail to do what it says, we are, James says, like a person who casually looks at his "natural" face, the one he was born with, in a mirror, and then quickly walks away, making no changes in his appearance. Phillips translates the verse like this: "He sees himself, it is true, but he goes off without the slightest recollection of what sort of person he saw in the mirror" (1:24). This casual approach to God's Word produces what Howard Hendricks calls *functionally illiterate* Christians:

> Have you ever seen a Bible "parked" in the rear window
> of someone's car? That's common where I come from.

> A guy will come out of church, hop into his car, toss
> his Bible in the back, and leave it there until the next
> Sunday. That's quite a statement of the value he places
> on God's Word. In effect, when it comes to Scripture,
> he's functionally illiterate six out of seven days a week.[8]

There are many Christians today who refuse to look into the perfect law of liberty because they do not want to face the truth about their lives. They would rather live in deception than to know the truth. They are like the African princess that George Sweeting tells about in one of his books:

> She lived in the heart of the uncivilized jungle, and for
> years this chieftain's daughter had been told by all that
> she was the most beautiful woman in the entire tribe.
> Although she had no mirror to view herself, she had
> been convinced of her unparalleled beauty. One day
> when an exploring party traveled through that part of
> Africa, the princess was given a mirror as a gift. For the
> first time in her life she was able to see her own reflec-
> tion. Her immediate reaction was to smash the mirror
> on the nearest rock. Why? Because f   or the first time
> in her life she knew the truth. What other people had
> told her all those years was of little importance. What
> she had believed about herself made no difference. She
> saw for the first time that her beauty was not genuine.
> It was false.[9]

The Careful Approach

The forgetful hearer simply glances at the Word of God and goes his way, but the true hearer gazes at God's Word. To denote this careful look, James uses a Greek word that means "to look at something that is out of the normal line of vision." It is the same word that was used to denote the way Peter, John, and Mary stooped down to look into the empty tomb on resurrection morning (Luke 24:12; John 20:5, 11). It is also found in 1 Peter 1:12 where we are told that the angels desire "to look into" the glories of salvation that are outside of their personal experience. The careful look intently examines the truth and meaning of the Word because there is a desire to put into practice everything that God is saying.

As James pictures this careful student of the Word, he sees him doing what he hears. The word for "doing," the Greek *poieetai,* is found only six times in the entire New Testament, four of them in the book of James. It conveys far more than routine observance of commands. From *poieetai* we get our word "poet," and it speaks of creative obedience:

> A poet is one who puts words together in order to express a thought or feeling in a beautiful manner. That is what God wants us Christians to be—poets, creators of the beautiful. We are to be creative in life. We are to take all the experiences, pleasant and unpleasant, and present them as attractive poems to the world around us.[10]

STEP FOUR—MEDITATION

There is yet another step beyond personal application of the Word. "But he who looks into the perfect law of liberty and continues in it."

There is a basic difference between an explorer and a tourist. The tourist travels quickly, stopping only to observe the highly noticeable or publicized points of interest. The explorer, on the other hand, takes his time to search out all that he can find.

Too many of us read the Bible like tourists and then complain that our devotional times are fruitless. Geoffrey Thomas warns us against such an approach to the Scriptures:

> Do not expect to master the Bible in a day, or a month, or a year. Rather expect often to be puzzled by its contents. It is not all equally clear. Great men of God often feel like absolute novices when they read the Word. The apostle

Peter said that there were some things hard to understand in the epistles of Paul (2 Peter 3:16). I am glad he wrote those words because I have felt that often. So do not expect always to get an emotional charge or a feeling of quiet peace when you read the Bible. By the grace of God you may expect that to be a frequent experience, but often you will get no emotional response at all. Let the Word break over your heart and mind again and again as the years go by and imperceptibly there will come great changes in your attitude and outlook and conduct.[11]

It is crucial that we take the time to explore the Bible if we are to grow. Here are some key Scriptures that extol the virtues of meditation:

This Book of the Law shall not depart from your mouth, but you shall meditate in it day and night, that you may observe to do according to all that is written in it. For then you will make your way prosperous, and then you will have good success. (Josh. 1:8)

Blessed is the man who walks not in the counsel of the ungodly, nor stands in the path of sinners, nor sits in the seat of the scornful; but his delight is in the law of the Lord, and in His law he meditates day and night. (Ps. 1:1–2)

Oh, how I love Your law! It is my meditation all the day. (Ps. 119:97)

Let the words of my mouth and the meditation of my heart be acceptable in Your sight, O Lord, my strength and my Redeemer. (Ps. 19:14)

If you haven't meditated on God's Word in a long time, maybe Donald Whitney's words will set you free to begin anew:

Because meditation is so prominent in many spiritually counterfeit groups and movements, some Christians are uncomfortable with the whole subject and suspicious of those who engage in it. But we must remember that meditation is both commanded by God and modeled by the godly in Scripture.... The kind of meditation encouraged in the Bible differs from other kinds of meditation in several ways. While some advocate a kind of meditation in which you do your best to empty your mind, Christian meditation involves filling your mind with God and truth. For some, meditation is an attempt to achieve complete mental passivity, but biblical meditation requires constructive mental activity. Worldly meditation employs visualization techniques intended to "create your own reality." ... We link meditation with prayer to God and responsible, Spirit-filled human action to effect changes.[12]

STEP FIVE—MEMORIZATION

The casual Bible student is a forgetful student, but the careful Bible student commits to memory the things on which he meditates. Lorne Sanny of the Navigators looked back over his life and evaluated why he took the time to memorize the Bible (NIV). In an abbreviated form, this is what he said:

Deliverance from Sin. The act of memorizing Scripture doesn't keep me from sin. God's Word does: "I have hidden your word in my heart that I might not sin against you" (Ps. 119:11).

Victory over Satan. We are told in Ephesians 6:17 to combat him with "the sword of the Spirit, which is the word of God." (See also Matt. 4:1–11.)

Spiritual Prosperity. Meditating—thinking, chewing, letting the Word of God linger in our minds day and night—brings spiritual prosperity (Ps. 1).

Personal Guidance. Psalm 119:24 says, "Your statutes are my delight; they are my counselors."

Helping Others. "Have I not written thirty sayings for you, sayings of counsel and knowledge, teaching you true and reliable words, so that you can give sound answers to him who sent you?"
(Prov. 22:20–21).[13]

STEP SIX—DEMONSTRATION

James concludes this section of his letter by giving three concrete examples of behaviors that will flow from the life of the person who has taken God's Word seriously. For the third time in this first chapter, he warns his readers about the danger of deception (1:16, 22, 26). It is possible, according to James, to think you are living the Christian life when, in actuality, you are just fooling yourself. The three tests he offers to his first-century readers are just as important for us today.

The Test of Self-Control

When James addresses the subject of the tongue later in this letter, he describes it as "a restless evil, full of deadly poison" (3:8 NIV). He says that if a man is able to control his tongue, "he is a perfect [mature] man" (3:2). Now he ties this matter of self-control to the reality of one's religious claims: "If anyone among you thinks he is religious, and does not bridle his tongue but deceives his own heart, this one's religion is useless" (James 1:26).

The unruly tongue engages in lying, cursing, and swearing, slander, and filthy language. From man's point of view the hasty word, shading of the truth, the subtle innuendo, and the questionable joke are shrugged off as insignificant. Yet from God's perspective they are a violation of the command to love the Lord God and to love one's neighbor as oneself. A breach of this command renders man's religion of no avail.[14]

The Test of Spiritual Compassion

The second acid test of real religion is one's attitude toward those in distress. Here James mentions two groups of people: the widows and the orphans. The social conditions in the first century were very hard on such people, for there were not agencies to protect or aid them. Their only help was to be found among their brothers and sisters in Christ. Old Testament law demanded that they be cared for by God's people: "... the stranger and the fatherless and the widow who are within your gates, may come and eat and be satisfied, that the Lord your God may bless you in all the work of your hand which you do" (Deut. 14:29).

The Lord Jesus went so far as to equate His followers' treatment of the distressed with their treatment of Him. He said:

"For I was hungry and you gave Me food; I was thirsty and you gave Me drink; I was a stranger and you took Me in; I was naked and you clothed Me; I was sick and you visited Me; I was in prison and you came to Me." Then the righteous will answer Him, saying, "Lord, when did we see You hungry and feed You, or thirsty and give You drink? When did we see You a stranger and take You in, or naked and clothe You? Or when did we see You sick, or in prison, and come to You?" And the King will answer and say to them, "Assuredly, I say to you, inasmuch as you did it to one of the least of these My brethren, you did it to Me." (Matt. 25:35–40)

I read about a minister who preached a Sunday sermon about heaven. Next morning, as he was going to town, he met one of his wealthy members who stopped him and said, "Pastor, you preached a good sermon on heaven, but you didn't tell me where heaven is." "Ah," said the preacher, "I am glad of the opportunity this morning. I have just returned from the hilltop up yonder. In that cottage there is a member of our church. She is a widow with two little children. She is sick in one bed and her two children are sick in the other bed. She doesn't have anything in the house—no coal, no bread, no meat, and no milk. If you will buy a few groceries, then go up there yourself and say, 'My sister, I have brought these provisions in the name of the Lord Jesus.' Then ask for a Bible and read Psalm 23, and then go down on your knees and pray—and if you don't see heaven before you get through, I'll pay the bill." The next morning the man said, "Pastor, I saw heaven and spent fifteen minutes there as sure as you are listening."[15]

The Test of Social Corruption

In regard to society, the believer is to walk a fine line. He is to be completely and compassionately involved with the social problems of his day, but he is not to allow the culture that produced those problems to have any impact upon his holy life. In James' words, he is to "keep [himself] unspotted from the world."

When James speaks of the world, he is talking about the system that is under the control of Satan and in opposition to the purpose of God. John Henry Jowett said, "It is life without high callings, life devoid of lofty ideals. Its gaze is always horizontal, never vertical. Its motto is 'forward,' never 'upward.' It has ambition, but no aspiration."[16]

The Christian is to conduct his life in the world in such a way that he will not be ashamed to face His Lord. Peter says that we must be *diligent* in this regard: "Therefore, beloved, looking forward to these things, be diligent to be found by Him in peace, without spot and blameless" (2 Peter 3:14).

When we come to the hearing or reading of the Word of God with the proper preparation of heart, with a careful examination of its truth, with a determined application of its message, when we meditate upon it and hide its words in our hearts, something dramatic will happen in our lives. We will be changed! This is the promise of God Himself: "So shall My word be that goes forth from My mouth; it shall not return to Me void, but it shall accomplish what I please, and it shall prosper in the thing for which I sent it" (Isa. 55:11).

Probably there is no more sensational example of the life-transforming power of the Bible than the legendary story of *Mutiny on the Bounty*. In 1788 the *Bounty*, under Captain William Bligh, set sail for the island of Tahiti in the South Seas. After a voyage of ten months, the ship reached the Friendly Islands in Tonga, and the sailors became attached to the native girls. Upon receiving the order to embark, in April 1789 they mutinied, set the captain and a few men adrift in an open boat, and returned to the island.

Captain Bligh survived his ordeal and eventually arrived home in England. A punitive expedition was sent out, which captured fourteen of the mutineers. But nine of them had transferred to another island, where they formed a new colony. Here they degenerated so fast and became so fierce as to make the life of the colony a hell on earth. The chief reason for this was the distillation of whiskey from a native plant. Quarrels, orgies, and murders were a common feature of their life. Finally, all the men except one were killed or had died off.

Alexander Smith was left alone with a crowd of native women and half-breed children. Then a strange thing happened. In a battered chest, he found a Bible. He read it, believed it, and began to live it. Determining to make amends for his past evil life, he gathered the women and children around him and taught them too. Time rolled on. The children grew up and became Christians. The community prospered exceedingly. Nearly twenty years later, an American ship visited the island and brought back to Europe and England word of its peaceful state. This island was a Christian community. There was no disease, no insanity, no crime, no illiteracy, and no strong drink. Life and property were safe, and the moral standards of the people were as high as anywhere in the world. It was a veritable utopia on a small scale. What had brought about this astounding transformation? Just the reading of a book. That book was the Bible.[17]

WHAT TO DO WHEN JUSTICE ISN'T BLIND
(JAMES 2:1–13)

If you show partiality, you commit sin,
and are convicted by the law as transgressors.

Joel Engel, a Los Angeles–based author who writes frequently for the *New York Times,* tells of an experience he once had aboard a Los Angeles bus:

> Considering the large crowd inside, the lack of voices startled me; only a rustle of newspapers and the groaning diesel engine broke the silence. Several well-dressed men stood in the aisle, so I assumed all seats were taken. But as I moved to the rear, I spotted an empty aisle seat on a double bench—and fathomed at once why it remained unoccupied.
>
> The young man next to the window was breathtakingly ugly, his grotesque face apparently the victim of fibroid tumors. Yet it wasn't only his face that made him so unappealing. His long, filthy, matted hair and tattered clothing warned others away. He was obviously homeless, and it was easy to guess why. He sat with shoulders hunched and eyes fixed through the window ... truly the image of a beast—forlorn and excruciatingly alone.
>
> Nearly paralyzed by pity, I gave silent thanks that my young daughter wasn't with me, asking her inevitable questions about him in a none-too-discreet voice—or

worse, uttering revulsion. But it was because of her that I finally sat down. The kind of man I want my daughter's father to be sits on a bus next to someone whose only crime is extreme ugliness.

I can't pretend I relaxed. My left shoulder and arm scrunched involuntarily, and my entire torso leaned Pisa-like away from him. Continuing to stare out the window, he didn't acknowledge my presence.

The bus made one more stop before entering the freeway. Several people boarded. An elderly woman walked toward the rear. I waited for anyone else, male or female, to offer her a seat. None did, so I stood and motioned to her. "No, I don't want to sit there," she said loudly, "next to him."[1]

It is painful to read this story. We feel anger as we think of this unfortunate man being rejected. We are appalled at the insensitivity of the elderly woman! We are shocked that this could happen in our country, on a public city bus. But what if I told you that this sometimes happens in church?

In fact, it was happening so much in the small churches to which James addressed his letter that he had to devote an entire section of his epistle to the problem. As he confronts social discrimination, his focus is on the rich and the poor, but the principles he gives us are much broader in their application. Rick Warren suggests at least five areas where we as believers can be tempted to discriminate:

- We can discriminate on the basis of *appearance*.
- We can discriminate on the basis of *ancestry*.
- We can discriminate on the basis of *age*.
- We can discriminate on the basis of *achievement*.
- We can discriminate on the basis of *affluence*.[2]

Lewis Smedes in his book *A Pretty Good Person* reminds us that we can all be guilty of sinful discrimination unless we develop the kind of love that sees through the labels we like to put on one another:

We put labels on people the way designers sew labels on their clothes. And then we let the labels tell us what people are and what they are worth. If we value intelligence in children, we label them as fast learners or slow learners, and the first question we ask about any child is how he or she is doing at school. If we value money, we label people as well-to-do, or poor, and the first thing we wonder about people is how much money they make. If we value physical appearance, we label people as attractive or unattractive, and the first thing we ask about a person is what he or she looks like. Here is a church group that puts a premium on stable families and lasting marriages: When a woman in that church gets a divorce, the church labels her a divorced woman, and blinds itself to her reality, to her pains, to her gifts, to her needs.... When people come along who are physically disabled, we label them disabled, and we thereby blind ourselves to the infinite treasure they have to offer us.[3]

In this chapter, James' reasons for rejecting a discriminatory spirit are set forth in a clear and compelling manner. They challenge us to examine our hearts to see if perhaps we are harboring a secret prejudice or hatred.

SOCIAL DISCRIMINATION IS INCOMPATIBLE WITH THE CHRISTIAN FAITH

James addresses his readers as "my brothers," reminding us that the problem he is about to discuss is a family concern. Whenever he uses that term to identify his readers, he is getting ready to point out something that needs to be changed in their lives. Here he is about to unleash a scathing denunciation against all forms of prejudice, favoritism, snobbery, and respect of persons. For many of his Jewish readers, this would be a familiar subject since they would have been

well acquainted with the warnings against discrimination found in the
Old Testament:

> You shall not be partial to the poor, nor honor the person
> of the mighty. (Lev. 19:15)

> You shall not show partiality in judgment; you shall hear
> the small as well as the great. (Deut. 1:17)

> For the Lord your God is God of gods and Lord of lords,
> the great God, mighty and awesome, who shows no partial-
> ity nor takes a bribe. (Deut. 10:17)

> You shall not pervert justice; you shall not show partial-
> ity, nor take a bribe. (Deut. 16:19)

> These things also belong to the wise: It is not good to
> show partiality in judgment. (Prov. 24:23)

> To show partiality is not good, because for a piece of
> bread a man will transgress. (Prov. 28:21)

James' word *partiality* literally means "to receive a face." It portrays
the undue favoritism that was being shown to the wealthier visitors to
the assembly, while little attention was being paid to the poorer ones.
According to James, such conduct was dishonoring to the Lord, who is
never a respecter of persons.

Partiality is mentioned several times in the New Testament. Most
of these occurrences refer to the absence of partiality in God's dealings
with men:

> Then Peter opened his mouth and said, "In truth I perceive
> that God shows no partiality." (Acts 10:34)

> For there is no partiality with God. (Rom. 2:11)

> And you, masters, do the same things to them,
> giving up threatening, knowing that your own Master
> also is in heaven, and there is no partiality with Him.
> (Eph. 6:9)

> But he who does wrong will be repaid for what he has
> done, and there is no partiality. (Col. 3:25)

> And if you call on the Father, who without partiality
> judges according to each one's work, conduct yourselves
> throughout the time of your stay here in fear. (1 Peter 1:17)

James' reference to Jesus Christ as the Lord of Glory draws a dramatic contrast between the true glory of the Lord Jesus Christ and the false glory of the glittering riches that had so captured the attention of the ushers in the assembly.

It is the Lord Jesus Christ Himself who showed us that He was willing to leave the refinements of heaven to sojourn upon this earth. The fact that He became man and then went to the cross should humble and disarm anyone who would entertain the thought of class prejudice in the church (Phil. 2:5–8). The cross itself is a visual demonstration of our need to love all men:

> Consider that cross this way! The vertical beam is longer
> than the horizontal beam, for the vertical beam is reaching
> high and upward to God; the horizontal beam reaches
> outward to the level of all mankind. In the cross, we reach
> high, but we stay on the level to minister to all mankind.
> When we come to believe in the Christ of this cross, our
> concern, our love, our service must be willing to reach
> outward to all mankind as we level with one another,
> without the thought of status in life or of race.[4]

SOCIAL DISCRIMINATION IS INSENSITIVE
TO THE CHURCH'S CALLING

J. B. Phillips's paraphrase of these verses makes this problem sound like it could have occurred last Sunday:

> Suppose one man comes into your meeting well-dressed and with a gold ring on his finger, and another man, obviously poor, arrives in shabby clothes. If you pay special attention to the well-dressed man by saying, "Please sit here, it's an excellent seat," and say to the poor man, "You stand over there, please, or if you must sit, sit on the floor," doesn't that prove that you are making class distinctions in your mind and setting yourselves up to assess a man's quality?[5]

Here comes a man into the local assembly. We see he is a stranger because he doesn't know where to sit. He could be a Christian or a non-Christian, since both attended the services of the early church (1 Cor. 14:23–24). The man is golden fingered and is wearing fine clothes. As soon as it is apparent that he is wealthy, he is given the royal treatment and ushered to the prominent seat in the assembly. The poor man who follows him into the meeting place is shoved to one side and treated with disdain.

The word for assembly in verse 2 is the Greek word *synagogen*, which is the usual term for the Jewish synagogue. This is the only time in the New Testament where the word is used of a Christian gathering. It is a reminder of the overtly Jewish nature of these church services, in which the scribes and the Pharisees occupied the most important seats: "They love the best places at feasts, the best seats in the synagogues" (Matt. 23:6; see also Mark 12:39; Luke 11:43; 20:46).

James' question to those showing favoritism is rhetorical and anticipates an affirmative answer: "Have you not shown partiality among yourselves, and become judges with evil thoughts?" If a judge in a court of law were to allow himself to be affected by the clothing of the defendant, would he not be violating justice? Just so, for a Christian to accept or reject someone on the basis of his outward appearance is no less wrong!

James will have some strong words for the wealthy man later on in his letter, but at this point he is chiding the people in the assembly for the way they handled him when he came into their midst. The issue went far deeper than preferential treatment. It was a barometer of the hearts of the people in the congregation—they were more concerned about money and possessions than people. Instead of being caught up with the glory of the Lord, they were staring at the splendor of the gold ring and the fine clothes. Instead of honoring Jesus Christ, they were paying respect to the rich and despising the poor. Instead of accepting people on the basis of their faith in Christ, they were showing favoritism based on appearance and status.

I read about a woman living on the wrong side of the tracks who wanted to join a very fashionable church. She talked to the pastor about it, and he suggested she go home and think about it carefully for a week. At the end of the week she came back. He said, "Now, let's not be hasty. Go home and read your Bible for an hour every day this week. Then come back and tell me if you feel you should join." Although she wasn't happy about this, she agreed. The next week she was back, assuring the pastor she wanted to become a member of the church. In exasperation he said, "I have one more suggestion. You pray every day this week and ask the Lord if He wants you to come into our fellowship." The pastor did not see the woman for six months. Then he met her on the street one day and asked her what she had decided. She said, "I did what you asked me to do. I went home and prayed. One day while I was praying, the Lord said to me, 'Don't worry about not getting into that church. I've been trying to get into it Myself for the last twenty years.'"

I can't vouch for the accuracy of that story, but Tom Eisenman recalls something that actually did happen one Sunday in the Bel Aire Presbyterian Church:

> When in attendance, Governor Ronald Reagan and Nancy
> usually sat in the same seats just off the center aisle about

two-thirds of the way into the sanctuary. On this particular morning the governor and his wife were late and by the time they got there, two college students had occupied those seats. An usher came down the aisle and asked the students if they would take different seats off to the side. They moved, and Ron and Nancy Reagan were brought in and seated. To his credit the pastor got up from his place in the chancel, walked down and over to the college students and said, "As long as I am pastor of this church, that will never happen to you again."[6]

SOCIAL DISCRIMINATION IS INCONSIDERATE OF GOD'S CHOICES

James makes the point that by their rejection of the poor in favor of the rich, the Christians have dishonored the very people God has singled out for special blessing. The poor are precious in the sight of the Lord. The Scriptures are clear about that:

> The Spirit of the Lord GOD is upon Me, because the LORD has anointed Me to preach good tidings *to the poor.* (Isa. 61:1)

> Jesus answered and said to them, "Go and tell John the things you have seen and heard: that the blind see, the lame walk, the lepers are cleansed, the deaf hear, the dead are raised, *the poor have the gospel preached to them.*" (Luke 7:22)

> Then He lifted up His eyes toward His disciples, and said: "*Blessed are you poor*, for yours is the kingdom of God." (Luke 6:20)

> But *He saves the needy from the sword*, from the mouth of the mighty, and from their hand. So *the poor have hope*, and injustice shuts her mouth. (Job 5:15–16)

For the needy shall not always be forgotten; *the expectation of the poor shall not perish forever.* (Ps. 9:18)

"For *the oppression of the poor*, for the sighing of the needy, now I will arise," says the Lord; "I will set him in the safety for which he yearns." (Ps. 12:5)

He who oppresses the poor reproaches his Maker, but he who honors Him has mercy on the needy. (Prov. 14:31)

He who has pity on the poor lends to the Lord, and He will pay back what he has given. (Prov. 19:17)

Whoever shuts his ears *to the cry of the poor* will also cry himself and not be heard. (Prov. 21:13)

Do not rob the poor because he is poor, nor oppress the afflicted at the gate; for the Lord will plead their cause, and plunder the soul of those who plunder them. (Prov. 22:22–23)

Better is the poor who walks in his integrity than one perverse in his ways, though he be rich. (Prov. 28:6)

Neither James nor the Old Testament writers are saying that God saves only the poor, nor are they saying that the poor are automatically to be understood as righteous and the rich as unrighteous. But they are consistent with the words of Paul written to the Corinthian believers:

For you see your calling, brethren, that not many wise according to the flesh, not many mighty, not many noble, are called. But God has chosen the foolish things of the world to put to shame the wise, and God has chosen the weak things of the world to put to shame the things which are mighty; and the base things of the world and the things

which are despised God has chosen, and the things which
are not, to bring to nothing the things that are, that no
flesh should glory in His presence.... As it is written, "He
who glories, let him glory in the Lord." (1 Cor. 1:26–31)

God does not love the poor more than He loves the rich, but many
more of the poor have responded to the gospel than have the rich and
powerful. This was so widely recognized that among the Jews, "the
poor" was often a designation for "the pious."

> The Gospel has always made a strong appeal to those who
> are poor in earthly goods.... That should not be construed
> to mean that all the poor will be saved, nor does it mean
> that there is anything meritorious in poverty; but it does
> affirm that the poor are not at a disadvantage to accept the
> salvation provided by the Lord. It vividly demonstrates that
> those so often rejected by man have been chosen by God.[7]

SOCIAL DISCRIMINATION IS INCONGRUOUS, GIVEN THE CONDUCT OF THE RICH

James continues his argument by reminding his friends that they are
showing special treatment to the very class of people who are abusing
them. In order to make his point, he asks three questions.

Who Is Oppressing You?

James begs his readers to look at the suffering they are experiencing and to identify the major source of that suffering. "Are not the
instigators of your pain the very class of people that you are fawning all
over in your church services?" he asks.

According to the Old Testament, the oppression of the poor by the
rich was a common occupation in Israel:

> Hear this, you who swallow up the needy, and make the
> poor of the land fail. (Amos 8:4)

> They covet fields and take them by violence, also
> houses, and seize them. So they oppress a man and his
> house, a man and his inheritance. (Mic. 2:2)

> Do not oppress the widow or the fatherless, the alien or
> the poor. Let none of you plan evil in his heart against his
> brother. (Zech. 7:10)

The writer of Hebrews acknowledges that this kind of treatment had been the experience of many who had lived for Christ in New Testament times as well:

> But recall the former days in which, after you were illumi-
> nated, you endured a great struggle with sufferings; partly
> while you were made a spectacle both by reproaches and
> tribulations, and partly while you became companions of
> those who were so treated; for you had compassion on me
> in my chains, and joyfully accepted the plundering of your
> goods, knowing that you have a better and an enduring
> possession for yourselves in heaven. (10:32–34)

Who Is Dragging You into Court?

Not only did the rich oppress the believers, but they also litigated them and tried to rob them through legal means. They dragged them into court to sue them. In the trial of Stephen that led to his martyrdom, we are told that his accusers "set up false witnesses" against him (Acts 6:13). Jesus warned His disciples that this kind of treatment could be expected from the world. "But beware of men, for they will deliver you up to councils and scourge you in their synagogues. You will be brought before governors and kings for My sake, as a testimony to them and to the Gentiles" (Matt. 10:17–18).

Without thinking, these early believers were actually pandering to the very people who were causing them so much harm. Later on in his letter, James scolds the rich for this kind of mistreatment of the poor:

Come now, you rich, weep and howl for your miseries
that are coming upon you! Your riches are corrupted, and
your garments are moth-eaten. Your gold and silver are
corroded, and their corrosion will be a witness against
you and will eat your flesh like fire. You have heaped up
treasure in the last days. Indeed the wages of the laborers
who mowed your fields, which you kept back by fraud,
cry out; and the cries of the reapers have reached the
ears of the Lord of Sabaoth. You have lived on the earth in
pleasure and luxury; you have fattened your hearts as in a
day of slaughter. You have condemned, you have murdered
the just; he does not resist you. (5:1–6)

It is probable that the recipients of James' letter were neither rich
nor poor, but middle class. They were guilty of oppressing the poor
while they themselves were being oppressed by the rich. In other
words, they were experiencing the same kind of treatment they were
dishing out.

Who Blasphemes That Noble Name by Which You Are Called?

Not only did the rich oppress the Christians and drag them into
court, but they also spoke with contempt against the One whom the
Christians loved and served. As we look back over these three questions
posed by James, Homer Kent's summary is very helpful:

James was not denouncing wealth per se as evil. Neither
was he advocating reverse discrimination, whereby the
poor are to be favored at the expense of the rich. He
was arguing against favoritism of any kind. At this point
he was showing how logically and morally inappropriate his readers' particular kind of discrimination was.
It may be helpful to understand that James may have
been using the term "the rich" with the same definition
that Jesus did as "those who trust in riches" (Mark 10:24
nkjv), not merely those who possess money.[8]

SOCIAL DISCRIMINATION IS INDIFFERENT TO THE CHARACTER OF THE LAW

In this section of James' argument, he removes the problem of social discrimination from the category of a simple oversight and places it squarely in the circle of transgression. He emphatically states that the wrong treatment of the poor is a violation of God's law. He identifies this law with the Scripture and brands any violation of it as sin and transgression (2:9). In other words, those who practice prejudice and discrimination are not just inconsiderate; they are lawbreakers and sinners.

James refers to the royal law and defines it like this: "You shall love your neighbor as yourself." This law of love is the law of the kingdom of God, which was stressed by the Lord Jesus Christ throughout His earthly ministry. On one occasion, a Pharisee, who also happened to be a lawyer, asked Jesus a penetrating question designed to trip Him up. "Teacher, which is the great commandment in the law?" Here was Jesus' answer:

> "You shall love the Lord your God with all your heart, with all your soul, and with all your mind." This is the first and great commandment. And the second is like it: "You shall love your neighbor as yourself." On these two commandments hang all the Law and the Prophets. (Matt. 22:36–40)

James' definition of the royal law is a direct quote from the words of Jesus Christ. And our Lord took His words from two great summary statements of the law found in the Old Testament. The first statement outlines man's vertical responsibilities: "Hear, O Israel: The Lord our God, the Lord is one! You shall love the Lord your God with all your heart, with all your soul, and with all your might" (Deut. 6:4–5).

The first four of the Ten Commandments are covered by this summary statement. The man who loves the Lord God with all of his heart and soul and strength will

- not put any other god before Jehovah God—Commandment One;
- not make an idol—Commandment Two;
- not misuse the name of the Lord—Commandment Three;
- remember the Sabbath to keep it holy—Commandment Four.

The second statement outlines man's horizontal responsibilities: "You shall not take vengeance, nor bear any grudge against the children of your people, but you shall love your neighbor as yourself: I am the Lord" (Lev. 19:18).

This is repeated in the New Testament with strong emphasis:

> "You shall love the Lord your God with all your heart, with all your soul, with all your strength, and with all your mind," and "your neighbor as yourself." (Luke 10:27)

> For all the law is fulfilled in one word, even in this: "You shall love your neighbor as yourself." (Gal. 5:14)

The last six of the Ten Commandments are covered by this summary statement. The man who loves his neighbor as himself will
- honor his father and mother—Commandment Five;
- not commit murder—Commandment Six;
- not commit adultery—Commandment Seven;
- not steal—Commandment Eight;
- not give false testimony against his neighbor—Commandment Nine;
- not covet—Commandment Ten.

In the parable of the good Samaritan, Jesus explained that a neighbor was any needy human we have opportunity to help. He also elevated the standard of love for our neighbor from "loving as we love ourselves" to "loving as He has loved us" (see John 15:12).

This is truly the royal law, the supreme law of human relationships given by the King Himself. It includes all other commandments having to do with our relationships with others.

The Bible teaches that this law is a part of the entire law, which stands as a unified whole. Partiality, murder, and adultery are seen to be a part of the whole law. To fail to treat our neighbor as ourself is to be guilty of disregarding the law of God. James is not saying that all sins are the same in magnitude and result, but he is making the point that breaking one of the commandments puts the offender in the class of transgressors.

D. L. Moody compared God's law to a chain of ten links suspend-
ing a man over a precipice. If all ten links break, the man falls to his
doom. If five of the ten links break, the man falls to his doom. And if
only one link breaks, the man falls to his doom just the same.[9]

> The unity of the law emanates from the unity of the
> Lawgiver (2:11). The same God gave both the seventh com-
> mandment, "You shall not commit adultery" (Ex. 20:14),
> and the sixth one, "You shall not murder" (Ex. 20:13). To
> violate either is to violate the law of love toward one's
> neighbor. It is illogical to assume that a person by keeping
> one of the commandments is free to violate any of the
> others with impunity.... A person may not have murdered
> someone or been unfaithful to his spouse, but to harbor
> resentment against a brother or sister still makes one a
> transgressor. Prejudice toward the poor makes one guilty.[10]

> The larger truth James is teaching is that a person
> may in most respects appear to be a very good person
> and yet spoil it all before God by one fault, even a
> so-called respectable fault, a fault for which he may
> often be praised. He may appear moral in his action,
> pure in his speech, and faithful in worship; yet he
> may be judgmental and self-righteous; he may be
> rigid, without sympathy; and when this is the case,
> his so-called goodness is spoiled by his underlying
> faults.[11]

SOCIAL DISCRIMINATION IS IGNORANT
OF THE FUTURE JUDGMENT

The text literally says, "Keep on speaking, and keep on acting as those
who will be judged by the perfect law of liberty" (2:12). James once
again focuses our attention on his main theme of integrity. What we say
must be accompanied by corresponding actions (1:26–27).

We are reminded here that our judgment will be in three distinct areas of our life.

Our *words* will be judged! It was the words of the ushers to the rich and the poor that revealed their hearts.

Our *actions* will be judged! We must also conduct ourselves as those who will be judged some day by the perfect law of liberty.

Our *attitudes* will be judged! Either we have shown mercy, or we have not. Someday the truth about our words, our actions, and our attitudes will be known! The writer of Hebrews reminds us that no creature is "hidden from His sight, but all things are naked and open to the eyes of Him to whom we must give account" (4:13).

The standard of our future judgment is identified as the "law of liberty" or "the law that makes us free." This term was used earlier by James as a synonym for the Word of God (1:25 NEB). At first look, this seems to be a contradiction in terms. How could this law be called the "law of liberty"? Isn't the law a restricter of freedom? Not for the sincere believer.

> In the freedom of the law of love the child of God flourishes. Therefore, the Christian lives not in fear of the law but in the joy of God's precepts. As long as he stays within the boundaries of the law of God, he enjoys complete freedom. But the moment he crosses one of those boundaries, he becomes a slave to sin and loses his freedom.[12]

James ends his sermon on discrimination with a triumphant note in verse 13: "For judgment is without mercy to the one who has shown no mercy. Mercy triumphs over judgment." Jesus taught this truth also:

> Blessed are the merciful, for they shall obtain mercy.
> (Matt. 5:7)

> For if you forgive men their trespasses, your heavenly Father will also forgive you. But if you do not forgive men

their trespasses, neither will your Father forgive your
trespasses. (Matt. 6:14–15)

Judge not, that you be not judged. For with what
judgment you judge, you will be judged; and with the
same measure you use, it will be measured back to you.
(Matt. 7:1–2)

Obviously, James is not talking about believers being rejected by
God at some future judgment. When the Christian stands before God
at the judgment seat of Christ, his salvation is not in question! But
he must still answer for the works done in the flesh, whether they are
good or bad (2 Cor. 5:10).

This is not a presentation of salvation by works! It simply falls in line
with the entire argument of this book. James' point made on almost
every page is that we demonstrate the reality of our faith by the way
we live. Those of us who have truly been changed by the grace of God
have had a dramatic shift in attitude toward others. We no longer see
people in class distinctions; the miracle of the new birth has radically
changed our outlook.

We began this chapter on a busy Los Angeles bus. We shall end
it on a subway in New York City. In his book *The 7 Habits of Highly
Effective People*, Stephen Covey tells about an experience he had that
caused a major "paradigm shift," a major attitude adjustment.

I remember one Sunday morning on a subway in New
York. People were sitting quietly—some reading newspapers, some lost in thought, some resting with their eyes
closed. It was a calm, peaceful scene.

Then suddenly, a man and his children entered the
subway car. The children were so loud and rambunctious
that instantly the whole climate changed.

The man sat down next to me and closed his eyes,
apparently oblivious to the situation. The children were
yelling back and forth, throwing things, even grabbing

people's papers. It was very disturbing. And yet, the man sitting next to me did nothing.

It was difficult not to feel irritated. I could not believe that he could be so insensitive as to let his children run wild like that and do nothing about it, taking no responsibility at all. It was easy to see that everyone else on the subway felt irritated, too. So finally, with what I felt was unusual patience and restraint, I turned to him and said, "Sir, your children are really disturbing a lot of people. I wonder if you couldn't control them a little more?"

The man lifted his gaze as if to come to a consciousness of the situation for the first time and said softly, "Oh, you're right. I guess I should do something about it. We just came from the hospital where their mother died about an hour ago. I don't know what to think, and I guess they don't know how to handle it either."[13]

We blush for Stephen Covey and for all those times when we too have made insensitive judgments!

WHAT TO DO WHEN FAITH DOESN'T WORK
(JAMES 2:14–26)

For as the body without the spirit is dead,
so faith without works is dead also.

James Patterson and Peter Kim conducted a monumental survey that resulted in *The Day America Told the Truth*. In that book they surveyed the American people about many issues, including the relevance of their religious belief. In a chapter entitled "Who Really Believes in God Today?" they wrote:

> What is going on in congregations, parishes, and synagogues across America? The news is good—and bad.
>
> God is alive and very well. But right now in America, fewer people are listening to what God has to say than ever before.
>
> Ninety percent of the people we questioned said that they truly believe in God. It would be the logical conclusion then to think that God is a meaningful factor in today's America. But we reached a different conclusion when we dug deeper with our questions.
>
> In every single region of the country, when we asked how people make up their minds on issues of right and wrong, we found that they simply do not turn to God or religion to help them decide about the seminal or moral issues of the day.
>
> For most people, religion plays virtually no role in shaping their opinions on a long list of important public

questions. This is true even for questions that seem closely related to religion: birth control, abortion, even teaching creationism and the role of women in the clergy.

On not one of those questions did a majority of people seek the guidance of religion in finding answers. Most people do not even know their church's position on the important issues....

Only one American in five ever consults a minister, a priest, or a rabbi on everyday issues.

Half of us haven't been to a religious service for a minimum of three months. One in three haven't been to a religious service for more than a year.

More than half of us (58 percent) went to services regularly while growing up, but less than half of those (27 percent) do so today.

Only one in ten of us believe in all of the Ten Commandments. Forty percent of us believe in five or fewer Commandments.[1]

Charles Colson sees the impact of this shallow faith reflected in our churches today:

People flit about in search of what suits their taste at the moment. It's what some have called the "McChurch" mentality. Today it might be McDonald's for a Big Mac; tomorrow it's Wendy's salad bar; or perhaps the wonderful chicken sandwiches at Chick-fil-A.... Spiritual consumers are interested not in what the church stands for but in the fulfillment it can deliver.... The result is an age of mix'em match'em, salad bar spirituality.[2]

Apparently there were also some in James' day who spoke the language of Christianity without reflecting the reality of its truth in their lives. This section of his letter addresses that problem, and it is not the first time that he has raised the issue:

His entire epistle consists of the tests of true faith, all of which are the practical fruits of righteousness in the life of a believer: perseverance in trials (1:1–12); obedience to the Word (vv. 13–25); pure and undefiled religion (vv. 26–27); impartiality (2:1–13); righteous works (vv. 14–26); control of the tongue (3:1–12); true wisdom (vv. 13–18); hatred of pride and worldliness (4:1–6); humility and submission to God (vv. 7–17); and right behavior in the body of believers (5:1–20).[3]

Faith and works are mentioned together ten times in the thirteen verses of this section. James is about to set forth in very clear tones the major premise of his letter. In his words "Faith without works is dead" the whole of this epistle can be summarized. Faith that is not evidenced by a life of integrity is not biblical faith at all. To James, works are not "an added extra to faith, but an essential expression of it."[4]

The lesson is clear: If we say we have faith, there needs to be some evidence in our lives to back up our claim. The writer asks us to take a look at some of the spurious kinds of faith so that we might be better able to discern real faith—faith with integrity!

REAL FAITH IS MORE THAN VERBAL AFFIRMATION

This is one of the most controversial texts in the New Testament. If it is not carefully understood, it can lead to serious error in a most important area of doctrine. In verse 14 and again in verse 16, James refers to what people "say" about their faith. As he rejects the false say-so faith, he points out several reasons for the failure of this verbal-affirmation faith.

Verbal Faith Does Not Save

James here uses two rhetorical questions to make his point. First, he asks, "What does it profit, my brethren, if someone says he has faith but does not have works? Can faith save him?" In the case of both of these questions, the expected answer is in the negative. A. T. Robertson explains, "The question of James 2:14, introduced by the

Greek participle *me,* grammatically presumes a negative answer: 'Can that faith save him? Of course not!'"[5]

In other words, a faith that does not demonstrate its genuineness in works is not genuine. A few verses later James writes, "For as the body without the spirit is dead, so faith without works is dead also" (2:26). In this regard, John MacArthur is accurate when he concludes:

> Not all faith is redemptive. James 2:14–26 says faith without works is dead and cannot save. James describes spurious faith as pure hypocrisy, mere cognitive assent, devoid of any verifying works—no different from the demons' belief. Obviously, there is more to saving faith than merely conceding a set of facts.[6]

James is simply saying that if one has been truly born anew, his life will be changed. "James was addressing himself to the ever-present conflict between mere assent to a creed and a vital faith which displays itself in action."[7]

> The one thing that James and those close to Christ simply could not accept was the idea that one could make a great profession with words but produce no constructive action. The watching world cannot accept such hypocrisy today either.[8]

Part of the confusion over the second question in verse 14 results from an inadequate translation in the King James Version of the New Testament. When the scholars translated this verse, they chose to ignore the Greek article in front of the word *faith.* In other words, the question is not "Can faith save him?" but "Can *that* faith save him?" James is not contradicting Paul and creating a new means of justification before God. Here is his question:

> "If a man says that he has faith and it is not demonstrated through his works, can that kind of faith save him?"

Answer expected, "No." He was not talking about faith
in general but about "the faith" which the person in his
illustration was claiming to possess.[9]

Alexander Maclaren makes a valid observation when he writes,
"The people who least live their creeds are … the people who shout the
loudest about them. The paralysis which affects the arms does not, in
these cases, interfere with the tongue."[10]

Verbal Faith Does Not Serve

Because verbal faith is powerless to save, it is also incapable of
serving. Once again, James uses a stirring illustration to drive home
his point. He recites a little parable that many believe represented
a common occurrence in the early church. James asks his readers
to imagine a situation in which they are confronted by a Christian
brother or sister who is destitute of food and without adequate
clothing. This person shows up at the door of the believer asking
for help.

If, instead of helping the needy brother, the Christian says to
him, "Depart in peace, be warmed and filled," and does not give him
the things that he needs, that professing Christian has cast doubt
upon the integrity of his own faith. It is this point that the apostle
John makes in his first epistle, "But whoever has this world's goods,
and sees his brother in need, and shuts up his heart from him, how
does the love of God abide in him? My little children, let us not love
in word or in tongue, but in deed and in truth" (3:17–18).

So if faith is not expressed in one's lifestyle, then, according
to James, it may not be genuine faith. The following satire etched
James' lesson into my heart. Perhaps it will have the same impact
on you:

I was hungry, and you formed a humanities club and
discussed my hunger.

I was imprisoned, and you crept off quietly to your
chapel in the cellar and prayed for my release.

I was naked, and in your mind you debated the morality
of my appearance.

I was sick, and you knelt and thanked God for your health.

I was homeless, and you preached to me the spiritual
shelter of the love of God.

I was lonely, and you left me alone to pray for me.

You seem so holy, so close to God, but I'm still very
hungry and lonely, and cold.[11]

The hungry man needs bread and the homeless man needs a roof;
the dispossessed need justice and the lonely need fellowship; the undisciplined need order and the slave needs freedom. To allow the hungry man
to remain hungry would be blasphemy against God and one's neighbor,
for what is nearest to God is precisely the need of one's neighbor. It is
for the love of Christ, which belongs as much to the hungry man as to
myself, that I share my bread with him and that I share my home with
the homeless. If the hungry man does not attain faith, then the guilt
falls on those who refused him bread. To provide the hungry man with
bread is to prepare the way for the coming of grace.[12]

Verbal Faith Does Not Survive

James makes a very strong summary statement in verse 17 when
he writes that faith unaccompanied by works is dead. In other words,
it was never alive, and the lack of any fruit in the life is the proof of a
"profession only" faith. Adamson says, "Having form, this faith lacks
force. It is outwardly inoperative, because it is inwardly dead."[13] James
says that we have the right to see the evidence that one's faith is genuine. Jesus said the same thing:

You will know them by their fruits. Do men gather grapes
from thornbushes or figs from thistles? Even so, every
good tree bears good fruit, but a bad tree bears bad fruit.
A good tree cannot bear bad fruit, nor can a bad tree
bear good fruit. Every tree that does not bear good fruit
is cut down and thrown into the fire. Therefore by their

fruits you will know them. Not everyone who says to Me,
"Lord, Lord," shall enter the kingdom of heaven, but he
who does the will of My Father in heaven.
(Matt. 7:16–21)

Even Martin Luther, who is sometimes cited as an enemy of James'
teaching, wrote the following:

> Oh, it is a living, quick, mighty thing, this faith.... It does
> not ask whether good works are to be done, but before
> the question could be asked it does them, and is always
> doing them. He who does not these good works is a man
> without faith.... Yea, it is impossible to separate works
> from faith, as impossible to separate burning and shining
> from fire.[14]

Before changing directions, James proposes one more hypotheti-
cal situation. He imagines someone stepping forward with a liberal
approach to the entire issue and reasoning like this, "I know that you
are into works, but I'm more into faith. We are both all right ... we
just have a different emphasis in our spiritual lives." While this is a very
loose paraphrase, it is a very accurate representation of what this person
is saying.

Tasker says this unidentified speaker is suggesting that "one
Christian may claim the gift of faith and another the gift of perform-
ing good works ... that the two aspects can be divided and that each
position is legitimate."[15]

James explodes in his reaction to such logic. He says, "Show me
your faith without your works, and I will show you my faith by my
works." *The New American Standard Bible* translates this verse this
way: "You have faith and I have works. I can demonstrate my faith by
my works, but I challenge you to exhibit your faith without works."

> In effect, James says here: "You claim to have 'faith' and
> I claim to have 'works,' actions, behavior. I can prove the

existence and quality of my 'faith' by my works (actions
and behavior) but I defy you to prove to me or any of
the rest of mankind the existence and or quality of your
faith. For I do not believe that without works, actions, and
behavior you can possibly have any genuine faith."[16]

James is not arguing with the importance of faith in the Christian
experience, but he is attacking the validity of a "professed faith" that
produces no outward result in conduct.

REAL FAITH IS MORE THAN MENTAL ASSENT

James' second point about faith is this: Real faith is more than just
mental assent to a system of facts. He uses the demons as his example:
"You believe that there is one God. You do well. Even the demons
believe—and tremble!"

According to James, there are no atheists among the demons. They
tremble and shudder and bristle when they think of the one true God.
Jesus encountered persons possessed by demons during His ministry
as did his disciples, and the demons always recognized Jesus' deity
and spoke respectfully (Matt. 8:29; Mark 1:24; 5:7; Luke 8:28; Acts
16:17). They were sincere, but it was not enough!

In the story of the Gerasene demoniac (Mark 5:1–10;
Luke 8:26–33), we have a clear illustration of such a faith
on the part of the demons. These malicious supernatural
spirits, engaged in seeking to possess and torment men,
readily confessed God's existence and omnipotence;
further, they know that as such He is totally and consis-
tently their enemy. But their "faith" does not transform
their character and conduct or change their prospects for
the future. They establish the sad truth that "belief may
be orthodox, while character is evil."[17]

William Barclay reminds us,

> There is a belief which is purely intellectual. For
> instance, I believe that the square on the hypotenuse of
> a right-angled triangle equals the sum of the squares on
> the other two sides; and if I had to, I could prove it—but
> it makes no difference to my life and living. I accept
> it, but it has no effect upon me.... There is another
> kind of belief I believe that five and five make ten, and,
> therefore, I will resolutely refuse to pay more than ten
> pence for two fivepenny bars of chocolate. I take that
> fact not only into my mind but into my life and action.
> What James is arguing against is the first kind of belief,
> the acceptance of a fact without allowing it to have any
> influence upon life.[18]

No one illustrates the futility of mental-assent faith better than
John Wesley:

> Before John Wesley was a believer, he was a clergyman
> and a missionary who worked with all he had. He
> memorized most of the Greek New Testament. He had
> a disciplined devotional life. As a missionary to the
> American Indians, he slept on the dirt to increase his
> merit and hopefully be accepted by God. But then came
> that celebrated day when he trusted in Christ alone
> for his salvation. It was then that he began a works-
> filled life.... He preached in Saint Mary's in Oxford; he
> preached in the churches, he preached in the mines, he
> preached in the streets, he preached on horseback. He
> even preached on his father's tombstone. John Wesley
> preached 42,000 sermons. He averaged 4,500 miles a
> year. He rode sixty to seventy miles a day and preached
> three sermons a day on an average. When he was
> eighty-three, he wrote in his diary, "I am a wonder to
> myself. I am never tired, either with preaching, writing
> or traveling."[19]

REAL FAITH IS MORE THAN A POSITIVE ATTITUDE

James continues to make his case that faith without action is useless. There are many today who have defined faith as a "positive mental attitude." But faith is more than an attitude; faith is an action. According to James, faith is made perfect by works. This is not a contradiction of Paul's doctrine of justification by faith. Manfred George Gutzke integrates the concepts of faith and works when he writes:

> Faith is significant only when it promotes action. Faith without action is useless. This is the basic principle for everything everywhere, and it is true in every case. It would be true in the matter of farming. It would be true in the matter of insuring a home. It would be true in the matter of conducting a business. If we say that we have faith in anything and we do nothing about it, our faith does not amount to a thing. Faith without action is useless.[20]

Now James appeals to two well-known Old Testament personalities: Abraham the patriarch and Rahab the prostitute.

Abraham the Patriarch

> Was not Abraham our father justified by works when he offered Isaac his son on the altar? Do you see that faith was working together with his works, and by works faith was made perfect? And the Scripture was fulfilled which says, "Abraham believed God, and it was accounted to him for righteousness." And he was called the friend of God. You see then that a man is justified by works, and not by faith only. (James 2:21–24)

Abraham was the most powerful example that James could have chosen. Father Abraham was revered as a man of faith who enjoyed a close relationship with God. Nothing would be considered legitimate truth that was contradicted by Abraham's experience. In Genesis 15 we read of God's promise to the patriarch concerning his future and a son. Showing him the stars of the heavens, God told him that his seed would be as numerous. And Genesis 15:6, quoted by James, says, "And he believed in the Lord, and he accounted it to him for righteousness." That was the first use of the word *believe* in the Bible!

Abraham demonstrates that we are justified by faith alone. But our faith is never alone, for it is always accompanied by works. When he was told by God to take the son of promise, Isaac, and go to Mount Moriah and there sacrifice him upon the altar, Abraham did what God told him to do! How did he do this? And why is he so honored for doing it?

> In his life, Abraham had shown trust and confidence in God by traveling to the promised land, waiting decades for his promised son, Isaac, and finally demonstrating his obedience by being willing to sacrifice him. The supreme test was not so much in his traveling or waiting but in preparing to sacrifice Isaac. Killing his own son meant that the promise would end. But as the writer of Hebrews sums it up, "Abraham reasoned that God could raise the dead, and figuratively speaking, he did receive Isaac back from death" (Heb. 11:19 NIV).[21]

Abraham had to come to some conclusions, and it is in his conclusions that the nature of his faith is found. In the Genesis passage, we are told that he believed that he and Isaac would return from the mountain. "Then on the third day Abraham lifted his eyes and saw the place afar off. And Abraham said to his young men, 'Stay here with the donkey; the lad and I will go yonder and worship, and we will come back to you'" (Gen. 22:4–5).

If Abraham had said, "I believe God," but had refused to obey His commands, he would have had mental-assent faith but not real faith. It was his trip to the mountain, his obvious intention to go through with the sacrifice, that made the difference. We are justified by faith alone, but not by faith that is alone.

James' statement about works has often been used to illustrate the differences between James and Paul. Here James clearly says that Abraham was justified by works, and he quotes Genesis to prove his point. Paul also refers to Genesis and uses it to conclude that Abraham was not justified by works.

> What then shall we say that Abraham our father has found according to the flesh? For if Abraham was justified by works, he has something to boast about, but not before God. For what does the Scripture say? "Abraham believed God, and it was accounted to him for righteousness." Now to him who works, the wages are not counted as grace but as debt. But to him who does not work but believes on Him who justifies the ungodly, his faith is accounted for righteousness. (Rom. 4:1–5)

> … just as Abraham "believed God, and it was accounted to him for righteousness." Therefore know that only those who are of faith are sons of Abraham. (Gal. 3:6–7)

While this may seem to be a contradiction, it is not, when we understand what both writers are saying:

> Paul and James cite different incidents in Abraham's life which illustrate the point each is making. Paul is referring to Abraham's absolute reliance on God's promise, however improbable it seemed (Rom. 4:1–12). Abraham's faith was reckoned or counted to him as righteousness (Gen. 15:6), resulting in a right standing with God. James (v. 21) is referring to the time when Abraham was prepared to sacrifice Isaac, the miraculous son of promise, on Mt. Moriah (Gen. 22). In Paul's example, Abraham had righteousness and salvation reckoned or counted to him as righteousness (Gen. 15:6), resulting in a right standing with God. In the example used by James, Abraham demonstrated the life-changing nature of his earlier experience by his action

of preparing to offer his son in obedience to God. To put
it another way, Paul views the matter from the heavenly
or divine perspective and asserts that we are justified in a
legal, positional sense and that faith is the ground of that
justification. James views the situation from the earthly or
human perspective and asserts that works are the evidence
before men that salvation indeed has occurred. A faith that
saves will result in good works. Ephesians 2:8–10 reveals
clearly the agreement in theology which exists between
Paul and James. We are not saved by faith plus works, but
we are saved by a faith that does work.[22]

Because of this passage, Martin Luther rejected the entire Epistle
of James and called it "a right strawy epistle" and without evangelical
character.[23] But there are few today who see any conflict between the
teaching of Paul and the teaching of James. "They are not antagonists
facing each other with crossed swords; they stand back to back, con-
fronting different foes of the Gospel."[24] Paul was attacking the belief
that works were necessary for salvation. James was attacking a verbal
faith that did not produce godliness in life. They both agreed that
works were the proof of salvation and not the path to salvation.

There is no question ... as some seem to imagine of setting
"works" in opposition to faith as the ground of justification.
No man can, by general busyness or specific good deed ...
merit salvation. Activity is never a rival to faith. We cannot
gain God's commendation by presenting to Him—as Cain
desired—the work of our hands. Faith alone is His requirement: the sole condition upon which He justifies the ungodly.
Such faith always goes hand-in-hand with obedience ...
it is ever fruitful. Relationship to God never leaves the life
unchanged.... Men and women of God will manifest that fact
in godly acts. Faith ever finds expression in works—works of
faith, not the mere doing of good. What these works should
be in individual lives, God will reveal in each case.[25]

Rahab the Prostitute

The second example of faith is Rahab. There could be no greater contrast between two people than between Abraham and Rahab:

> Abraham is a Hebrew, called by God to become the father
> of believers. Rahab is a Gentile, an inhabitant of ancient
> Jericho, destined for destruction by the Israelite army. As a
> man, Abraham is the representative head of God's cov-
> enant people (Gen. 15:17). Rahab is a woman, known only
> as a prostitute.... Abraham ... gave proof of his obedience
> to God for at least three decades.... Rahab knew about
> Israel's God only by hearsay, yet she displayed her faith by
> identifying herself with God's people.[26]

John Calvin believed that James put together "two persons so different in their character in order more clearly to show that no one, whatever may have been his or her condition, nation, or class in society, has ever been counted righteous without good works."[27]

James returns to a rhetorical question as he inquires about Rahab. His question implies a positive answer: "Likewise, was not Rahab the harlot also justified by works when she received the messengers and sent them out another way?" (2:25).

What James fails to mention in his statement is the content of Rahab's faith. She truly had come to believe in God. She said,

> I know that the Lord has given you the land, that the
> terror of you has fallen on us, and that all the inhabit-
> ants of the land are fainthearted because of you. For
> we have heard how the Lord dried up the water of the
> Red Sea for you when you came out of Egypt, and what
> you did to the two kings of the Amorites who were on
> the other side of the Jordan, Sihon and Og, whom you
> utterly destroyed. And as soon as we heard these things,
> our hearts melted; neither did there remain any more
> courage in anyone because of you, for the Lord your

God, He is God in heaven above and on earth beneath.
(Josh. 2:9–11)

Because of her faith, Rahab went into action. She hid the spies and advised them where to flee. She risked her life for them. Because of her active faith, she was spared from death when the walls of Jericho came tumbling down: "By faith the harlot Rahab did not perish with those who did not believe, when she had received the spies with peace" (Heb. 11:31).

Rahab's works were very different from Abraham's, but they had the same effect—they proved that she had a living, working faith, that she was a woman of spiritual integrity.

James' summary statement is yet another vivid illustration of the interrelationship between faith and works. He concludes, "For as the body without the spirit is dead, so faith without works is dead also" (2:26).

The human body is a perfect example for James' concluding argument. Just as the body without the spirit is dead, so faith that does not demonstrate itself with works is also dead. "An inactive faith, entombed in an intellectually approved creed, is of no more value than a corpse. A saving faith is an active faith."[28]

Frank Gaebelein reminds us of the relevancy of this test of faith for this generation of believers, describing it as "a greatly needed corrective to the unreal, verbalistic kind of religion that claims allegiance to high doctrine but issues in living on a low and selfish level."[29]

Gaebelein wrote his warning before a survey of mainline denomination members found that only 32 percent believed their faith had anything to do with their life outside of church.[30]

Many have thought that James 2:14–26 is the hardest passage in the New Testament to interpret. I do not argue with their assessment, but I cannot help but wonder if the difficulty lies in a different direction. As I have pondered these words of our Lord's half brother, I have found that the difficulty for me is in what I clearly do understand. The Christian life must have integrity! As followers of Jesus Christ, we must be set apart from the lifestyle of our contemporary world. Most of all, if we understand James' key illustration, we must be men and women of compassion. We must not turn our brothers and sisters away when they stand at our door in need of that which we are able to supply.

Our message to the watching world must be more than what we say. In the words of Francis of Assisi, "Preach the Gospel all of the time; if necessary, use words." Charles Haddon Spurgeon, in a sermon preached on September 7, 1867, reminded his congregation that the Christian

> serves his Lord simply out of gratitude; he has no salvation to gain, no heaven to lose ... now, out of love to the God who chose him, and who gave so great a price for his redemption, he desires to lay out himself entirely to his Master's service.... The child of God works not *for* life, but *from* life; he does not work to be saved, he works *because* he is saved.[31]

With clear direction Os Guinness sends us marching out of this chapter with a deep commitment to the integrity of our faith:

> Stress obedience apart from faith and you produce legalism. Stress faith apart from obedience and you produce cheap grace. For the person who becomes a Christian, the moment of comprehension leads to one conclusion only— commitment. At that point the cost has been counted ... and a contract for discipleship has been signed. The decision is irreversible. It is not faith going a second mile; it is faith making its first full step, and there is no going back.[32]

WHAT TO DO WHEN YOUR TONGUE ISN'T TIED
(JAMES 3:1–12)

But no man can tame the tongue. It is an unruly evil, full of deadly poison.

A deacon was briefed beforehand on what his role would be at an upcoming missionary banquet and was told to be sensitive to the fact that there would be guests from foreign countries who were not accustomed to American culture.

During the banquet, the deacon found himself seated next to an African man who was hungrily devouring his portion of chicken. Trying to think of some way to communicate with the man, the deacon leaned over and said, "Chomp, chomp, good, huh?" The man, gazing back at the deacon, simply replied, "Mmmmmm, good!"

A few minutes later, as the African man savored a delicious cup of coffee, the deacon leaned over and commented, "Glug, glug, glug, good, huh?" The man, a little uncertain, replied, "Mmmmm, good!"

To the deacon's dismay, when the speaker for the evening was announced, it happened to be the African man next to him. The man got up and delivered a flawless message in Oxford-accented English. Upon concluding, the speaker headed toward the deacon, whose face was aglow with red. The speaker simply said, "Blab, blab, blab, good, huh?"

Does that remind you of the most embarrassing thing you ever said? Isn't it incredible the kind of trouble our tongues can create for us? That little bit of muscle can start wars and stop them, create stress and then relieve it, express love and renounce it, build up friendships and then tear them down again. With our tongues we can praise and worship God, and with those same instruments we can curse God and deny His existence. It is a true proverb that says, "Death and life are in the power of the tongue" (Prov. 18:21).

Dr. Criswell graphically describes the potential for evil that resides in the tongue when he writes:

> There are many people who have never set fire to a man burned at the stake; they have never clapped their hands at the shrieks of those who in agony were being torn apart by a ferocious lion in some colosseum. There are people who have never beat the drums to drown out the agonizing cry of those who were offered to the fiery god of Moloch; but there are people without number who assassinate friends, neighbors, and acquaintances by untrue tale-bearing, vicious and evil words.... I do not think there is anyone of us but has felt the sting of unkind words.[1]

Curtis Vaughan adds these insightful thoughts about the tongue:

> It can sway men to violence, or it can move them to the noblest actions. It can instruct the ignorant, encourage the dejected, comfort the sorrowing, and soothe the dying. Or it can crush the human spirit, destroy reputations, spread distrust and hate, and bring nations to the brink of war.[2]

Of course the problem is not the tongue itself but, rather, man's ability to control it properly. Joseph Butler views the tongue as a renegade member of our bodies and defines lack of control as:

> the disposition to be talking, abstracted from the consideration of what is to be said, with little regard to or thought

of doing either good or harm. As such persons cannot
go on forever talking about nothing, they will go on to
defamation, scandal and gossip rather than be silent. It is
like a torrent which must and will flow and the least thing
imaginable will give it either this or that direction.[3]

Roxane S. Lulofs labels the undisciplined talker as a HARM, an
acrostic for Hit-and-Run Mouth:

a person who, for whatever reason, feels compelled to tell
you just what he thinks of you and your actions, regardless of how well he knows you. His desire is to be heard
without hearing, to be known without knowing. He doesn't
care about getting his facts straight; what he wants is
attention.[4]

Even many of our biblical heroes struggled to control their
tongues:

Moses. They angered Him also at the waters of strife, so
that it went ill with Moses on account of them; because
they rebelled against His Spirit, so that he spoke rashly
with his lips. (Ps. 106:32–33)

Isaiah. So I said: "Woe is me, for I am undone! Because
I am a man of unclean lips, and I dwell in the midst of a
people of unclean lips; for my eyes have seen the King,
the Lord of hosts." Then one of the seraphim flew to me,
having in his hand a live coal which he had taken with the
tongs from the altar. And he touched my mouth with it,
and said: "Behold, this has touched your lips; your iniquity
is taken away, and your sin purged." (Isa. 6:5–7)

Job. Behold, I am vile; what shall I answer You? I lay my
hand over my mouth. (Job 40:4)

Peter. This disciple of the Lord one day boasted: "Even if all are made to stumble because of You, I will never be made to stumble" (Matt. 26:33). But that night Peter sinned with his tongue when he denied the Lord and cursed (Matt. 26:69–75).

Now we know, when Paul lists the five different organs of the body that are the most common vehicles of sin (throat, tongue, lips, mouth, and feet—Romans 3:13–15), why four of them relate to speech!

On a windswept hill in an English country churchyard stands a drab gray slate tombstone. The faint etching reads:

> Beneath this stone, a lump of clay,
> Lies Arabella Young,
> Who, on the twenty-fourth of May,
> Began to hold her tongue.

If James is correct, there are many who will not gain control over their tongues until they, like Arabella, lie cold in the ground. But there is hope! It is possible to learn how to manage our mouths. In each of the five chapters of James' letter, including this extended section in chapter 3, he has something to say about the tongue:

> So then, my beloved brethren, let every man be swift to hear, slow to speak, slow to wrath. (1:19)

> If anyone among you thinks he is religious, and does not bridle his tongue but deceives his own heart, this one's religion is useless. (1:26)

> So speak and so do as those who will be judged by the law of liberty. (2:12)

> Do not speak evil of one another, brethren. He who

speaks evil of a brother and judges his brother, speaks evil
of the law and judges the law. But if you judge the law, you
are not a doer of the law but a judge. (4:11)

But above all, my brethren, do not swear, either by
heaven or by earth or with any other oath. But let your
"Yes" be "Yes," and your "No," "No," lest you fall into
judgment. (5:12)

Since many have referred to James' letter as the Proverbs of the
New Testament, we should not be surprised to find much additional
material on the use of the tongue in that Old Testament book:

In the multitude of words sin is not lacking, but he who
restrains his lips is wise. (10:19)

Lying lips are an abomination to the Lord, but those who
deal truthfully are His delight. (12:22)

He who guards his mouth preserves his life, but he who
opens wide his lips shall have destruction. (13:3)

A soft answer turns away wrath, but a harsh word stirs
up anger. (15:1)

These are just a few of the many references to the tongue in the
book of Proverbs. We might greatly increase our discipline of the
tongue if we would make an extensive study of Solomon's wisdom in
Proverbs. But for now, we need to focus our attention on James' words
of instructions to his scattered Christian friends.

THE POWER OF THE TONGUE TO INFLUENCE MANY

James begins right at the top of the Jewish religious hierarchy. His
first words are for teachers, who are prominent for using their tongues.

By making this statement first, James demonstrates that this issue is a menace for everyone, from the top down. He warns that there is a stricter judgment awaiting those who teach, because they have the power to influence so many others. How often I have read that statement and felt a twinge of fear in my heart. Look at Jesus' words about the responsibility of influence: "But whoever causes one of these little ones who believe in Me to sin, it would be better for him if a millstone were hung around his neck, and he were drowned in the depth of the sea" (Matt. 18:6).

William Barclay believes that a teacher struggles all of his life to avoid two pitfalls:

> He must have every care that he is teaching the truth, and not his own opinions or even his own prejudices. It is fatally easy for a teacher to distort the truth and to teach not God's version, but his own. He must have every care that he does not contradict his teaching by his life.... He must never get into the position when his scholars and students cannot hear what he says for listening to what he is.[5]

This caution about teaching reflects the New Testament principle that greater knowledge means greater responsibility: "For everyone to whom much is given, from him much will be required; and to whom much has been committed, of him they will ask the more" (Luke 12:48).

THE POTENTIAL OF THE TONGUE TO INDICATE MATURITY

James says that we all stumble in many things. We can all say amen to that! But he points out that if we do not stumble in the use of our tongue, we are *perfect* and able to bridle the whole body.

In other words, if we can control our tongues, then we will not have any trouble in controlling the rest of the body. The control of the tongue is the most difficult assignment! The word *perfect* here means "maturity." A true mark of Christian maturity is the control of the tongue! Since a teacher uses his tongue more than most, he is very vulnerable in this regard:

> The more we say, the more we are likely to stumble. The more we do for Christ, the more mistakes we are likely to make, and the more criticisms we are likely to incur. The most criticized person in the house of God is the most active one in both words and deeds. The person who does nothing is seldom criticized.[6]

THE PICTURES OF THE TONGUE THAT ILLUSTRATE MEANING

In an earlier chapter, we pointed out James' fondness of illustrations. Each section of his letter is salted with down-to-earth pictures. In order to press home his point about the tongue, he employs four examples.

The Horse and the Bridle

James' first illustrations are from the two most obvious things guided or steered by man in that day—the horse and the ship. He says, "We put bits in horses' mouths that they may obey us, and we turn their whole body" (3:3).

Without direction a horse can serve no useful purpose to man. It is only when a bit is placed in the horse's mouth that it becomes disciplined and directed. And the horse cannot bridle itself; this must be done by man. When the bit is placed in the horse's mouth, then the horse can become useful to man's purposes.

A. B. Simpson, founder of the Christian and Missionary Alliance Church, captures James' argument:

> Just as a man's mouth is the test of his character, so the horse's mouth is the place to control him. We put bits in their mouths, and by these turn about their whole body, so that a little bit of steel and a little thong of leather will

hold a fiery steed, and turn him at the touch of a woman's
hand. So the tongue is like a bridle, which can be put upon
us. With a fiery horse you put a curb in his bit. The idea is
to hurt him, if he pulls against the bit. So God has given to
us checks upon our tongue, making it hurt us, if we speak
unadvisedly.[7]

So too, a man with an unbridled tongue can serve no useful purpose to God. He stumbles in many things, especially in the misuse of
his mouth. Someone has noted that almost every sin is in some way
related to the abuse of the tongue. So when the tongue is brought
under the control of God, then man is brought under control as well.
The Greek construction in this paragraph goes way beyond the idea of
restraining the horse or the man. The concept of bridling describes the
process of being led and directed toward a positive goal.

The Ship and the Rudder

James now turns from the horse to the ship. "Look also at ships:
although they are so large and are driven by fierce winds, they are
turned by a very small rudder wherever the pilot desires" (3:4).

Most of James' readers would have seen the large cargo ships of that
day, since Israel bordered on the Mediterranean Sea. They probably
would have felt the same awe that we feel when we stand on the dock
and look up at a giant cruise ship. Perhaps they would have thought, as
we do, "How does something that massive stay afloat?"

Of course, the ships of that day were not nearly as large as ours, but
they were still large. The Egyptian grain ship on which Paul was shipwrecked carried 276 passengers in addition to its cargo (Acts 27:37).
Since these were true sailing vessels, it was not only the size of the ship
but also the power of the wind that made them difficult to control.
And yet that control was wielded by the tiny rudder!

On May 21, 1941, the "unsinkable" German battleship the *Bismarck*
was sighted in the North Atlantic. Immediately planes and ships from
the British navy sped to the scene. As the *Bismarck* headed toward the
German-controlled French coast where it would be safe from attack, to

the astonishment of all, the massive battleship suddenly swung around and reentered the area where the British ships were massed in greatest strength. At the same time, she began to steer an erratic zigzag course, which made it much easier for the British to overtake her. You see, a torpedo had damaged her rudder, and without its control, the "unsinkable" *Bismarck* was sunk. As the rudder controls a ship, so the tongue controls a person.

The Forest Fire and the Spark

Just as the giant horse is controlled by the tiny bit and the massive ship is governed by the little rudder, so a gigantic fire is started by the tiny spark. In other words, the tongue may not be very big, but we should not let its size cause us to underestimate its potential!

Here are some of James' most direct words of warning: "And the tongue is a fire, a world of iniquity. The tongue is so set among our members that it defiles the whole body, and sets on fire the course of nature; and it is set on fire by hell" (3:6).

The great Chicago Fire in 1871 burned down almost one-half of the city, destroying 1,700 buildings; killing over 250 people; and leaving 125,000 persons homeless. In 1953 a pan of rice boiled over onto a charcoal stove in a small home in Korea. Before twenty-four hours had passed almost 3,000 buildings were completely destroyed within an area covering one square mile. Those of us who live in Southern California have discovered that thousands of acres of land can be destroyed very quickly because of one small spark from a careless camper. Simon J. Kistemaker writes:

> One spark is sufficient to set a whole forest ablaze: stately oaks, majestic cedars, and tall pine trees are reduced to unsightly stumps of blackened wood. And that one spark usually can be attributed to human carelessness and neglect. When we calculate the annual damage done to our forests by devastating fires, the amount runs into the millions in addition to the untold

suffering and death inflicted on the wildlife of the
stricken areas.[8]

When James writes that the tongue "sets on fire the course of
nature," he uses a very unique expression. *The New American Standard
Bible* translates that phrase, "sets on fire the course of our life." Vernon
Doerksen explains, "Our whole life cycle from birth to death is set on
fire by our tongue—the cycles or routines of everyday life are set on fire
by the vicious, uncontrolled tongue."[9]

According to James, this fire in the tongue is ignited from hell!
The word that is translated "hell" is *gehenna*, which Christ describes
in Matthew 5:22 as "hell fire." James is the only place where *gehenna*
is used outside of the Gospels. Zodhiates graphically elaborates on the
meaning of the word:

> This is a Chaldean word, which was the name of a valley
> on the southeast of Jerusalem where Moloch, an idol
> having a form of a bull, dwelt and received into his fiery
> arms little children thrown there as part of heathen
> sacrifice. The word actually means "the valley of lamenta-
> tion," and the Jews so abhorred this place because of these
> horrible sacrifices that, after they had been abolished by
> King Josiah (2 Kings 23:10), they cast into it not only all
> manner of refuse, but even the dead bodies of animals
> and of unburied criminals who had been executed. And
> since fires were always needed to consume dead bodies,
> the place came to be known as "the gehenna of fire." In
> the Gospels the word occurs some ten times from the lips
> of the Lord Jesus Christ, describing the place of the future
> punishment of the wicked, "where their worm dieth not,
> and the fire is not quenched" (Mark 9:48 kjv).
>
> And as someone has said, "Hell is the rubbish heap of
> the universe." James is most careful in the presentation
> of symbolic figures. He tells us that the evil tongue defiles
> the whole body. When the whole body is defiled, what

good is it but to be thrown on the refuse heap and burned? All evil talk, James says, has its beginning in hell and will cause the whole body, the whole personality, to burn in hell. These are serious words, and we shall do well to heed them. The fire that we start with our tongues has been borrowed from hell and it is going to lead us and others there.[10]

The Animal and the Animal Trainer

Now we come to the final illustration. James says that we are able to control every kind of beast and animal, but that we have not yet learned how to control the tongue. The backdrop of this statement is creation. Man was to rule over the fish, birds, cattle, and every creeping thing (Gen. 1:26). When Noah came out of the ark, God reiterated His purpose: "And the fear of you and the dread of you shall be on every beast of the earth, on every bird of the air, on all that move on the earth, and on all the fish of the sea. They are given into your hand" (Gen. 9:2).

Today, the nature of the animal has been tamed by the nature of man. We have dancing bears, trained seals, talking dolphins, acrobatic birds, charmed snakes, dogs jumping through hoops, lions with their mouths open wide and the trainer's head inside. We have elephants that march in line behind one another with riders perched on top. All of these things happen, but the tongue is untamed and untamable without God's help. When man fell into sin, he lost his ability to govern himself.

THE POISON OF THE TONGUE THAT INFECTS THE MOUTH

The final indictment of the tongue is given by James in verse 8: "It is an unruly evil, full of deadly poison." "The picture is that of a poisonous snake whose tongue is never at rest and whose fangs are filled with lethal venom. Man's tongue is unstable, elusive, restless. Besides, it is full of a death-bringing poison."[11]

The Greek word translated "poison" also means "arrow." How

often the tongue is used to shoot arrows at others, with deadly results. Someone has calculated that for every word in Hitler's *Mein Kampf*, 125 lives were lost in World War II. The psalmist reminds us that we must never underestimate the damage that can be done by the tongue:

> Your tongue devises destruction, like a sharp razor, working deceitfully. You love evil more than good, lying rather than speaking righteousness. You love all devouring words, you deceitful tongue." (52:2–4)

> The words of his mouth were smoother than butter, but war was in his heart; his words were softer than oil, yet they were drawn swords." (55:21)

> Who sharpen their tongue like a sword, and bend their bows to shoot their arrows—bitter words, that they may shoot in secret at the blameless; suddenly they shoot at him and do not fear. (64:3–4)

> They sharpen their tongues like a serpent; the poison of asps is under their lips. (140:3)

Here are two types of poison that can infect the mouth.

The Poison of Gossip

Gossip has been dubbed the favorite indoor sport of many who call themselves Christians. Only we don't call it gossip; we say we are "sharing prayer requests." Sportswriter Morgan Blake writes about gossip in these chilling words:

> I am more deadly than the screaming shell from the howitzer. I win without killing. I tear down homes, break hearts, and wreck lives. I travel on the wings of the wind. No innocence is strong enough to intimidate me, no purity

pure enough to daunt me. I have no regard for truth,
no respect for justice, no mercy for the defenseless. My
victims are as numerous as the sands of the sea, and often
as innocent. I never forget and seldom forgive. My name is
Gossip.[12]

John Dryden, a seventeenth-century British dramatist and poet, once commented on man's propensity to gossip:

> There is a lust in man no charm can tame,
> Of loudly publishing his neighbor's shame.
> Hence, on eagle's wings immortal scandals fly,
> While virtuous actions are but born and die.[13]

Here is just a sampling of the indictment of this ugly pastime in Proverbs:

> An ungodly man digs up evil, and it is on his lips like a
> burning fire. A perverse man sows strife, and a whisperer
> separates the best of friends. (16:27–28)

> He who repeats a matter separates friends. (17:9)

> The words of a talebearer are like tasty trifles, and they
> go down into the inmost body. (18:8)

> Like a madman who throws firebrands, arrows, and
> death, is the man who deceives his neighbor, and says, "I
> was only joking!" Where there is no wood, the fire goes
> out; and where there is no talebearer, strife ceases.... The
> words of a talebearer are like tasty trifles, and they go
> down into the inmost body. (26:18–22)

One woman gossiped about another to such an extent that the second woman was almost destroyed. The first woman later discovered that the things she had been saying were not true. She went to her wise pastor to ask him what she should do to make things right. Her pastor told her to take a pillow of feathers and scatter them up and down the streets of the city and then come back and see him the next day.

Though this seemed like strange advice, she followed his instructions. When she returned, he told her to go back through the streets of the city and gather up all the feathers that she had scattered the day before. The woman protested, "I could never find those feathers again, because the wind has blown them all over the place." To which her pastor replied, "Nor can you gather back all the words that you said about the other woman."

Before we leave the subject of gossip, we need to be reminded that the person who listens to gossip also has a responsibility. Gossip would soon die out if we all refused to entertain it in our conversations.

The Poison of Flattery

"If gossip is saying behind a person's back what you would never say to his face, flattery is saying to a person's face what you would never say behind his back."[14] And once again the Psalms reinforce the warning:

> For there is no faithfulness in their mouth; their inward
> part is destruction; their throat is an open tomb; they
> flatter with their tongue. (5:9)

> They speak idly everyone with his neighbor; with
> flattering lips and a double heart they speak. May the Lord
> cut off all flattering lips, and the tongue that speaks proud
> things. (12:2–3)

James brings a powerful conclusion to his sermon on the tongue. He cannot conceive of men using the tongue to praise the Lord in one moment and then to destroy each other in the next. "With it we bless our God and Father, and with it we curse men, who have been made in the similitude of God. Out of the same mouth proceed blessing and cursing. My brethren, these things ought not to be so" (3:9–10).

Robert Brow thinks the key to understanding these verses lies in the use of the word *logos* in James 3:2. "If any man offend not in word (*logos*) and tongue, he is a perfect man, and able to bridle the whole body." He explains that in classical Greek, *logos* was both the spoken word and the inward thought behind that spoken word. He believes that "you can't control the tongue, if your logos is wrong."[15]

It is said that General George Patton was violently profane and yet deeply religious. He prayed before battles and knelt beside the beds of the wounded to intercede for them. But if he was in the presence of a coward, or if the tide of the war went wrong, he flew into a tirade of blasphemy and foul language that would curl the ears of the Devil himself. Whatever concept of manhood you might associate with Patton, one thing is for sure—he was not a godly man. His *logos* was essentially evil.

> Some people go through life cursing their luck, their boss, their spouse, Jews or Arabs, women's lib or male chauvinism, big business or the unions. When the logos of cursing infects your mind, there is no way your tongue can be sweet. The cursing will show in your scowl.
>
> The alternative is the logos of blessing. You praise God for what He will do in your nation; you praise God that even the politicians are under His ultimate control; you praise Him for every member of your family, and for every thorn in your flesh at work. You even bless God for those hypocrites and self-willed nuisances in church.
>
> If you are praising for something or someone, your tongue is very unlikely to say a wrong word.[16]

According to James, just as a spring cannot produce both fresh and bitter water at the same time, neither should our tongues be capable of blessing and cursing. "To utter forth blessing and cursing from the same source is incongruous.... It indicates that something completely out of character, something utterly incongruous, which ought not to happen, was happening."[17]

Blessing and cursing are no more compatible than fig trees and olive berries, than a vine and figs, than salt water and sweet water coming from the same source. Jesus expressed this thought on one occasion: "You will know them by their fruits. Do men gather grapes from thornbushes or figs from thistles?" (Matt. 7:16).

Dietrich Bonhoeffer was a German Lutheran pastor and theologian who openly criticized Hitler and his anti-Jewish policy and, because of that, was executed by Hitler on April 9, 1945. Although he used his tongue as a powerful weapon against the evils of the Nazi rule, he also spoke out against Christians who used their tongues to unfairly wound one another. In his classic *The Cost of Discipleship*, he penned words that could have been born in the third chapter of James:

> Every idle word we utter betrays our lack of respect for our neighbor, and shows that we place ourselves on a pinnacle above him and value our own lives higher than his. The angry word is a blow struck at our brother, a stab at his heart; it seeks to hit, to hurt and to destroy. A deliberate insult is even worse, for we are then openly disgracing our brother in the eyes of the world, and causing others to despise him. With our hearts burning with hatred, we seek to annihilate his moral and material existence. We are passing judgment on him, and that is murder. And the murderer himself will be judged.[18]

WHAT TO DO WHEN WISDOM IS FOOLISH
(JAMES 3:13–18)

Who is wise ... among you? Let him show by good conduct that his works are done in ... wisdom.

In an article entitled "America's Last Men and Their Magnificent Talking Cure," Os Guinness tells about a secret moment in history that may have been a harbinger of some of Christianity's most volatile current struggles:

> In 1909, at the height of one of the busiest periods of immigration in American history, two arrivals from Europe stood at the rail of their ship as it passed the Statue of Liberty and entered New York harbor. The older one, a fifty-three-year-old Jew born in Moravia, poked the younger man from Switzerland in the ribs and said with excitement, "Won't they get a surprise when they hear what we have to say to them?"
>
> ... The speaker was Sigmund Freud. His companion was his friend and disciple Carl Gustav Jung. And in the form of psychoanalysis and its legacy, "What we have to say to them," has had as much impact on the United States in the twentieth century as any one set of human ideas and words.... Within six years of their arrival their ideas had set up a reverberation in human thought and conduct of which few as yet dare to predict the consequences.

... What were once the esoteric ideas of a small and
controversial European elite have mushroomed in America
into a dominant academic discipline and a vast, lucrative
industry. More than five hundred brand-name therapies now
jostle to compete for millions of clients in an expanding
market of McFreud franchises and independent outlets that
pull in more than $4 billion a year.... The couch has become
as American as the baseball diamond and the golden arches.

... In the process, the United States became the world
capital of psychological-mindedness and therapeutic
endeavor.... Although America had only 6 percent of the
world's population, it boasted over a third of the world's
psychiatrists and over half the world's clinical psychologists.... Eighty million Americans have now sought help from
therapists. An estimated ten million are doing so every year.[1]

While this chapter is not a tirade against psychiatry and psychology, it is an honest look at James' strong censure of the world's wisdom.
Certainly many of the ideas put forth by Freud and Jung would qualify
as examples. In a positive way, James wants to make the point that the
wisdom necessary for a solid life foundation is not the wisdom of the
world. It is the wisdom that comes from God alone. The apostle Paul
wrote that the world by its wisdom cannot know God (1 Cor. 1:21).
It is God's wisdom that leads a man to his Creator and enables him
to see life from an eternal perspective. Lloyd John Ogilvie helps us to
understand the special nature of God's wisdom when he writes:

Wisdom is the special gift of the Lord for our quest to
know His will. It is beyond intellect and knowledge. In a
willing mind, wisdom enables a person to hear with God's
ears and see with His eyes. Wisdom is inspired depth-per-
ception into people and situations. It is the vertical thrust
of the mind of God into our minds, making discernment
possible on the horizontal level of human affairs. With wisdom we can penetrate the mysteries of God—His nature,

plan, and purpose.... If we long to know God's maximum
for our lives, wisdom is the gift we need and want in order
to do the will of God.[2]

In the last chapter we examined James' warnings concerning our use
of the tongue. We learned that the tongue reflects the heart, that our
speech demonstrates the inner quality of our life. Now James addresses
that inner reality as he presents the dramatic contrast between earthly
wisdom and heavenly wisdom. Here is his assessment of the world's
wisdom:

> Who is wise and understanding among you? Let him
> show by good conduct that his works are done in the
> meekness of wisdom. But if you have bitter envy and
> self-seeking in your hearts, do not boast and lie against
> the truth. This wisdom does not descend from above, but
> is earthly, sensual, demonic. For where envy and self-
> seeking exist, confusion and every evil thing are there.
> (3:13–16)

As we examine earthly and heavenly wisdom, we shall do so by
carefully looking at their origin, operation, and outcome.

THE ORIGIN OF WORLDLY WISDOM

Wisdom consists of having insight and expertise in order to draw conclusions that are correct. An old proverb sums it up this way, *Foresight is
better than hindsight, but insight is best.* The best insight that the world
can offer is defined by James as earthly, sensual, and demonic.

Earthly Wisdom

> Where is the wise? Where is the scribe? Where is the
> disputer of this age? Has not God made foolish the wisdom
> of this world? For since, in the wisdom of God, the world

through wisdom did not know God, it pleased God through the foolishness of the message preached to save those who believe. (1 Cor. 1:20–21)

These words of the apostle Paul echo the appraisal of wisdom presented by James. In the first two chapters of his first letter to the Corinthian church, Paul provides a contrast of the world's wisdom and God's wisdom. Note the differences:

The world's wisdom is the wisdom of words (1:17–24).
God's wisdom is the wisdom of power (2:4–5).

The world's wisdom operates by man's word (2:4). God's wisdom operates by the Spirit's words (2:13).

The world's wisdom is championed by the spirit of the world (2:12). God's wisdom is championed by the Spirit of God (2:12).

The world's wisdom is foolishness to God (1:20). God's wisdom is foolishness to the world (2:14).

The world's wisdom is declared by the philosopher (1.20). God's wisdom is declared by the preacher (1:21; 2:4).

The world's wisdom brings ignorance (1:21). God's wisdom brings knowledge (2:12).

The world's wisdom leads to condemnation (1:18). God's wisdom leads to salvation (1:18; 2:7).

From the beginning, man has been trying to reach up to God by his own wisdom, but, as Paul explains in the book of Romans, it has always backfired: "Although they knew God, they did not glorify Him as God, nor were thankful, but became futile in their thoughts, and their foolish hearts were darkened. Professing to be wise, they became fools" (Rom. 1:21–22).

Even Christians must fight the temptation to build their lives on the foundation of the world's wisdom. Paul warned the Colossians, "Beware lest anyone cheat you through philosophy and empty deceit, according to the tradition of men, according to the basic principles of the world, and not according to Christ" (2:8).

Whenever man has tried to construct his life on a foundation of the world's wisdom, he has ended up defeated, discouraged, and disappointed. Think back to the beginning of biblical history, and take note of the consistent pattern of failure.

The Tower of Babel was man's attempt to reach God through his own wisdom. The result was total confusion.

Abraham followed the wisdom of the world when he left God's appointed place during a time of famine. It made human sense to go to Egypt, but the result for Abraham was his sinful relationship with the Egyptian woman, Hagar, and ultimately the birth of Ishmael.

Lot followed the wisdom of the world and chose all the good land. His choice made sense on paper, but the result was his own spiritual demise and the loss of his wife.

We could go on through the pages of the Old and New Testaments and cite example after example of the world's wisdom and its evil effects. Instead of going forward in the Scripture, however, I want you to join me as we turn backward to the very beginning of the Bible—to the beautiful garden of Eden, the birthplace of man's wisdom.

This event recorded in Genesis 3 provides the first mention of the world's wisdom. Here are the words of Satan, the Tempter, as he promises Eve this new kind of wisdom, and here is her response as she embraces his promise:

> Then the serpent said to the woman, "You will not surely die. For God knows that in the day you eat of it your eyes will be opened, and you will be like God, knowing good and evil." So when the woman saw that the tree was good

for food, that it was pleasant to the eyes, and a tree desirable *to make one wise*, she took of its fruit and ate. She also gave to her husband with her, and he ate. (vv. 4–6)

The wisdom Adam and Eve received when they disobeyed God in favor of Satan's promise was the wisdom of the world, which James says is earthly, natural, and demonic.

Natural Wisdom

The word "sensual" is the Greek word *pseuke*. It means "natural," or "soulish," and is translated in 1 Corinthians 2:14 as "the natural man." The words *psychology* and *psychiatry* are derivatives of this word. When *pseuke* is used to describe the wisdom of the world, it means "natural" as opposed to "spiritual." Dr. James Boyer says there are four things that are always true of the natural man:

1. He has a limited nature. His spirit is dead and therefore he cannot respond to God.
2. He has a prejudiced disposition. The things of God are not welcomed in his life.
3. He has a distorted judgment. The things of God are moronic to him.
4. He has inadequate abilities. He lacks the necessary equipment to examine spiritual things. He is like a blind man in an art gallery ... like a deaf man at a symphony.[3]

Demonic Wisdom

When the word "demonic" is used to describe the world's wisdom, it settles once and for all the identity of the mastermind behind this world's system. It is Satan himself.

Satan's wisdom is alive and well, and you and I are more affected by it than we know. It is the dominating influence in our world. It is piped into our homes on the average of seven hours per day, and without constant vigil we are intimidated by its principles.

The apostle John explains how the world's wisdom can undermine the integrity of the believer:

Do not love the world or the things in the world. If
anyone loves the world, the love of the Father is not in
him. For all that is in the world—the lust of the flesh,
the lust of the eyes, and the pride of life—is not of the
Father but is of the world. And the world is passing
away, and the lust of it; but he who does the will of God
abides forever. (1 John 2:15–17)

The wisdom of the world operates through "the lust of the
flesh, the lust of the eyes, and the pride of life." It was this threefold
approach that Satan used on Eve (Gen. 3:1–7). It was the same
strategy he tried to implement when he tempted Jesus Christ (Matt.
4:1–11). And it is still his battle plan for you and me today.

The crucial thing to keep in mind, if you are a believer, is this:
The wisdom of the world belongs to the old life, the life BC, before
Christ. It should not characterize the new you because you are to
live in a new realm. That's what Paul was trying to get across to the
Ephesian believers when he wrote:

And you He made alive, who were dead in trespasses
and sins, in which you once walked according to the
course of this world, according to the prince of the
power of the air, the spirit who now works in the sons of
disobedience, among whom also we all once conducted
ourselves in the lusts of our flesh, fulfilling the desires
of the flesh and of the mind, and were by nature children of wrath, just as the others. But God, who is rich
in mercy, because of His great love with which He loved
us, even when we were dead in trespasses, made us alive
together with Christ (by grace you have been saved).
(2:1–5)

THE OPERATION OF WORLDLY WISDOM

James now presents four distinct characteristics of the world's wisdom.

Jealous Anger

The wisdom of the world exalts man and tries to glorify him. The person who operates on the basis of the world's wisdom is always seeking to promote himself. It is reminiscent of the argument among the apostles over the place of honor in the kingdom. The number one ploy of such a person is the age-old game of pushing oneself up by pushing someone else down.

The secular booksellers are not even trying to cover up this self-centered philosophy anymore. They've gone public! Books on how to be number one ... how to intimidate your opponent ... your employees ... your wife ... or your date are best sellers. It's the world's wisdom, packaged and ready to market, and people are buying not only the books but also the ideas.

Selfish Ambition

The word "strife" is the translation we read in most of our Bibles. This word was used in New Testament times to describe a politician who was canvassing for his job. Later the word came to mean "a party spirit." Today we would call this "manipulation." We manipulate to get our man in office. We manipulate to get ourselves elected. We try to befriend influential people, so we can manipulate others through them. In opposition to the wisdom of God, which is pure and peaceable, this wisdom of the world has a hidden agenda. Don't forget, such practices find their source in Satan. William Barclay reminds us:

> You can tell what a man's relationship with God is by looking at his relationship with other people. If a man is at variance with his fellowman and if he's a quarrelsome, competitive, argumentative troublemaking creature, he may be a diligent church attender, he may even be a church officebearer, but he's not a man of God. If a man is distant from his fellowman, it is good proof that he is distant from God. If he is divided from his fellowman, he is divided from God.[4]

Paul settles the issue for Christians everywhere when he writes, "Let nothing be done through selfish ambition or conceit, but in lowliness of mind let each esteem others better than himself" (Phil. 2:3).

Proud Arrogance

The phrase "glory not" (James 3:14 KJV) is a warning against arrogance and bragging. The wisdom of the world is identified by the arrogance of the one who is under its spell. Pride loves to boast.

Paul was dealing with this as he wrote his second letter to the Corinthians. He wrote it because he was being constantly attacked by the Corinthian people. In this moving passage, he explains why some people boast and then points out why it is such an absurd thing to do: "For we dare not class ourselves or compare ourselves with those who commend themselves. But they, measuring themselves by themselves, and comparing themselves among themselves, are not wise" (10:12).

According to Paul such boasting is unwise because it is based on the absurdity of self-comparison. The whole concept makes me think of a prayer that was jokingly written by Glenda Palmer, one of the women in our church, after she heard me preach on the problem of pride. Her poem drips with sarcasm, but it is not far from the attitude James describes:

> I thank You, Lord, for giving me
> terrific looks, a brilliant mind,
> and sparkling personality
> that's spiritually inclined.

> I love my kids and Christian mate,
> our friendly church and Sunday school,
> our ranch-style home with patio
> and solar-heated swimming pool.

> I know my talents come from You;
> I'm praised for my angelic voice

that sings and teaches weaker ones
the way to make a godly choice.

And thanks for my prestigious job
and giving me an added gift—
that anything my pen jots down
becomes indeed, inspired script.

You ought to bless every Christian;
some lives seem ready to crumble,
but I am proud that You blessed me—
I guess it's just that I'm so humble.

Deceitful Actions

Now watch closely how all of these characteristics fit together. Selfish ambition leads to a party spirit or an attempt to elevate oneself. In order to be elevated, arrogant boasting must be utilized. Arrogant boasting inevitably leads to deceit and lying.

The Outcome of Worldly Wisdom

The two consequences of the world's wisdom are clearly marked out for us: "confusion and every evil work" (3:16 KJV).

Confusion

The word "*confusion*" means "to disturb." It is sometimes used to describe anarchy. Let's look at the two other occasions where the word is used in James.

"He is a double-minded man, unstable in all his ways" (1:8). The word "unstable" is the same word as the word "confusion" in the text we are studying.

"But no man can tame the tongue. It is an unruly evil, full of deadly poison" (3:8). The word "unruly" is the same word as the word "confusion" in our text.

Wherever the wisdom of the world operates, the result is instability, chaos, and convulsive conditions.

Every Evil Work

The word "*evil*" here does not mean "bad"; it literally means "worthless" or "good for nothing." The wisdom of the world comes to nothing; it is without any value. The prophet Isaiah states, "For the wisdom of their wise men shall perish, and the understanding of their prudent men shall be hidden" (29:14).

William Barclay summarizes this passage in James, when he writes:

> James describes this arrogant and bitter wisdom in its
> effects. The most notable thing about it is this, that it
> issues in disorder. That is to say, instead of bringing
> people together, it drives them apart. Instead of producing
> peace, it produces strife. Instead of producing a fellow-
> ship, it produces a disruption in personal relationships.
> There is a kind of person who is undoubtedly clever. He
> has an acute brain and skillful tongue. But the effect in
> any committee, in any church, in any group, is to cause
> trouble, to drive people apart, to foment strife, to disturb
> personal relationships. It is a sobering thing to remember
> that what that man possesses is devilish rather than
> divine. And that such a man is engaged in Satan's work
> and not in God's work.[5]

Paul feared that this was the kind of wisdom that was operating in Corinth, and when he wrote to them, he said so:

> For I fear lest, when I come, I shall not find you such as
> I wish, and that I shall be found by you such as you do
> not wish; lest there be contentions, jealousies, outbursts
> of wrath, selfish ambitions, backbitings, whisperings,
> conceits, tumults. (2 Cor. 12:20)

The apostle John described another church where such wisdom was operative—the church of Laodicea:

> So then, because you are lukewarm, and neither cold
> nor hot, I will vomit you out of My mouth. Because you
> say, "I am rich, have become wealthy, and have need of
> nothing"—and do not know that you are wretched, miser-
> able, poor, blind, and naked. (Rev. 3:16–17)

This "pseudowisdom" we have examined is divisively envious, selfishly ambitious, arrogantly boastful, and outwardly deceitful. The product of this imitation of God's wisdom is confusion and every evil work. A man who chooses the world's wisdom over God's wisdom will spend his life in futility and frustration.

Guy King in his commentary on this passage warns:

> When Mr. Worldlywise is allowed to be in the church, the
> tide of spiritual revival has been stayed. The holy task of
> soulwinning has been impaired. The commanding voice
> of Christian testimony has been silenced. And the growing
> experience of blessed intimacy with God has been arrested.
> Yes, and many more deplorable effects have ensued when
> worldly wisdom has been allowed to have its way.[6]

When James asks, "Who is wise and understanding?" (3:13), he is asking a very important question. He answers it by saying that such a man shows by his life that he has a right relationship with God. In other words, his life will reflect that his wisdom is not the wisdom of the world but the wisdom of God.

THE ORIGIN OF HEAVENLY WISDOM

"The wisdom ... is from above" (3:17). James uses a present tense participle to make his point. He says, "Wisdom is coming from above." Wisdom from above is not available in onetime allotments, nor is it to be procured on the installment plan. James pictures it as a steady flow from God to His children that just keeps on coming. The supply of God's wisdom never runs dry. It comes to us continually from above to meet the demands of each hour.

James 1:5 teaches us that wisdom comes from God in response to our prayer: "If any of you lacks wisdom, let him ask of God, who gives to all liberally and without reproach, and it will be given to him."

James 1:17 further amplifies that by reminding us, "Every good gift and every perfect gift is from above, and comes down from the Father of lights, with whom there is no variation or shadow of turning."

This wisdom is manifested through God's Son. It is made available through God's Holy Spirit, and it is written down in God's Holy Book, the Bible.

The wise individual is the one who has given himself to Jesus Christ and who by the help of the Holy Spirit keeps his intellect in submission to the will of God.

THE OPERATION OF HEAVENLY WISDOM

James' inventory of the characteristics of heavenly wisdom is similar to other lists in the New Testament that speak of the Christian way of life:

> the description of true love (1 Cor. 13:4–7), the fruit of the Spirit (Gal. 5:22–23), the godly mind-set (Phil. 4:8), and the lifestyle of the new man (Col. 3:12–15). Our Lord, 'who became to us wisdom from God' (1 Cor. 1:30), exemplified perfectly these characteristics.[7]

Heavenly Wisdom Is Pure

Purity is first in James' list because God's wisdom, like His nature, is based upon His holiness. In the command of James 4:8, we are instructed to purify our hearts and turn from duplicity.

There are no hidden motives in God's wisdom. It is transparent and clean. There is nothing under the surface. It is all up front. The wisdom of God, which is shown out of our good behavior, is first pure.

Heavenly Wisdom Is Peaceable

This characteristic is important to the argument of the book of James because of the dissension that is addressed in chapters 3 and 4. True peace is always an outgrowth of purity. Peace is blessing conferred upon us by God, and it is available to us from Him alone. Purity always brings peace. The absence of purity will always be accompanied by the absence of peace. Look at Isaiah's warning: "But the wicked are like the troubled sea, when it cannot rest, whose waters cast up mire and dirt. 'There is no peace,' says my God, 'for the wicked'" (57:20–21).

When the peace of God follows the purity of God's wisdom into our hearts and lives, it will affect those around us. We will be able to "follow peace with all men" (Heb. 12:14 KJV). For Christ, who is our peace, who came into this world as the Prince of Peace, will be on the throne of our hearts. The "sweet reasonableness" of this peace will cause us to be approachable, to allow discussion, to be willing to yield to others. Such peaceableness will not permit us to drag in personalities or allow us to make excuses when we are dealing with problems.

John White believes that someone exhibiting this kind of peace will stand out in this world:

> Peace is a kind of lighthouse in the midst of a storm.
> Winds shriek, waves crash, and lightning flickers all
> around it, but inside, the children are playing, while
> their parents go about their work. They may look out the
> window to marvel at the powers that rage around them,
> but they have peace. It is the peace of knowing that the
> strength that surrounds them is stronger than the strength
> of the storm.[8]

The prophet Isaiah had this in mind when he wrote, "You will keep him in perfect peace, whose mind is stayed on You, because he trusts in You" (26:3).

And Paul communicates the same idea when he describes this tranquility to the Philippians as "the peace of God, which surpasses all understanding" (4:7). The psalmist takes us back to the source of peace when he says, "Great peace have those who love Your law, and nothing causes them to stumble" (119:165).

Heavenly Wisdom Is Gentle

The wisdom of God is first pure and then peaceable and then gentle. According to Matthew Arnold, "Gentleness is sweet reasonableness." Homer Kent describes the quality of gentleness as

> being considerate of others and making allowance for their feelings, weaknesses, and needs. Such qualities as being equitable, fair, reasonable, and forbearing ... not insisting on the letter of the law but showing a willingness to yield. It was commonly used of God, kings, or slavemasters who showed moderation or lenience to someone beneath them when it was actually within their power to insist upon their rights.[9]

Gentleness is a characteristic of servants. Jesus spoke of Himself as being "gentle and humble in heart" (Matt. 11:29 NIV). Paul wrote of "the meekness and gentleness of Christ" (2 Cor. 10:1), and he instructed Titus concerning gentleness when he told him "to speak evil of no one, to be peaceable, gentle, showing all humility to all men" (Titus 3:2). He said the same thing to Timothy: "And a servant of the Lord must not quarrel but be gentle to all, able to teach, patient" (2 Tim. 2:24).

Strife is the world's wisdom, but gentleness is a property of the wisdom from above. Aristotle put it this way:

> Gentleness is equity to pardon human failings, to look to the law giver and not to the law, to the spirit and not to the letter, to the intention and not to the action, to the whole and not to the part, to the character of the person in the long run, and not to the present moment, to remember the good and not the evil.[10]

Carl Sandburg once described Abraham Lincoln as a man of "velvet steel." So a man who operates in the wisdom of God may be a strong, aggressive person, but he will exhibit a sweet gentleness as he deals with people.

Heavenly Wisdom Is Willing to Yield

God's wisdom has a conciliatory spirit and listens to reason. The Greek term translated by the phrase "willing to yield" is found only in this verse in the New Testament. It is a military term that means "to be willing to take instructions." When the spiritually wise man is in command, he must be "gentle." When he is under authority, he must be willing to yield, willing to take instruction.

Heavenly Wisdom Is Full of Mercy and Good Fruits

This characteristic of God's wisdom reminds us that our wisdom is demonstrated by our behavior (James 3:13). Our godly wisdom must be like our love ... demonstrated in word and in truth. Our lives must back up our testimonies.

When James mentions good works, he touches on an emphasis much needed among God's people today. In our determination to keep "good works" out of the gospel message, we have almost removed the term from our vocabularies. But "good works" is an important doctrine for the Christian to understand and practice. There is a consistent emphasis on this truth in the New Testament:

> And God is able to make all grace abound toward you, that you, always having all sufficiency in all things, may have an abundance for every good work. (2 Cor. 9:8)

> That you may walk worthy of the Lord, fully pleasing Him, being fruitful in every good work and increasing in the knowledge of God. (Col. 1:10)

> Now may our Lord Jesus Christ Himself, and our God and Father, who has loved us and given us everlasting

consolation and good hope by grace, comfort your hearts
and establish you in every good word and work.
(2 Thess. 2:16–17)

In like manner also, that the women adorn themselves
in modest apparel ... which is proper for women professing godliness, with good works. (1 Tim. 2:9–10)

Do not let a widow under sixty years old be taken into
the number, and not unless she has been the wife of one
man, well reported for good works.
(1 Tim. 5:9–10)

Those who are rich in this present age ... let them do
good, that they be rich in good works.
(1 Tim. 6:17–18)

All Scripture is given by inspiration of God ... that the
man of God may be complete, thoroughly equipped for
every good work. (2 Tim. 3:16–17)

In all things showing yourself to be a pattern of good
works. (Titus 2:7)

Who gave Himself for us, that He might redeem us from
every lawless deed and purify for Himself His own special
people, zealous for good works. (Titus 2:14)

Remind them to be subject to rulers and authorities, to
obey, to be ready for every good work. (Titus 3:1)

This is a faithful saying, and these things I want you
to affirm constantly, that those who have believed in God
should be careful to maintain good works. These things are
good and profitable to men. (Titus 3:8)

> And let us consider one another in order to stir up love
> and good works. (Heb. 10:24)

The consistent message of the Epistle of James is this: "Faith without works is dead" (James 2:20).

Heavenly Wisdom Is without Partiality

The term used here describes someone who is not discriminatory toward others nor uncertain within himself. He does not take a position in one circumstance and then change his position when the circumstances alter. Chapter 4 of this book is devoted to the issue of partiality as it plays out in the prejudicial treatment of others (James 2:1–13). R. W. Dale describes one who has worldly wisdom:

> It makes him as shifty as a politician. He sets his sails
> to the prevailing wind. He speaks well of a man one day
> whom he spoke ill of yesterday. Not because the man has
> changed, but yesterday there was no gain by speaking well
> of him, and today there is.[11]

Heavenly Wisdom Is without Hypocrisy

Hypocrisy is a word that comes from the world of drama. In New Testament days, when a person played a part onstage with a mask, he was called a *hypocrite*. The term gradually became associated with folks who played a role offstage as well. Today, a hypocrite is someone who is not real, who is phony, and does not truly represent himself.

When Paul wrote to the Romans, he admonished them to love without hypocrisy (12:9).

THE OUTCOME OF HEAVENLY WISDOM

The comparison of heavenly and earthly wisdom is instructive. The world's wisdom results in "confusion" (James 3:16), but God's wisdom brings "peace" (v. 18). The result of the world's wisdom is "every evil work" (v. 16 KJV). We pointed out earlier that this phrase means "every good-for-nothing work." But God's wisdom brings forth fruit. In the fruit of God's wisdom are the seeds of more fruit. As the fruit of righteousness is sown in righteousness (v. 18), God's wisdom automatically multiplies.

At the Rockefeller Center in New York City are four large murals. The first painting is of a primitive man laboring with his hands, attempting to survive his alien environment. Next is the portrayal of man having become the creator of tools, and the comforts of civilization have been multiplied. The third mural shows man to be both master and servant of the machine. The vast forces of the material world are now under his direction and his control. Our eyes move to the last painting with a sense of overwhelming surprise. It seems so out of context with the other three. Jesus Christ is the theme of this presentation, and He is seen in the setting of His Sermon on the Mount. Struggling to reach Him are masses of men and women and children. Underneath the fourth mural, the mural of Christ, are inscribed these words:

> Man's ultimate destiny depends not on whether he can learn new lessons or make new discoveries or conquests, but on his acceptance of the lesson that was taught him over 2,000 years ago.[12]

And I can hear Jesus saying amen.

8

WHAT TO DO WHEN WORSHIP TURNS TO WAR

(JAMES 4:1–12)

God resists the proud, but gives grace to the humble.

Readers of the *Chicago Tribune* were surprised recently by this off-beat headline: "Tennessee Church Destroyed by Fire after Members Come to Blows at Meeting." The story was of a church in Tazewell, Tennessee, that had problems. The conflict flared during a church service, leading to a fistfight. "It just all broke loose," recalled one member. The church later burned to the ground and the police are investigating. The saddened pastor told a television station, "That's God's house. It's no place to throw fists, or shoot people, or talk about shooting people, it's for blessing the Lord."

The congregation is now meeting in a church member's garage.[1]

Unfortunately, this kind of story has cropped up many times in Christian history. Visitors to St. Giles Cathedral in Edinburgh, Scotland, linger at the spot where an irate woman named Jenny Geddes threw a milk stool at the bishop while he was reading a prayer book printed in England. That was four hundred years ago, but the story has endured.

Many of us have attended tense meetings at church, and we know how unpleasant they can be. Spiritual issues are emotional, and most churches are made up of people with varying levels of maturity. We come from diverse backgrounds. We view things differently. We sometimes get our feelings hurt, express ourselves badly, get angry with the pastor, feel slighted by the staff, or worry that our opinions aren't heard.

And don't forget about the devil! He attends church regularly with an armful of firewood to throw on any controversy. When I think of all this, I recall a parable someone gave me once, reminding us that faith and fisticuffs are not always mutually exclusive.

> The wedding guests have gathered in great anticipation; the ceremony to be performed today has long been awaited. The orchestra begins to play an anthem, and the choir rises in proper precision. The bridegroom and his attendants gather in front of the chancel. One little saint, her flowered hat bobbing, leans to her companion and whispers, "Isn't he handsome?" The response is agreement, "My, yes. The handsomest...."
>
> The sound of the organ rises, a joyous announcement that the bride is coming. Everyone stands and strains to get a proper glimpse of the beauty. Then a horrible gasp explodes from the congregation. This is a bride like no other.
>
> In she stumbles. Something terrible has happened! One leg is twisted; she limps pronouncedly. The wedding garment is tattered and muddy; great rents in her dress leave her scarcely modest. Black bruises can be seen welting her bare arms; the bride's nose is bloody. An eye is swollen, yellow and purple in its discoloration. Patches of hair look as if they had actually been pulled from her scalp.
>
> Fumbling over the keys, the organist begins again after his shocked pause. The attendants cast their eyes down. The congregation mourns silently. Surely the bridegroom deserved better than this! That handsome prince who has kept himself faithful to his love should find consummation with the most beautiful of women—not this. His bride, the church, has been fighting again.[2]

Our new awareness of the many contemporary church fights should not lead us to conclude that this is something unique to our generation. When Paul wrote this second letter to the church in Corinth, he mentioned the kinds of problems that can often erupt in a church:

> For I fear lest, when I come, I shall not find you such as I wish, and that I shall be found by you such as you do not wish; lest there be contentions, jealousies, outburst of wrath, selfish ambitions, backbitings, whisperings, conceits, tumults. (12:20)

Yes, there have always been conflicts among God's people, and James obviously had firsthand knowledge of such division in the churches to which he writes his letter.

It is important to make the connection between James 3 and 4. "Now the fruit of righteousness is sown in peace by those who make peace. Where do wars and fights come from among you? Do they not come from your desires for pleasure that war in your members?" (3:18—4:1).

James has documented for us the results of God's wisdom at work in our lives. It is peace and righteousness and other godly virtues. But the wisdom of the world also has a by-product. When it is set free in the church of Jesus Christ, it will bring about all the evil results we are about to unfold.

THE CAUSE OF CONFLICT IN THE CHURCH

In his introductory statement, James uses two questions to probe his readers, and the second question answers the first. He asks his readers first to identify the source of their quarrels and disputes. "Where do wars and fights come from among you?" Then, before they can respond, he gives them the answer: "Do they not come from your desires for pleasure that war in your members?" (4:1).

Some scholars have translated the phrase "among you" as "in you." They insist that this is not a struggle *between* people but a struggle *within* people. The two ideas, however, cannot be completely detached, because external struggles are often the symptoms of internal struggles. "A person not at peace with himself can surely not be at peace with his associates."[3]

When he suggests that these struggles come from within man himself, James steps on the toes of many psychologists who have been attempting to blame man's hostility on everything from heredity to environment.

When he says that the problem lies in man's desires for pleasures, he uses the Greek word *hedone.*

> Desires (*hedonon*), the term from which we derive our
> English term *hedonism*, denotes the enjoyment derived
> from the fulfillment of one's desires or ... the craving for
> the pleasures itself. This hedonism, "the playboy philoso-
> phy that makes pleasure mankind's chief end," still wages
> battle in people's hearts.[4]

It is impossible to overstate the power of this force within people:

> Lust is the "atomic energy" within human personality.
> It defies precise definition, for "lust" embraces a vast
> range of desires and yearnings, aspirations and strivings,
> pleasures and emotions.... It ... conveys the suggestion of
> volcanic potentialities; the terrible capacities inherent in a
> lion crouched ready to spring upon his prey.[5]

The Bible has some strong things to say about seeking pleasure as the ultimate good. Moses learned that the afflictions of God were better than the "passing pleasures of sin" (Heb. 11:24–25). Jesus said that the "pleasures of life" are thorns that choke out the Word of God in a man's heart (Luke 8:14). The apostle Paul said that "various lusts and pleasures" characterize the life of the unbeliever (Titus 3:3). Peter said that one of the ways to identify a false teacher was if he considered it "pleasure to carouse in the daytime" (2 Peter 2:13).

THE CHARACTERISTICS OF CONFLICT IN THE CHURCH

Vernon Doerksen rewrites verses 2 and 3 to show the cause-and-effect cycle:

> You lust
>
> and do not have.
>
> You kill and envy
>
> and you are not able to obtain.
>
> You fight and quarrel
>
> [and] you do not have because you do not ask.
>
> You ask and you do not receive,
>
> because you ask amiss,
>
> that you may spend it on your pleasures.[6]

If we follow Doerksen's organization of this passage, we can clearly see four characteristics of conflict among God's people.

Unsatisfied Pleasure—"You Lust and Do Not Have"

Three times in verse 2 we are told that those who sought for pleasure were frustrated in the process. Pleasure never gives full satisfaction:

> If we have two cars, we want a third one. If we have one,
> we want a second one. If we are affluent enough to have
> a beautiful townhouse, we would like to have one also out
> in the country. If we have a million dollars, we want two. If
> we have 500 million dollars, we want a billion. The people
> who are the most avaricious and grasping for money are
> rich people. They just expand and expand, and the more
> they have, the more they want.[7]

Uncontrolled Passion—"You Kill and Envy and You Are Not Able to Obtain"

In spite of the slugfest in Newton, Massachusetts, it is still difficult to comprehend murder actually taking place in a church fellowship. Because of this, many commentators have tried to lessen the impact of

this verse by retranslating it. Vernon Doerksen explains their argument
and then rejects it:

> "You commit murder" does not fit the passage, therefore it
> is best to change the text from "you kill," (phoneuete), to
> "You are envious" (phthoneite). Moffatt gives this transla-
> tion: "You crave and miss what you want: you envy and
> covet, but you cannot acquire: you wrangle and fight." *There
> is, however, absolutely no textual support for that conjecture.*[8]

But history has proved that an insatiable desire for more can often
lead to murder. David murdered Uriah because of his lust for Bathsheba
(2 Sam. 11:2–17), and Ahab murdered Naboth because of his desire
for a vineyard (1 Kings 21:1–13). Murder is the extreme to which frustrated desire may lead!

> The steps of the process are simple and terrible. A man
> allows himself to desire something. That thing begins to
> dominate his thoughts; he finds himself involuntarily think-
> ing about it in his waking hours and dreaming of it when he
> sleeps. It begins to be what is aptly called a ruling passion.
> He begins to form imaginary schemes to obtain it; and these
> schemes may well involve ways of eliminating those who
> stand in his way. For long enough all this may go on in his
> mind. Then one day the imaginings may blaze into action;
> and he may find himself taking the terrible steps necessary
> to obtain his desire. Every crime in this world has come from
> desire which was first only a feeling in the heart, but which
> being nourished long enough, came in the end to action.[9]

Untapped Potential—"You Fight and War, Yet You Do Not Have Because You Do Not Ask"

The spiritual condition of those to whom James is writing is summarized in this statement: "[They did] not have because [they did] not

ask." Instead of turning to God as the giver of every perfect gift, they tried to get what they wanted through their own schemes. In the process of their self-efforts, they further eroded their own practice of prayer.

> The Bible is repeatedly clear that a driving desire for pleasure is ruinous to the prayer life.... The way this works is that first, the pleasure-mad Christian, who has some spiritual sensitivity, realizes his prayers are inappropriate. Somehow he senses that his desire for a Maserati may not be a spiritual essential. So he asks for nothing. In fact he doesn't pray much at all because few of the things he wants are high on the divine priority list.[10]

Unanswered Prayer—"You Ask and You Do Not Receive, Because You Ask Amiss"

In the first case, there is no receiving because there has been no asking. In this instance, there is no receiving because the asking is done with the wrong motive. There is a certain way that we must pray if we are to be heard and responded to by God. Dr. Criswell reminds us:

> When it comes to praying and getting our prayers answered, we have to follow the directions that God has set down for success. God has put this world together in such a way that it runs according to certain principles and certain laws. If we obey those principles and those laws we find a response, a return; but if we do not, we do not find a response and we do not find a return.... If we have a problem in mathematics, the answer to whether or not we did it right is the sum of it. Is it correct? If we have a machine, the answer to whether the thing is put together right or not is whether it does what we want it to do. Does it run and does it produce? So it is in the matter of prayer—of getting things from God. If we do it right we have to use the instrument in a correct way.[11]

Simon J. Kistemaker adds,

> God refuses to listen to men who eagerly pursue selfish
> pleasures. Greed is idolatry and that is an abomination in
> the sight of God. God does not listen to prayer that comes
> from a heart filled with selfish motives. Covetousness and
> selfishness are insults to God.[12]

There are some principles in the New Testament that provide guidelines for getting our prayers answered. Here are five basic things that the New Testament teaches about proper praying. As we look through this checklist, we might be surprised to discover the cause of our own unanswered petitions:

> When we pray, we are to ask in faith. "But let him ask in
> faith, with no doubting, for he who doubts is like a wave of
> the sea driven and tossed by the wind" (James 1:6).

> When we pray, we are to pray in Jesus' name. "Until now
> you have asked nothing in My name. Ask, and you will
> receive, that your joy may be full"
> (John 16:24).

> When we pray, we are to pray according to God's will.
> "Now this is the confidence that we have in Him, that
> if we ask anything according to His will, He hears us"
> (1 John 5:14).

> When we pray, we are to be in right relationship with
> others. "Husbands, likewise, dwell with them with under-
> standing, giving honor to the wife, as to the weaker vessel,
> and as being heirs together of the grace of life, that your
> prayers may not be hindered" (1 Peter 3:7).

> When we pray, we are to have no unconfessed sin in

our lives. "If I regard iniquity in my heart, the Lord will not hear" (Ps. 66:18).

The Condemnation of Conflict in the Church

James calling his readers "adulterers and adulteresses" would not have been nearly as shocking to them as it is to us today. Because of their Jewish background, they would have associated his words with the many passages in the Old Testament that use the metaphor of marriage to depict the relationship of Jehovah God to His people, Israel:

> For your Maker is your husband, the Lord of hosts is His name; and your Redeemer is the Holy One of Israel. (Isa. 54:5)

> "Surely, as a wife treacherously departs from her husband, so have you dealt treacherously with Me, O house of Israel," says the Lord. (Jer. 3:20)

> Do not rejoice, O Israel, with joy like other peoples, for you have played the harlot against your God. You have made love for hire on every threshing floor. (Hos. 9:1)

Jesus also used this figure of speech in His teaching:

> But He answered and said to them, "An evil and adulterous generation seeks after a sign, and no sign will be given to it except the sign of the prophet Jonah." (Matt. 12:39; see also Matt. 16:4)

> For whoever is ashamed of Me and My words in this adulterous and sinful generation, of him the Son of Man also will be ashamed when He comes in the glory of His Father with the holy angels. (Mark 8:38)

The New Testament uses marital metaphors to describe the relationship between the Christian and Christ. Husbands are instructed to love their wives as Christ loved the church (Eph. 5:25). Believers are described as chaste virgins, espoused to Jesus Christ (2 Cor. 11:2).

Friendship with the World Destroys Our Fellowship with God

James' strong words are a rebuke to his Christian friends who have allowed their love for the world to take the place of their love for Christ. They have become "lovers of pleasure rather than lovers of God" (2 Tim. 3:4).

What does James mean when he scolds his readers for loving the world? *World* has several distinct meanings, and almost all of them are illustrated in the book of James. In the first chapter, James speaks of keeping oneself unspotted from the world (1:27). Here he is speaking of the "world system," the evil principles of the world. In chapter 2 he writes of God's choice of "the poor of this world" (v. 5). This is a reference to the "world of men." In chapter 3 he says, "The tongue is a fire, a world of iniquity" (v. 6). This use of the word is one that is commonly employed today. It is in the universal sense or global sense that we describe a car dealership as "car world" or a furniture store as "furniture world," etc. In this way James is describing the vast damage that can be done by the misuse of the tongue.

Here in chapter 4, James uses *world* two more times to speak of a system that is in opposition to God. If you are unclear about the nature of the world system, here is one of the best descriptions I have ever read:

> The world is human nature sacrificing the spiritual to the material, the future to the present, the unseen and the eternal to that which touches the senses and perishes with time. The world is a mighty flood of thoughts, feelings, principles of action, conventional prejudices, dislikes, attachments, which have been gathering around human life for ages, impregnating it, impelling it, molding it, degrading it.[13]

The apostle John warns the caring believer against loving the world:

> Do not love the world or the things in the world. If anyone
> loves the world, the love of the Father is not in him. For all
> that is in the world—the lust of the flesh, the lust of the
> eyes, and the pride of life—is not of the Father but is of the
> world. And the world is passing away, and the lust of it; but
> he who does the will of God abides forever. (1 John 2:15–17)

It is not too strong to say that friendship with the world is enmity with God. The line is drawn that straight in other places in the New Testament as well. "No servant can serve two masters; for either he will hate the one and love the other, or else he will be loyal to the one and despise the other. You cannot serve God and mammon" (Luke 16:13).

In sadness, Paul wrote of his friend Demas, "For Demas has forsaken me, having loved this present world" (2 Tim. 4:10).

Friendship with the World Denies Our Faith in God's Word

One of the problems with verse 5 is the reference to the scriptural quotation, "The Spirit who dwells in us yearns jealously." First of all, if this is supposed to be a reference to some particular Old Testament passage, no one, from that time to this, has been able to locate it.

The best way to understand this reference is to view it in the same way we would view a preacher who might say, "The Bible says," and then refer to some concept that is generally taught in the Word of God. James is simply saying that the whole tenor of Scripture teaches us that the Holy Spirit who lives within the believer jealously desires to completely possess that believer and control his life. Here are some passages where that truth is evident:

> You shall not make for yourself a carved image—any
> likeness of anything that is in heaven above, or that is in
> the earth beneath, or that is in the water under the earth;
> you shall not bow down to them nor serve them. For I, the
> Lord your God, am a jealous God. (Ex. 20:4–5)

> For you shall worship no other god, for the Lord, whose name is Jealous, is a jealous God. (Ex. 34:14)

> For the Lord your God is a jealous God among you. (Deut. 6:15)

THE CURE FOR CONFLICT IN THE CHURCH

What is the cure for conflict in the church? How do we overcome the fightings and quarrels among us? According to James, the cure may be found in understanding the grace of God. The believer is not left to the cycle of unsatisfied pleasures, uncontrolled passions, untapped potential, and unanswered prayers. He does not have to be an enemy of God, a spiritual adulterer. The same grace that initiates a believer into fellowship with God is able to sustain that fellowship in spite of the pressures of the world. The good news is that God "gives more grace" and "gives grace to the humble." The consistent message of the New Testament is that God's grace is available for our deepest needs.

> And He said to me, "My grace is sufficient for you, for My strength is made perfect in weakness." Therefore most gladly I will rather boast in my infirmities, that the power of Christ may rest upon me. (2 Cor. 12:9)

> Let us therefore come boldly to the throne of grace, that we may obtain mercy and find grace to help in time of need. (Heb. 4:16)

> But where sin abounded, grace abounded much more. (Rom. 5:20)

Joni Eareckson Tada expressed her appreciation for the adequacy of God's grace when she wrote:

I feel that He will never give us a burden we cannot
bear. You know, I look at some of my friends who are
more disabled than I and I say, "I couldn't handle it."
I have a friend, Vicki, who at best can only move her
head from side to side. I at least can flail my arms and
shrug my shoulders. She's far more disabled than I. I've
said to her, "Vicki, I don't know how you do it," and she
says, "Well, with God's grace I can." When Vicki looks
at some of her friends who are hooked up to breathing
machines, she doesn't know how they do it. All of us are
placed somewhere on this scale of suffering. Some of us
suffer more than others, but wherever God places you
and me on the scale, *He gives us accompanying grace to
handle it.*[14]

When the pressure is on, when the problems seem overwhelming,
when the resources are low, when health wavers, when family dreams are
shattered, when the spiritual flame is but a flicker, God gives more grace.

Annie Johnson Flint was inspired by that thought to give us this
great verse, which is also now a wonderful hymn:

> He giveth more grace when the burdens grow greater;
> He sendeth more grace when the labors increase;
> To added afflictions He addeth His mercy,
> To multiplied trials His multiplied peace.

> When we have exhausted our store of endurance,
> When our strength has failed ere the day is half done;
> When we reach the end of our hoarded resources,
> Our Father's full giving is only begun.

> His love has no limits, His grace has no measure,
> His power has no boundary known unto men;
> For out of His infinite riches in Jesus,
> He giveth, and giveth, and giveth again.[15]

When James quotes the words, "God resists the proud, but gives grace to the humble," he is citing a passage in Proverbs 3:34: "Surely He scorns the scornful, but gives grace to the humble." This is also quoted by Peter: "God resists the proud, but gives grace to the humble" (1 Peter 5:5).

However, if we are to be the recipients of God's grace, pride will have to die:

> Those who proudly turn from God and choose to be friends of the world must face God's opposition. The world with its more immediate rewards ministers to their pride, and its wisdom can foster human egos and often advance their ambitions. God however, ministers His grace to the humble. Those who are willing to acknowledge their need, repudiate selfish ambition, and let God's wisdom guide them will find that God's provision of grace for each day will be their greatest resource.[16]

PRINCIPLES FOR APPROPRIATING GRACE

Now, on the heels of this great promise of grace, James outlines a program that will enable the believer to appropriate the grace of God. Through this grace these first-century believers would be able to withstand the gravitational pull of the world system. In verses 7 through 12, James uses a series of Greek imperatives to communicate nine key principles of God's grace for the believer. As you read through these principles, please allow the Holy Spirit to measure your own life.

Grace Principle One: Relinquish Control of Your Life

Therefore submit to God.

The word *submit* means to "take rank under." The proud person will find this to be the ultimate challenge. He will struggle with the carefully rehearsed lifestyle of controlling everything himself. He will want to do it his way. But if a believer is unwilling to submit to the control of God in his life, he will never be open to the grace of God that has been promised. If I am trying to earn my own way, what do I need with the grace of God? Stevenson defines this submission to Christ as

> a surrender of the right to run our own life, to think and say and do as we please; and a continuing dependence and obedience. It is a recognition that only God can deal with this rebellious tyrant self, and a readiness for Him to do so.... It means acknowledging Him in all our ways, that He might direct our paths.[17]

Grace Principle Two: Resist the Devil

> Resist the devil and he will flee from you.

James instructs his friends to resist the Devil, and he promises them that their resistance will cause the Devil to flee. Peter makes a very similar statement in his first letter: "Be sober, be vigilant; because your adversary the devil walks about like a roaring lion, seeking whom he may devour. Resist him, steadfast in the faith" (5:8–9).

We must implement the armor of God (Eph. 6:10–18)! We must saturate ourselves with God's Word (Matt. 4:4)! And we must pray (John 15:7; 1 John 5:14–15; Eph. 6:18)!

Grace Principle Three: Restore Worship to a Priority

> Draw near to God and He will draw near to you.

We have already been commanded to submit to God as servants. Now we are admonished to draw near to God as worshippers. The verb "draw near" is the way the Old Testament describes the Levitical priests approaching God with their sacrifices:

> Also let the priests who come near the Lord consecrate themselves, lest the Lord break out against them. (Ex. 19:22)

> And Moses said to Aaron, "This is what the Lord spoke, saying: 'By those who come near Me I must be regarded as holy; and before all the people I must be glorified.'" (Lev. 10:3)

In the book of Hebrews, which exalts the high priesthood of Jesus Christ as superior to the Old Testament priesthood, the believer is encouraged with these words: "For the law made nothing perfect; on the other hand, there is the bringing in of a better hope, through which we draw near to God" (7:19).

The promise associated with this command has been experienced by every true worshipper. When we draw near in worship, God always draws near to us. I have sensed the closeness of God in times of personal and congregational worship. In those special moments, the grace of God is truly appropriated.

It is also important to understand that in the very act of calling us to draw near to Him, God has initiated our response. Through His grace, He has wooed us to Himself. John Calvin wrote, "But if anyone concludes from this passage that the first part of the work belongs to us, and that afterwards the grace of God follows, the apostle meant no such thing ... but the very thing [the Spirit of God] bids us do, He Himself fulfills in us."[18]

Grace Principle Four: Renounce Sinful Actions

> Cleanse your hands, you sinners.

This instruction is reminiscent of the terminology of the tabernacle. The priest had to wash his hands before he could approach the Holy Place of almighty God. The psalmist incorporates this thought into one of his hymns: "Who may ascend into the hill of the Lord? Or who may stand in His holy place? He who has clean hands and a pure heart, who has not lifted up his soul to an idol, nor sworn deceitfully" (24:3–4).

As we continue to experience God's grace in our lives, we will not be able to hold on to those actions we know are a violation of His holy standards and righteousness.

Grace Principle Five: Reject Sinful Attitudes

Purify your hearts, you double-minded.

James calls the readers "double-minded," a term that expresses fickleness and vacillation. It fits the person who loves God and the world. It is this attitude that will keep the grace of God from flowing in the life of the Christian.

Grace Principle Six: React to Sin with Sorrow

Lament and mourn and weep!

James is like an Old Testament prophet who calls his people to repentance by having them grieve over their sins and in a sense "sit in sackcloth and ashes." When Paul was dealing with the sin in his life, he cried out, "O wretched man that I am! Who will deliver me from this body of death?" (Rom. 7:24).

Grace Principle Seven: Refrain from a Frivolous Attitude toward Evil

Let your laughter be turned to mourning and your joy to gloom.

James is not saying that a Christian should dress in black clothing and walk around with a somber face and preach gloom and doom. A Christian ought to be happy in the Lord, thankful for the gift of salvation, and obedient in doing the will of God. When he has fallen into sin and responds to God's call for repentance, a change must occur in his life. Laughter and joy are silenced. When he realizes what he has done, he cannot but be saddened![19]

Grace Principle Eight: Respond Humbly to Success

Humble yourselves in the sight of the Lord,
and He will lift you up.

Someone has calculated that this concept occurs over fifty times in the Word of God. Here are some representative passages:

For the Lord ... will beautify the humble with salvation. (Ps. 149:4)

Surely He ... gives grace to the humble. (Prov. 3:34)

Exalt the humble, and humble the exalted. (Ezek. 21:26)

Whoever exalts himself will be humbled, and he who humbles himself will be exalted. (Matt. 23:12)

Therefore humble yourselves under the mighty hand of God, that He may exalt you in due time. (1 Peter 5:6)

Grace Principle Nine: Refuse to Slander Your Brother

Do not speak evil of one another, brethren.

In one of his psalms, David links slander to a lack of humility: "Whoever secretly slanders his neighbor, him I will destroy; the one who has a haughty look and a proud heart, him I will not endure" (101:5).

In verse 7, James says that we are to resist the Devil. In the original, the noun "devil" is the Greek word *diabolos* and is sometimes translated "slanderer" (1 Tim. 3:11; 2 Tim. 3:3; Titus 2:3). The chief work of the Devil is to slander God's people. Peter uses this word twice in his first epistle to describe the way unbelievers talked about believers (2:12; 3:16). While most of us would never set out knowingly to do the work of the Devil, that's exactly what we are doing when we speak evil of our brothers. Mark Littleton pictures how this can happen in the church:

> We "speak against" our brothers and sisters when we complain about them, carry stories that make them look bad, judge their motives, and condemn them. Anything we say that tears them down instead of building them up is speaking against them. And such speech is one of the most common problems among Christians today.[20]

In Paul's letter to the Ephesians, he gave strong advice to those who would be tempted to tear down a brother: "Let no corrupt word proceed out of your mouth, but what is good for necessary edification, that it may impart grace to the hearers" (4:29).

When the warring church members from the Emmanuel Baptist Church in Newton, Massachusetts, were hauled into court, the judge, who was a member of the local Temple Beth Shalom, looked over the police report of the incident and dismissed the case from his courtroom with these stinging words:

> No charges will be pressed at this point, but I urge you to work this out within your own church. Your Jesus Christ may allow this sort of thing in His followers, but the Commonwealth of Massachusetts will not permit fistfights as a regular order of church service.[21]

As we have examined James' words in these twelve verses, we have been strongly reminded that God's standards are much higher than man's. Our Jesus Christ does not allow fightings within the community of believers, and if we will take seriously the instruction given by our Lord's brother, we can restore unity to our war-torn churches.

WHAT TO DO WHEN YOUR GOALS ARE NOT GOD'S
(JAMES 4:13–17)

You do not know what will happen tomorrow.
For what is your life? It is even a vapor.

Russell Chandler, former religion writer for the *Los Angeles Times*, recalls an event that took place in the midseventies while he was still writing for the newspaper:

> A bearded young man made repeated trips to the Los Angeles Times' lobby, seeking to be interviewed. After several polite refusals by this religion writer, Messiah Ron grew more insistent. One morning he again showed up in the lobby and by telephone told me he was delivering an important handprinted document that "must be published at once."
>
> An alert copy messenger was dispatched to the lobby. "See if you can discourage this guy from coming back," I told her.
>
> "This may come as quite a surprise to you," Messiah Ron began, handing the copy messenger a scroll. "I am the Messiah."
>
> "Well," the young lady replied with aplomb, "this may come as quite a surprise to you, but you're the third messiah we've had here today."[1]

Many non-Christians are still laughing because of Edgar C. Whisenant's *88 Reasons Why the Rapture Will Be in 1988*. This book, distributed to almost every pastor in America, predicted that the rapture was to take place September 11, 12, or 13, 1988.

On those three days, the Trinity Broadcasting Network (TBN) changed its regular programming and ran selected videotapes that instructed nonbelieving viewers what to do if their loved ones suddenly disappeared.

> Charles Taylor planned his 1988 tour of Israel to coincide with Whisenant's date, with the possibility of being raptured from the Holy Land as a sales incentive ... "only $1975 from Los Angeles or $1805 from New York (and return if necessary)," said his *Bible Prophecy News*. In a later pitch for the tour, he stated: "We stay at the Intercontinental Hotel right on the Mount of Olives where you can get the beautiful view of the Eastern Gate and Temple Mount. And if this is the year of our Lord's return, as we anticipate, you may even ascend to Glory from within a few feet of His ascension."[2]

Self-proclaimed prophets like Whisenant and Taylor create a great deal of interest. Over three million copies of Whisenant's book were distributed. As I write this chapter, a new book has been published here in California, setting yet another date for Christ's return. How people wish they could know what the future holds! How foolish they are willing to become just to speculate about it! But God has not allowed us that clear view. He has given us the ability to recall the past, but not to know the future.

According to Augustine, God was wise in His decision to veil the future from our eyes. "God will not suffer man to have the knowledge of things to come, for if he had prescience of his prosperity, he would be careless; and understanding his adversity, he would be senseless."[3]

More recently, W. A. Criswell has observed:

> There must have been a kindness and a goodness of God
> in thus veiling the future from our eyes; for if a man knew
> what the morrow would bring, he would live in constant
> fear and foreboding. Dying, he would die a thousand
> deaths before dying just once. Fainting, he would faint a
> thousand times under a stroke that was yet to be delivered.
> God hides the future from our eyes that we might live in
> confidence and in hope.[4]

In this concluding section of James 4, the author is reminding his readers that while they cannot predict the future, they must learn how to face it honestly. They should not plan the future without taking God into consideration or presume upon a future they cannot control. They must not postpone until the future what God has instructed them to do today. The three mistakes that these early Christians were making are often repeated by modern Christians. The warning to that generation will certainly be helpful to this one.

Mistake One: Planning the Future without God

James' readers have already been reproved for demonstrating a spirit of independence from God. They have sought the world's pleasures instead of loving God (4:1–10). By judging one another, they have attempted to evade the ultimate Judge—God Himself (4:11–12). Now the final indifference is uncovered. They have planned their business future and have omitted God from their plans. From a careful study of this passage, it is clear that their disregard of God is equal in substance to the first two sins. "By ignoring God, they show as much arrogance as does the person who slanders his neighbor. The sin of failing to come to God in prayer is one of the most common offenses a Christian commits."[5]

While not often recognized as such, this also qualifies as worldliness. "The form of worldliness of which he here speaks is a presumptuous confidence in the future, calculating on time to come without reference to God's providence, as if the future and all that it brings with it were in our hands."[6]

To introduce his thoughts, James uses an expression that is found in but one other place in the New Testament (James 5:1). The Greek expression is translated, "Come now." We might say it this way: "Now look here!" It usually implies disapproval and conveys a sense of urgency.

While these merchants are to be blamed for leaving God out of their plans, they are not faulted for planning. Nothing is said that would lead one to believe there is anything wrong in the planning process. In fact, in many ways, this is a model business plan.

1. The *plan* is constructed—"today or tomorrow." A good business plan needs to have some flexibility. This plan could have been executed either today or tomorrow.

2. The *place* is chosen—"we will go to such and such a city."

> This was an age of the founding of cities; and often when cities were founded and their founders were looking for citizens to occupy them, citizenship was offered freely to the Jews, for where the Jews came, money and trade followed. So the picture is of a man looking at a map. He points at a certain spot on it, and says, "Here is a new city where there are great trade chances. I'll go there; I'll get in on the ground floor; I'll trade for a year or so; I'll make my fortune and come back rich."[7]

3. The *period* is calculated—"spend a year there." They decided that their business could be completed in a year's time, and they assumed that they would be able to stay the course. They had no intention of permanently relocating.

4. The *purpose* is considered—"buy and sell." The Greek word used here is *emporeuomai*, from which we get our word "emporium." An emporium today is a commercial center. In this biblical context, the word means "to travel to a place for the purpose of doing business."

5. The *profit* is computed—"and make a profit."

> Profit-making had become a passion with these mer-
> chants. That was the only reason why they traveled, why
> they traded, why they lived.... Their aspirations were high,
> but they were not high enough. They stacked up profits,
> but not heavenly treasures while here on earth.[8]

As Christian businessmen, they should have considered eternity and consulted with the eternal God:

> It must not be concluded that James was condemning
> wise planning. Jesus taught His followers the folly of
> failing to calculate one's resources before beginning some
> enterprise (Luke 14:28–32). What is denounced is planning
> that leaves God out, planning that thinks human ingenuity
> alone is all that is necessary.[9]

We all know that it is wrong to *do* things without God, but now we are to understand that it is wrong to *plan* things without God. Some businessmen I have talked to leave God out of their plans because they fear the profit margin. They are afraid God will get in the way of their financial gain. If we are tempted along that line, we do well to remember God's promise to us:

> Therefore do not worry, saying, "What shall we eat?" or
> "What shall we drink?" or "What shall we wear?" For
> after all these things the Gentiles seek. For your heavenly
> Father knows that you need all these things. But seek first
> the kingdom of God and His righteousness, and all these
> things shall be added to you. (Matt. 6:31–33)

Robert Johnstone telescopes James' warning into this century when he writes:

> In an age like ours, when natural science is every day so
> greatly increasing the means of money-making, when

trade has so many ramifications, and connected with
it, so much that is exciting, there is very great peril of a
man's losing the thought of God, and, amid the whir of
commercial machinery, failing to hear the "still small
voice" which reminds us that "life, and breath, and all
things" are at His disposal. For our time, therefore, the
apostle's words have, if possible, even greater force than
they had for his own.[10]

It is good to have goals in business, but for the Christian businessman, the ultimate goal must be the glory of God and the service of
humanity.

Mistake Two: Presuming to Know the Future

In planning their future business growth, these men made three
errors:

They Failed to Comprehend the Complexity of Life

How many were the things that they counted on accomplishing ...
today, tomorrow, spend a year, buy and sell, make a profit. Each one
had in itself the seeds of great disappointment. How sure could one
ever be about tomorrow, to say nothing of a year from tomorrow? What
if there was no buyer? Suppose there was a price war and no margin for
profit? How could anyone presume to know the complexities of such
an enterprise?

I read something recently that reminded me again of man's inability
to know the future:

> Thirty years ago, futurists peering into their crystal balls
> predicted that one of the biggest problems for coming
> generations would be what to do with their abundant spare
> time. I remember hearing this prediction often. In 1967,
> testimony before a Senate subcommittee claimed that by
> 1985 people could be working just twenty-two hours a

> week or twenty-seven weeks a year or could retire at age
> thirty-eight....
>
> According to a Harris Survey, the amount of leisure time
> enjoyed by the average American has decreased 37 percent
> since 1973. Over the same period, the average workweek,
> including commuting has jumped from under forty-one
> hours to nearly forty-seven hours.[11]

No matter how hard he tries, man cannot comprehend the complexities of life so as to accurately predict what will happen in the future.

They Failed to Comprehend the Uncertainty of Life

They could not possibly have known what they needed to know to make so bold a prediction. Their statement was raw arrogance.

> The skillful use of the repetitive *we will go ... and stay ...
> and trade ... and make a profit* and the mention of a year's
> stay both suggest deliberate and calculated arrogance.
> They would go where they liked for as long as they liked.
> Their resolve, together with their refusal to reckon with
> death, has a modern ring.[12]

The foolishness of such planning has been illustrated for me through many conversations with people who tell me that life has thrown them some curves. Things have not always turned out the way they planned. "When I was young, I was poor; when old, I became rich; but in each condition I found a disappointment. When I had the faculties of enjoyment, I had not the means; when the means came, the faculties were gone."[13]

They Failed to Comprehend the Brevity of Life

James asks one of the most profound questions of the Bible when he inquires, "What is your life?" This is not a question about the origin or essence of life. It is apparent in James' answer that he is talking about the time between birth and death. In the Bible at least eighteen metaphors express the brevity and uncertainty of life. Among them are the following:

Our days on earth are as a shadow. (1 Chron. 29:15)

My days are swifter than a weaver's shuttle, and are spent without hope. (Job 7:6)

Oh, remember that my life is a breath! (Job 7:7)

As the cloud disappears and vanishes away, so he who goes down to the grave does not come up. (Job 7:9)

For we were born yesterday, and know nothing, because our days on earth are a shadow. (Job 8:9)

Now my days are swifter than a runner; they flee away, they see no good. They pass by like swift ships, like an eagle swooping on its prey. (Job 9:25–26)

Man who is born of woman is of few days and full of trouble. He comes forth like a flower and fades away; he flees like a shadow and does not continue. (Job 14:1–2)

Lord, make me to know my end, and what is the measure of my days, that I may know how frail I am. Indeed, You have made my days as handbreadths, and my age is as nothing before You; certainly, every man at his best state is but vapor. (Ps. 39:4–5)

For my days are consumed like smoke. (Ps. 102:3)

My days are like a shadow that lengthens, and I wither away like grass. (Ps. 102:11)

As for man, his days are like grass; as a flower of the
field, so he flourishes. For the wind passes over it, and it is
gone, and its place remembers it no more. (Ps. 103:15–16)

But, beloved, do not forget this one thing, that with the
Lord one day is as a thousand years, and a thousand years
as one day. (2 Peter 3:8)

An unknown writer has captured the way life slips through our
fingers with these words:

When as a child, I laughed and wept—time crept.
When as a youth, I dreamed and talked—time walked.
When I became a full-grown man—time ran.
When older still I grew—time flew.
Soon I shall find in passing on—time gone.

Jesus tells the story of a very wealthy farmer who looked into the
future and decided that he needed to build bigger barns so that he
would be able to become even wealthier. His ultimate goal was a lei-
surely retirement. "And I will say to my soul, 'Soul, you have many
goods laid up for many years; take your ease; eat, drink, and be merry'"
(Luke 12:19).

In the parable the man is called a fool, not because he was planning
for the future, but because he thought he was in total control of it. On
the very night when he had so carefully laid out his plans, he died and
became the fulfillment of the Old Testament proverb, "Do not boast
about tomorrow, for you do not know what a day may bring forth"
(Prov. 27:1).

MISTAKE THREE: POSTPONING WHAT SHOULD
BE DONE TODAY

There is a wonderful story about a man who was cleaning out his desk
one day when he found a shoe-repair ticket that was ten years old.

Figuring that he had nothing to lose, he went to the shop and gave the ticket to the repairman, who began to search the back room for the unclaimed shoes. After several minutes, he reappeared and gave the ticket back to the man.

"What's wrong?" asked the man. "Couldn't you find my shoes?"

"Oh, I found them," replied the repairman, "and they'll be ready next Friday."

We smile at the exaggeration of this story, but we cannot laugh at its intended message. Procrastination is at the root of much of our trouble. I read about a businessman who had these letters in a large frame—PITTOT. They meant "Procrastination Is the Thief of Time."

As we read the Old Testament, we discover that the destructive practice of procrastination has been around for a long time.

> "Come," one says, "I will bring wine, and we will fill
> ourselves with intoxicating drink; tomorrow will be as
> today, and much more abundant." (Isa. 56:12)

> Do not withhold good from those to whom it is due,
> when it is in the power of your hand to do so. Do not say
> to your neighbor, "Go, and come back, and tomorrow I will
> give it," when you have it with you.
> (Prov. 3:27–28)

But the Bible has written the word *now* in large letters in the gospel message. "Behold, *now* is the accepted time; behold, *now* is the day of salvation" (2 Cor. 6:2). The time for obedience is now! We cannot count on tomorrow, so we must take advantage of today. In business terms, *yesterday* is a canceled check. *Tomorrow* is a promissory note. *Today* is the only cash we have.

If we isolate James' words from this context, the whole idea of the sin of omission has never been given more pointed expression: "Therefore, to him who knows to do good and does not do it, to him it is sin" (4:17).

There is also another basic truth wrapped up in verse 17. James is making it very clear that knowledge and responsibility go hand in hand. To sin ignorantly is one thing. To sin in the face of known truth is something altogether different. Here are two statements to that effect: one from Peter and one from our Lord:

> For it would have been better for them not to have known the way of righteousness, than having known it, to turn from the holy commandment delivered to them. (2 Peter 2:21)

> And that servant who knew his master's will, and did not prepare himself or do according to his will, shall be beaten with many stripes. But he who did not know, yet committed things deserving of stripes, shall be beaten with few. For everyone to whom much is given, from him much will be required; and to whom much has been committed, of him they will ask the more. (Luke 12:47–48)

Earlier James had faulted the businessmen for leaving God out of their plans. Now he reminds them of a sin that is just as serious:

> Sin ought never to be taken lightly. This is especially true of the sin of omission which is often given the innocuous appearance of oversight. But this is not so. Consider the farewell speech of Samuel. He says to the Israelites, "As for me, far be it from me that I should sin against the Lord by failing to pray for you" (1 Sam. 12:23 NIV). Samuel shunned the sin of neglect. Neglect is the equivalent of ignoring God and the neighbor, and is therefore a sin against the law of God.[14]

Facing Up to Pride

The key to understanding why these businessmen were violating the future is found in verse 16. Simply put, the problem was pride. They planned without God because they thought they were the masters of their fate. They presumed about tomorrow because they thought that nothing could happen outside of their control. They procrastinated because they assumed that they would be able to do tomorrow what they chose not to do today. J. B. Phillips paraphrases verse 16 like this: "As it is, you take a certain pride in planning with such confidence. That sort of pride is all wrong."

Alec Motyer explains the two Greek words that are used to define their haughty spirit:

> The verb "to boast" (*kauchaomai*) is often used in the New Testament in a good sense for exultant, abounding joy in something, as when, for example, we are encouraged to boast in our hope of the glory of God (Rom. 5:2). But what an unholy, unacceptable thing this exulting becomes when it arises from your arrogance! Here is a word (*alazoneia*) used elsewhere only in 1 John 2:16, and translated "the pride of life." In other words, when even in little, secret, almost unrecognized ways we forget how frail we are, and stop short of conscious dependence on our God, it is an element of the proud, boastful, vaunting human spirit, flaunting its supposed independence and self-sufficiency.[15]

Because the word *boast* is in the plural, it is a reference to many outbursts of pride and bragging on the part of these merchants. Lewis Smedes says that this kind of pride comes in three basic models: pride of power, pride of knowledge, and pride of virtue:

> A person with *pride of power* believes that his power itself gives him the right to do anything with his power that he gets into his head to do. A person with *pride of knowledge* believes that he has the whole truth and nothing but the truth in his head and that anything that contradicts his truth is a lie. A person with the *pride of virtue* believes that he is God's model of virtue and that anybody whose way of life does not match his, is probably living in sin.[16]

All three models of pride are unbecoming to the Christian, but according to the apostle Paul, there can be a legitimate reason for a Christian to boast. For instance, we may boast in our weakness, for in our weakness the power of Christ becomes apparent:

> If I must boast, I will boast in the things which concern my infirmity. (2 Cor. 11:30)

> Of such a one I will boast; yet of myself I will not boast, except in my infirmities.... And He said to me, "My grace is sufficient for you, for My strength is made perfect in weakness." Therefore most gladly I will rather boast in my infirmities, that the power of Christ may rest upon me. (2 Cor. 12:5, 9)

One of my favorite passages from the Old Testament suggests another possibility for Christian boasting:

> "Let not the wise man glory in his wisdom, let not the mighty man glory in his might, nor let the rich man glory in his riches; but let him who glories glory in this, that he understands and knows Me, that I am the Lord, exercising lovingkindness, judgment, and righteousness in the earth. For in these I delight," says the Lord. (Jer. 9:23–24)

Deo Volente

If you have read letters that passed between Christians one hundred years ago, you have probably noticed the postscript D.V. These two letters stand for the Latin words *Deo volente*, which mean "if the Lord wills or God willing." James' proposed alternative to the presumptuous lifestyle of the businessmen is found in verse 15. "Instead you ought to say, 'If the Lord wills, we shall live and do this or that.'" "If the Lord wills" should have been an acknowledgment that the planners wanted God's direction and approval and would do nothing without it.

Deferring to the will of God is the example that is set before us in many of the narrative sections of the New Testament where human plans are mentioned:

> Paul told the Jews at Ephesus that he would return for a renewed ministry among them "*if God wills*" (Acts 18:21). He wrote to the Corinthians that he planned another visit to them "*if the Lord wills*" (1 Cor. 4:19), and that he would remain with them a considerable time "*if the Lord permits*" (1 Cor. 16:7). A similar thought is doubtless to be inferred from Paul's statement that he hoped "*in the Lord*" to go to Philippi himself in the near future (Phil. 2:24). The writer of Hebrews expressed the goal of reaching spiritual maturity with the readers "*if God permits*" (Heb. 6:3).[17]

What James is asking his readers to consider is this: Trust in God and not a well-thought-out plan for material gain is the only way to face the future. He is asking them to live in the recognition that God, not man, is in control.

As far as knowing God's will, there is general agreement among Christians that three basic issues are involved. First, there must be a willingness to do God's will when we find it. Second, we must realize that God's will is always in harmony with His Word. And third, we must come to Him earnestly in prayer, seeking guidance. If we will do these things, we can know the will of God.

When our goals have been set and a target date determined for those goals to be accomplished, we can depend upon the Lord to direct our steps. But let us be reminded again that to enjoy God's help, it is necessary to specifically plan what we believe to be God's will. As God is a part of the planning, He will help toward the goal He has determined. One thing ought to be clear to us as we absorb the truth of this passage: If our goals are God's goals, we are certain to reach them faster than going it on our own.

An article titled "The Art of Being a Big Shot" was written by

Christian businessman Howard Butt. Among many insightful things that he said was this statement about pride. It sounds like he might have written these words after reading James 4:13–17:

> It is my pride that makes me independent of God. It's appealing to me to feel that I am the master of my fate, that I run my own life, call my own shots, go it alone. But that feeling is my basic dishonesty. I can't go it alone. I have to get help from other people, and I can't ultimately rely on myself. I'm dependent on God for my next breath. It is dishonest of me to pretend that I'm anything but a man—small, weak, and limited. So, living independent of God is self-delusion. It is not just a matter of pride being an unfortunate little trait and humility being an attractive little virtue; it's my inner psychological integrity that's at stake. When I am conceited, I am lying to myself about what I am. I am pretending to be God, and not man. My pride is the idolatrous worship of myself. And that is the national religion of Hell.[18]

WHAT TO DO WHEN YOUR NET WORTH IS WORTHLESS
(JAMES 5:1–6)

*Come now, you rich, weep and howl for your
miseries that are coming upon you!*

My wife and I visited New York City recently, and while moving about the city in a cab, we drove past the Helmsley Palace. I was immediately reminded of one of the most bizarre stories of the 1980s. Who among us will ever forget the hotel baroness who was knee-deep in luxury but refused to pay her taxes and treated her employees like dirt? I don't know how you responded to that story, but as we watched the demise of Mrs. Helmsley, it was very difficult for us to keep our composure. There is something about a wicked wealthy person that causes the hair to stand up on the back of our necks. "With all of that money," we think, "the least she could do is treat people with a little decency."

But the fact is, as we will learn in this chapter, that there is something about the love of money for its own sake that brings out the worst in people:

> Achan's lust for money and possessions brought death
> to himself, his family, and dozens of men in battle (Josh.
> 7). The prophet Balaam would have cursed God's people
> for Balak's payment (Num. 22:4–25). Delilah betrayed
> Samson to the Philistines for a fee (Judg. 16). Solomon's

lust for more and more wealth led him to disobey
flagrantly the prohibitions of God's law concerning the
accumulation of large amounts of horses, gold, silver,
and wives (Deut. 17:16–17). To gain wealth, Gehazi lied
to Naaman and then to Elisha, for which he was afflicted
with leprosy (2 Kings 5:20–27). Ananias and Sapphira
withheld money they said was given to the Lord and were
struck dead for it (Acts 5:1–11). In the ultimate act of
treachery, the materialist Judas asked the chief priests,
"What are you willing to give me if I hand him over to
you?" and then betrayed the Son of God for thirty pieces
of silver (Matt. 26:14–16, 47–50; 27:3–10).[1]

Not only did the love of money have an evil effect on people we
read about in the Bible, but it is also at the root of much of the misery
we observe in present-day society. In one of the most provocative books
I have read in recent months, physician Richard A. Swenson, after list-
ing the gigantic strides we have taken through our prosperity, catalogs
some of the cost:

Unfortunately ... these benefits do not constitute the
whole story; luminous advancements often cast dark shadows. In the case of our economic prosperity, the shadows
of debt, vulnerability, and uncertainty extend far into the
future. For every positive economic indicator, there is a
corresponding dismal one. We are in troubled water on
nearly every financial front, and no one can confidently
suggest a way out. Serious economic experts make predic-
tions that come up inside out.[2]

As James focuses his attention on the wicked wealthy of his day,
his words are so strong that many commentaries pass over the first six
verses of chapter 5 with a simple summary statement. Other writers
honestly admit that they do not know what to do with such vitriolic
comments:

Upton Sinclair, the novelist and social reformer, once read
a paraphrase of this section to a group of ministers after
attributing it to Emma Goldman, an anarchist agitator. The
ministers were so enraged they declared she ought to be
deported.[3]

James has already mentioned the rich on three other occasions.
In 1:9–11, the rich are obviously believers. In 2:2–3 and 2:6, the rich
are nonbelievers. Here in 5:1–6, it is generally assumed that James is
addressing wealthy individuals outside of the Christian church:

> The words addressed to the rich are meant not primarily
> for their ears, but as an encouragement to Christians in
> times of unjust treatment, and to dissuade them from the
> folly of setting a high value upon wealth, or of envying
> those who possess it, or of striving feverishly to obtain it.[4]

As he speaks to those *outside* the church in a letter addressed to
those *inside* the church, James "employs a rhetorical device known
as *apostrophe,* a turning away from his real audience to address some
other group."[5]

No doubt some of these secular merchants were abusing members of the believing assembly and at the same time claiming some
relationship with God through their friendship with these godly followers of Christ.

Earlier, when he was teaching on the subject of favoritism, James
had reminded these same readers that the wealthy people they were
treating with preference were the very ones who were oppressing
them and dragging them into the courts of the land (2:6). Now,
James has had enough! His words here are some of the most biting
in the Bible.

This is not an indictment of wealth per se. There is no data from
the Bible to support the idea that it is wrong to be wealthy. In fact,
there is evidence to the contrary. In Proverbs we read, "The blessing of
the Lord makes one rich, and He adds no sorrow with it" (10:22).

There are many notable examples in the Bible of godly, wealthy people—Job, Abraham, Nicodemus, Mary, Martha, Lazarus, Joseph of Arimathea, Barnabas, and Philemon.

God does not disapprove of people with money, but He does speak out against those who "trust in riches." "He who trusts in his riches will fall" (Prov. 11:28). "But Jesus answered again and said unto them, 'Children, how hard it is for those who trust in riches to enter the kingdom of God!'" (Mark 10:24).

This uncontrolled desire for wealth is the target of James' sweeping statements. Like Paul he sees the danger not in wealth, but in so loving wealth that it blots out love for God and for others (1 Tim. 6:10).

Someone has said that God will not condemn a man for being wealthy, but He will ask him two questions. First, "How did you gain your wealth?" and second, "How did you use your wealth?"

THE DESPERATE ANGUISH OF THE WICKED WEALTHY

For the second time in just a few verses, James uses the strong exhortation, "Come now ..." (5:1; see 4:13). These wicked merchants are called upon to weep and howl. The tears are not tears of repentance but because of the judgment that is sure to fall on them. At the time they may think they are living well, but if they could only know what is to happen to them, they would begin at once to weep and mourn in sorrow.

John Calvin separates this kind of sorrow from the sorrow of repentance when he writes, "Repentance has indeed its weeping, but being mixed with consolation, it does not proceed to howling."[6]

Weep means "to sob aloud, to lament, to sob bitterly." It was used of wailing for the dead (Luke 7:13; John 11:31–33). Peter "wept bitterly" after he realized what he had done in denying Christ (Luke 22:62).

Howl is an expression of intense grief. The Greek expression is an onomatopoetic verb, meaning that the word sounds like what it means. The Greek word *ololuzontes* is found only here in all of the New Testament. The picture portrayed is that of open and vocal sobbing, with howls of agony, at the return of Christ in judgment.

THE DREADFUL JUDGMENT OF THE WICKED WEALTHY

James uses three expressions to illustrate the temporary nature of their wealth. In each case, the Greek construction anticipates their future demise as already happening. Your riches *are* corrupted. Your garments *are* moth eaten. Your gold and silver *are* corroded. You are being judged already!

Your Riches Are Corrupted

When we think of riches, we usually picture stocks and bonds, large bank accounts, and major real estate holdings. But wealth has always been a cultural expression. For instance, the wealth of Job was calculated in sheep, camels, oxen, and donkeys (Job 1:3). The wealth of the early New Testament church was apparently houses and lands (Acts 4:34–35). At the time of James' letter, the commodities were different yet.

Most commentators believe that James' mention of "riches" relates to foodstuffs … grains. In other words, their wealth was measured by the amount of grain and fruit and vegetables they had stored away for some future day.

But all these items are subject to decay, and James suggests to the wealthy that they are storing up wealth that has no way of enduring. It will rot!

Your Garments Are Moth Eaten

Another evidence of wealth was the wardrobe of the rich. They bought beautiful garments wherever they went and no doubt showed them off. It was the lure of the garment to which Achan confessed:

> When I saw among the spoils a beautiful Babylonian garment, two hundred shekels of silver, and a wedge of gold weighing fifty shekels, I coveted them and took them. And there they are, hidden in the earth in the midst of my tent, with the silver under it. (Josh. 7:21)

Jacob gave Joseph a coat of many colors (Gen. 37:3). Joseph gave Benjamin five changes of raiment (Gen. 45:22). Samson promised thirty changes of garments to the one who guessed his riddle (Judg. 14:12). Paul said, "I have coveted no one's silver or gold or apparel" (Acts 20:33).

As valuable as these garments were, when they were stored in the heat of the Orient, the moths would destroy them. There were no mothballs in those days, and the moths loved these rich garments.

Your Gold and Silver Are Corroded

It is obvious that pure gold and silver do not corrode. The figurative language is used to express the worthless nature of gold and silver that is stored up for the future. It might as well be a piece of corroded metal.

These three statements express the futility of keeping in storage those things that should be put into circulation for the glory of God and the welfare of mankind. The clothes could have been given to the poor; instead, they were given to the moths. The gold and silver could have purchased help and healing for the less fortunate; instead, they were allowed to corrode. This warning is in keeping with our Lord's words:

> Do not lay up for yourselves treasures on earth, where moth and rust destroy and where thieves break in and steal; but lay up for yourselves treasures in heaven, where neither moth nor rust destroys and where thieves do not break in and steal. For where your treasure is, there your heart will be also. (Matt. 6:19–21)

In AD 70, twenty-five years after James wrote this letter, Titus invaded Jerusalem and destroyed it. The wealthy and the poor alike were oppressed and stripped of everything that they owned. The riches that had been hoarded were taken by strangers and never returned.

Before we leave this discussion, perhaps I should anticipate your question. Is it wrong to save money for the future? Are the Christian financial advisers wrong when they instruct believers to put money aside? Here's the straight answer:

In the final analysis, the issue is not savings but hoarding. Modern saving is probably acceptable to God.... Hoarding, however, is never acceptable. He is trusting us with certain resources; He as owner and we as stewards. We should never pretend that we have rights to what is not ours.

God is honored by funnels and dishonored by sponges. Be a conduit of His blessing, not a dead end. Some increased savings for known future expenses and unknown contingencies seems acceptable. But dead-end hoarding or empire building is not.[7]

THE DEVASTATING FUTURE OF THE WICKED WEALTHY

The Old Testament preacher of Ecclesiastes had a similar word to that of James: "There is a severe evil which I have seen under the sun: riches kept for their owner to his hurt" (5:13).

The fact that the rich possess hoarded goods in the day of judgment will be presented as evidence that they have not followed God's directives for sharing with the poor. They are actually providing evidence to be used in their own indictment! Ezekiel has a parallel statement in his prophecy:

> They will throw their silver into the streets, and their gold
> will be like refuse; their silver and their gold will not be
> able to deliver them in the day of the wrath of the Lord;
> they will not satisfy their souls, nor fill their stomachs,
> because it became their stumbling block of iniquity. (7:19)

This graphic portrayal of their judgment is devastating. It will be as if their hoarded wealth is burning them with fire. In the loss of their property, their own personal loss is included.

The corrosive action of the rust on their hoarded gold and silver is now symbolically presented as eating the flesh of

the oppressive rich themselves in that day.... In the day of
Judgment their rusted wealth, like a rusty chain, will eat
into their pampered flesh like a festering sore. Its effect
will be like fire, torturing while it devours.[8]

To this promise of judgment the author adds a final note: "They
have treasured up their wealth in the last days." Peter Davids expresses
it this way: "These people have treasured up as if they would live and
the world would go on forever; but the end times, in which they have a
last chance to repent and put their goods to righteous uses, are already
upon them."[9]

The Christians of James' day firmly believed that Christ was soon
to come for judgment. Notice the three separate mentions of this in the
next section of chapter 5:

> Therefore be patient, brethren, until *the coming of the Lord.*
> See how the farmer waits for the precious fruit of the
> earth, waiting patiently for it until it receives the early and
> latter rain. You also be patient. Establish your hearts, for
> *the coming of the Lord* is at hand. Do not grumble against
> one another, brethren, lest you be condemned. Behold, *the
> Judge is standing at the door!* (vv. 7–9)

Homer Kent explains the mind-set of the people who would have
read James' letter:

> The "last days" was a designation for messianic times,
> which began with Christ's first coming (Acts 2:16–17;
> 1 Tim. 4:1–2; 2 Peter 3:3; 1 John 2:18). These rich men
> were oblivious to the momentous days in which they were
> living. They did not understand that the "last days' had
> already begun and that Christ's second coming could be
> at any moment. They were like the Babylonians, feasting
> and reveling in willful ignorance that disaster was about to
> strike their city (Dan. 5:1–31).[10]

THE DECEITFUL PRACTICES OF THE WICKED WEALTHY

German scholar Adolf Deissman wrote, "The Epistle of James will be best understood in the open air beside the piled sheaves of the harvest field."[11] Certainly this passage is one of the reasons for his comment. The picture presented here is of a rich absentee landowner who hires day laborers to care for his property in his absence. This was a common occurrence in ancient Israel. The practice of paying wages late or bilking the worker of his wages was also common in those times. James Adamson elaborates, "This scene is deliberately set after harvest: the owners of these Galilean 'estates' were well able to pay wages. The word *withheld* indicates not just delay but complete default."[12]

Many passages in the Old Testament deal with this wicked practice:

> You shall not cheat your neighbor, nor rob him. The wages of him who is hired shall not remain with you all night until morning. (Lev. 19:13)

> You shall not oppress a hired servant who is poor and needy, whether one of your brethren or one of the aliens who is in your land within your gates. Each day you shall give him his wages, and not let the sun go down on it, for he is poor and has set his heart on it; lest he cry out against you to the Lord, and it be sin to you. (Deut. 24:14–15)

> Woe to him who builds his house by unrighteousness and his chambers by injustice, who uses his neighbor's service without wages and gives him nothing for his work. (Jer. 22:13)

If James is referring to any of his Christian readers, he has already communicated to them that such indifference to the needs of the poor is proof of insincere religion:

> What does it profit, my brethren, if someone says he has faith but does not have works? Can faith save him? If a

> brother or sister is naked and destitute of daily food, and
> one of you says to them, "Depart in peace, be warmed
> and filled," but you do not give them the things which are
> needed for the body, what does it profit? (2:14–16)

Now James reminds his friends that the Lord hears the cries of those who have been cheated. In fact, he uses a special name for the Lord who hears. He calls Him *the Lord of Sabaoth*. *Sabaoth* is the Hebrew word for "hosts." It is used of human armies (Num. 1:3), angelic armies (1 Kings 22:19), and the stars of the heaven (Deut. 17:3). "The Lord of Hosts" is one of the majestic names for God and portrays Him as the commander of the heavenly army (Josh. 5:15). This phrase conveys the idea that the abuse of the poor gets the attention of the supreme Sovereign of the universe. Leslie Mitton reminds us, "It is the same God, who created the sun, moon and stars, and who orders their courses, who is also deeply concerned about the just treatment of the poor and insignificant."[13]

Alec Motyer adds that the name, Lord of Sabaoth, points to the Lord "who has within Himself and at His sovereign command, every potency and resource.... No power, however great or solid to the earthly eye, is beyond His capacity, no need, however pressing, is beyond His means, or outside His attention."[14]

Martin Luther incorporated this name for God into his great hymn "A Mighty Fortress Is Our God":

> Dost ask who that may be?
> Christ Jesus, it is He;
> Lord Sabaoth His name,
> From age to age the same,
> And He must win the battle.

When James employs this title, he is creating the clear image that the doom of these oppressors is near at hand. The Lord of Sabaoth is about to judge them. They have amassed their wealth at the expense of other people, and they will not escape God's judgment!

THE DELUXE LIFESTYLE OF THE WICKED WEALTHY

The Lifestyles of the Rich and Famous did not begin as a modern television series. It is as old as the prodigal son who "squandered his wealth in wild living" (Luke 15:13 NIV). It is characterized by Jesus in the description of the rich man as one "who was dressed in purple and fine linen and lived in luxury every day" (Luke 16:19 NIV).

This lifestyle is addictive! Randy Alcorn tells it like it is when he describes the modern version of this ancient depravity:

> Promising fulfillment in money and things and lands and houses and cars and clothes and boats and campers and hot tubs and world travel, materialism has left us bound and gagged, pathetically thinking what the drug addict thinks, that our only hope is getting more of the same. All the while the voice of God, so hard to hear through the clatter of our things, tells us that even if materialism did bring happiness in this life—which it clearly does not—it leaves us woefully unprepared for the next.[15]

And British writer Richard Holloway adds,

> It has been observed that if we pursue pleasure we fail to get it. Pleasure is a by-product of many activities.... The problem arises because of the mysterious tendency in our nature: we try to separate the pleasure from the act that gives it and go after it for its own sake. Unfortunately, it does not work for long ... because the pursuit of pleasure for its own sake is always ultimately unsatisfying ... and [becomes] addictive.[16]

Finally, listen to the words of A. W. Tozer:

> Before the Lord God made man upon the earth, He first prepared for him a world of useful and pleasant things for his sustenance and delight. In the Genesis account of the

creation these are called simply "things." They were made for man's use, but they were meant always to be external to the man and subservient to him. In the deep heart of the man was a shrine where none but God was worthy to come. Within him was God; without, a thousand gifts which God had showered upon him.

But sin has introduced complications and has made those very gifts of God a potential source of ruin to the soul. Our woes began when God was forced out of His central shrine and things were allowed to enter. Within the human heart things have taken over. Men have now by nature no peace within their hearts, for God is crowned there no longer; but there in the moral dusk, stubborn and aggressive usurpers fight among themselves for first place on the throne. This is not a mere metaphor, but an accurate analysis of our real spiritual trouble. There is within the human heart a tough, fibrous root of fallen life whose nature is to possess, always to possess. It covets things with a deep and fierce passion. The pronouns *my* and *mine* look innocent enough in print, but their constant and universal use is significant. They express the real nature of the Old Adamic man better than a thousand volumes of theology could do. They are verbal symptoms of our deep disease. The roots of our hearts have grown down into things, and we dare not pull up one rootlet lest we die. Things have become necessary to us, a development never originally intended. God's gifts now take the place of God, and the whole course of nature is upset by the monstrous substitution.[17]

When James mentions the "day of slaughter," he is using a prophetic term that likens the day of God's judgment to the day of the slaughter of His enemies (Isa. 34:5–8; Jer. 46:10; 50:25–27). Here are the ramifications of his words:

Unless we know how animals are prepared for food, we
might have trouble understanding James at this point. We
need to realize that steers are specially fed so that they
will make good steaks. Hogs are specially fed to make good
pork. Chickens and turkeys are specially fed to fatten them
up for the table. James is saying, "You have pampered
yourself in everything that you did. You have nourished
your hearts, as in a day of slaughter."[18]

Alec Motyer adds this:

They are like so many unthinking beasts, luxuriating in
their rich pasture day after day, growing fat by the hour
and careless of the fact that each day, each hour, brings
the butcher nearer. Only the thin beast is safe in that day;
the well-fed has made itself ready for the knife. In such a
way James saw the wealthy, blind alike to heaven and hell,
living for this life, forgetting the day of slaughter.[19]

THE DEADLY CRIMES OF THE WICKED WEALTHY

Whether the rich actually committed murder is not known. Perhaps by
dragging the poor into court and depriving them of the bare necessities
of life, they caused their deaths indirectly. In the second century before
Christ, Joshua ben Sira said, "The bread of the needy is the life of the
poor; whoever deprives them of it is a man of blood. To take away a
neighbor's living is to murder him; to deprive an employee of his wages
is to shed blood."[20]

When this section concludes with the phrase "he does not resist
you," the final indictment is leveled against the uncaring rich:

The very effective point of this climax plainly is that the
helplessness of their victims increases the damnation of
these rich.... The rich are represented, not as bold and

fearless champions, defending a cause against dangerous enemies, but as brutal bullies, picking as the victims of their outrages those who either cannot or will not resist.[21]

As we look back over the landscape of materialism and abuse, we must ask again this question, "What should be our attitude toward money?"

Earthly possessions are like the tides of the sea: they come and go. Therefore, we ought not to base our destiny on the instability of earthly riches. Rather, we should receive every good and perfect gift out of God's hand (James 1:17), and then wisely dispense the money God gives us. When we remember the needs of our fellowman and give generously, we reflect God's generosity toward us.[22]

If we place more importance on money than the Bible allows, we are destined for disappointment:

Picture 269 people entering eternity in a plane crash in the Sea of Japan. Before the crash there is a noted politician, a millionaire corporate executive, a playboy and his playmate, a missionary kid on the way back from visiting grandparents. After the crash they stand before God utterly stripped of MasterCards, checkbooks, credit lines, image clothes, how-to-succeed books, and Hilton reservations. Here are the politician, the executive, the playboy, and the missionary kid, all on level ground with nothing, absolutely nothing in their hands, possessing only what they brought in their hearts. How absurd and tragic the lover of money will seem on that day—like a man who spends his whole life collecting train tickets and in the end is so weighed down by the collection he misses the last train.[23]

Without meaning to, Henry Kissinger drives home the warning of James 5:1–6 when he writes:

> To Americans, usually tragedy is wanting something very badly and not getting it. Many people have had to learn in their private lives, and nations have had to learn in their historical experience, that perhaps the worst form of tragedy is wanting something badly, getting it, and finding it empty.[24]

WHAT TO DO WHEN YOU'RE IN A HURRY AND GOD ISN'T

(JAMES 5:7–12)

*Be patient.... Establish your hearts,
for the coming of the Lord is at hand.*

Some months ago, *Time* magazine published an article by Nancy Gibbs entitled "How America Has Run Out of Time." What she wrote about the escalating value of time coincides with my personal observations:

> There was once a time when time was money. Both could be wasted or both well spent, but in the end, gold was the richer prize. As with almost any commodity, however, value depends on scarcity. And these are the days of the time famine. Time that once seemed free and elastic has grown tight and elusive, and so our measure of its worth is dramatically changed. In Florida a man bills his ophthalmologist $90 for keeping him waiting an hour. In California a woman hires somebody to do her shopping for her—out of a catalog. Twenty bucks pays someone to pick up the dry cleaning, $250 to cater dinner for four, $1,500 will buy a fax machine for the car. "Time," concludes pollster Louis Harris, who has charted America's loss of it, "may have become the most precious commodity in the land."[1]

With time becoming so precious, is it any wonder that waiting has become the most hated and frustrating experience in life? We wait in bank lines, in supermarket lines, at the doctor's office, and on the freeway. And while we wait, we fret because we are wasting time.

Have you noticed how long we wait when we go out to eat? We wait to be seated. We wait for the menu. We wait to place our order. We wait for our food. We wait for the check. And finally we wait for the opportunity to pay the check. And the restaurant has the audacity to refer to the one who oversees all of this as "the waiter." The customer is the waiter. Believe me, I know!

A man's car stalled on the freeway, and no matter what he did, he could not get it started. Traffic was backing up, and most everyone was taking it pretty good-naturedly, except one guy in a pickup truck who was just laying on his horn. The driver of the stalled vehicle walked back to the driver of the pickup and said, "I'm sorry, but I can't get my car started. If you'll go up there and give it a try, I'll stay here in your truck and blow your horn for you."

I am told that the great New England preacher Phillips Brooks was known for his calmness and poise. His intimate friends, however, knew that he too suffered moments of frustration and irritability. One day a friend saw him pacing the floor like a caged lion. "What is the trouble, Dr. Brooks?" asked the friend. "The trouble is," replied Brooks, "that I'm in a hurry, but God isn't."

If you have ever felt like Phillips Brooks did, this section of James is for you! The words *patience, endurance,* and *perseverance* are mentioned no less than six times:

Be *patient* ... until the coming of the Lord. (5:7)

The farmer waits for the precious fruit of the earth, waiting *patiently* for it. (5:7)

Be *patient*. Establish your hearts, for the coming of the Lord is at hand. (5:8)

> My brethren, take the prophets, who spoke in the name
> of the Lord, as an example of suffering and *patience*. (5:10)

> Indeed we count them blessed who *endure*. You have
> heard of the *perseverance* of Job. (5:11)

Patience is the quality that the apostle Paul continually stressed as a requirement for a godly life:

> He mentions it in his first letter to the Corinthians, in his
> list of qualities that characterize love. He includes it as
> one of the nine traits which he calls the fruit of the Spirit
> in Galatians. When he describes to the Ephesians a life
> worthy of God's calling, he includes the trait of long-suf-
> fering. He also includes it when he gives the Colossians
> a list of godly qualities with which Christians should
> clothe themselves. He stresses it to the Thessalonians,
> and commends his own life to the Corinthians and to
> Timothy partly because patience is one of his character
> traits.[2]

Someone has said, "You can do anything if you have patience. You can carry water in a sieve, if you wait until it freezes."

WE NEED PATIENCE WHEN WE FACE DIFFICULTY

The people to whom James was writing were experiencing tremendous difficulty and persecution. As we learned in the first six verses of James 5, the wicked wealthy had committed all kinds of injustices against the believers.

Now James is going to remind his Christian readers that no matter what evil has done to them, they are not to retaliate against people or against God. In some ways he is returning to the theme with which he began his letter: "Count it all joy when you fall into various trials" (1:2).

The word for "patience" in Greek is *makrothumia,* which stresses nonretaliation. It means to hold one's spirit in check. W. E. Vine's *Expository Dictionary of Old and New Testament Words* gives this careful definition:

> MAKROTHUMIA (*makros* = long, *thumos* = temper) is usually rendered "long-suffering." Long-suffering is that quality of self-restraint in the face of provocation which does not hastily retaliate or promptly punish; it is the opposite of anger, and is associated with mercy, and is used of God, Exodus 34:6 (Sept.); Romans 2:4; 1 Peter 3:20.[3]

William Barclay adds:

> Chrysostom defined *makrothumia* as the spirit which could take revenge if it liked, but utterly refuses to do so. Lightfoot explained it as the spirit which will never retaliate. Now this is the very opposite of the Greek virtue. The Greek virtue was *megalopsuchia*, which Aristotle defined as the refusal to tolerate any insult or injury. To the Greek the big man was the man who went all out for vengeance. To the Christian the big man is the man who, even when he can, refuses to do so.[4]

Jerry Bridges explains how this concept works in everyday life:

> This aspect of patience is the ability to suffer a long time under the mistreatment of others without growing resentful or bitter. The occasions for exercising this quality are numerous; they vary from malicious wrongs all the way to seemingly innocent practical jokes. They include ridicule, scorn, insults, and undeserved rebukes, as well as outright persecution. The Christian who is the victim of office politics or organizational power plays must react with long-suffering. The believing husband or wife who is

rejected or mistreated by an unbelieving spouse needs this kind of patience.[5]

Jesus Christ is the perfect illustration of long-suffering. He was verbally and physically abused. He was spat upon, falsely accused, beaten, and nailed to the cross. He suffered much, but He did not retaliate. The apostle Peter captures the essence of our Lord's perseverance:

> For to this you were called, because Christ also suffered for us, leaving us an example, that you should follow His steps: "Who committed no sin, nor was deceit found in His mouth," who, when He was reviled, did not revile in return; when He suffered, He did not threaten, but committed Himself to Him who judges righteously.
> (1 Peter 2:21–23)

According to James, this long-suffering attitude is to control the believer until the Lord Jesus returns. In other words, until Jesus comes and rights all wrongs, the believer is to leave vengeance in His hands. For the early believers, the wait could not have seemed too long, for they expected that the Lord was coming back in their lifetime:

> Looking for the blessed hope and glorious appearing of our great God and Savior Jesus Christ. (Titus 2:13)

> Waiting for the revelation of our Lord Jesus Christ.
> (1 Cor. 1:7)

> For our citizenship is in heaven, from which we also eagerly wait for the Savior, the Lord Jesus Christ.
> (Phil. 3:20)

> When Christ who is our life appears, then you also will appear with Him in glory. (Col. 3:4)

> For they themselves declare concerning us what manner
> of entry we had to you, and how you turned to God from
> idols to serve the living and true God, and To wait for His
> Son from heaven, whom He raised from the dead, even Jesus
> who delivers us from the wrath to come. (1 Thess. 1:9–10)

> Beloved, now we are children of God; and it has not yet
> been revealed what we shall be, but we know that when
> He is revealed, we shall be like Him, for we shall see Him
> as He is. And everyone who has this hope in Him purifies
> himself, just as He is pure. (1 John 3:2–3)

> Let your moderation be known unto all men. The Lord is
> at hand. (Phil. 4:5 KJV)

Clement, the Greek church father (AD 150), informs us that James and his brother Jude were farmers. This explains why James so often uses vivid illustrations from farm life. He lived with the land from day to day. Now he admonishes his readers, "See how the farmer waits for the precious fruit of the earth, waiting patiently for it until it receives the early and latter rain" (5:7).

This illustration is drawn from Palestinian agriculture. The farmer sowed seed on ground that received no rain at all during much of the year. The fields were brown and the soil was dry. Modern irrigation techniques were unknown, and dependence upon the rains was crucial. Therefore, the farmer had to accept that fact and plan accordingly. He planned on two rainy seasons for the success of his crop. The "early and latter" rains refers to the fall rains in October and November which softened the ground after the blistering heat of summer, and to the spring showers of April and May, which caused the grain to ripen. The Bible often refers to these two seasons:

> Then I will give you the rain for your land in its season, the
> early rain and the latter rain, that you may gather in your
> grain, your new wine, and your oil. (Deut. 11:14)

> They do not say in their heart, "Let us now fear the Lord
> our God, who gives rain, both the former and the latter, in
> its season. He reserves for us the appointed weeks of the
> harvest." (Jer. 5:24)

> Be glad then, you children of Zion, and rejoice in the
> Lord your God; for He has given you the former rain
> faithfully, and He will cause the rain to come down for
> you—the former rain, and the latter rain in the first
> month. (Joel 2:23)

The point of the illustration is that the believer who is facing hostility must demonstrate a willingness to wait for vindication. As farmers wait for the rain for their crops, the believer must also learn to live in anticipation of the Lord's return and not get upset with circumstances that are difficult.

As they waited for the return of the Lord, the believers of James' day had no cause to worry—only thirty years had elapsed since Christ had promised to return. For us today, however, over 1,900 years have passed! Do we have the right to complain?

Think of how long it took for the first coming of Christ to arrive. In Genesis 3:15, we have what many consider to be the first gospel message. It is a prophecy of the first coming of Christ to the earth. No one knows exactly how many days passed between this promise and its fulfillment, but it is considerably more than 1,900 years. By the measurement of the most conservative scholars, it is more than twice that long. The great preacher G. Campbell Morgan declared:

> To me the second coming is the perpetual light on the path
> which makes the present bearable. I never lay my head on
> my pillow without thinking that, maybe before the morn-
> ing breaks, the final morning may have dawned. I never
> begin my work without thinking that perhaps He may
> interrupt my work and begin His own.[6]

The patience we are to exhibit in light of the Lord's return is not to be passive. In fact, James exhorts his readers, "Establish your hearts" (5:8). The text literally says, "Make firm your hearts."

> [James] ... urges them, as a decisive act, to strengthen and make firm their inner life. The verb conveys the thought of strengthening and supporting something so that it will stand firm and immovable. Instead of feeling agitated and shaken up by their experiences of oppression, they must develop an inner sense of stability. Williams paraphrases it, "You must put iron into your hearts," whereas the *New English Bible* calls upon them to be "stout-hearted." ... Here James calls upon the readers themselves to take this matter in hand. It is their personal duty to develop an attitude of courage and firmness in facing their circumstances.[7]

WE NEED PATIENCE WHEN WE FACE DISAPPOINTMENT

The next command seems almost out of place in this context until we stop and review our normal response to persecution and difficulty. What do we usually do when we begin to feel the heat? We complain to anyone who will listen! We lash out at each other because of the pressure that we are feeling. Now we can comprehend James' words, "Do not grumble against one another, brethren, lest you be condemned. Behold, the Judge is standing at the door!" (5:9).

Here are some other translations of this verse to upgrade our understanding:

> My brothers, do not blame your troubles on one another, or you will fall under judgment; and there stands the Judge, at the door. (NEB)

> Do not complain, brethren, against one another, so

> that you yourselves may not be judged; behold, the
> Judge is standing right at the door. (NASB)

> Don't make complaints against each other in the
> meantime, my brothers—you may be the one at fault
> yourself. The judge himself is already at the door. (PH)

James is now talking about how we are to act toward one another when we are facing difficulty. We are to exhibit this same long-suffering restraint in our relationships to other believers. If we think back to the illustration of the farm, we will gain added insight. I spent my growing-up summers on the farm, where I learned a valuable lesson: Farmers always help one another. In good times and in bad, they stick together. This is the goal James has in mind for the believers to whom he is writing. When pressures mount, there is a temptation to divide. It is at such a time, however, that the family of God must come together.

When we are experiencing the valleys of life and we look around at other Christians who seem to be sailing right along, what do we do? When we have lost our job and our best friend's husband just got a promotion, what do we do? Do we groan and grumble within? The word *groan* means "to sigh with an inner unexpressed feeling." There may be audible sounds, but actual words do not form. It is an inner sighing. James has already warned against overt complaining:

> Do not speak evil of one another, brethren. He who
> speaks evil of a brother and judges his brother, speaks
> evil of the law and judges the law. But if you judge the
> law, you are not a doer of the law but a judge. There is
> one Lawgiver, who is able to save and to destroy. Who
> are you to judge another? (4:11–12)

This letter was received by scattered believers, some of whom were suffering more than others. Not everyone was living at the same level of pain. Robert Johnstone imagines how it might have been in James' day:

Suppose one of these oppressed Jewish Christians is
summoned by some bigoted enemy of the cross ...
before a tribunal on some paltry pretext, but really,
as the accused and all around well know, because he
loves and honors Jesus.... The accused Christian then
suffers in his person or his goods, or both. While the
suffering is still fresh, his thoughts happen to turn to
a brother believer, one in every way as prominent a
member of the church as himself and in all respects
that he knows, as likely as himself to bring down upon
his head the vengeance of the unbelievers. Yet day
passes after day, month after month, and no evil comes
nigh him; he pursues his avocations and enjoys his
religious privileges in peace. Or he too is accused, and
tried—but allowed to go free. If the sufferer be off his
guard spiritually, grudging enters and gains strength
in his soul, withering his joys and energies.... And ...
on what does the grudging rest? Plainly on ... utterly
baseless suspicions that his Christianity, after all, is
not so pronounced and bright as it should be; that he
... contrives to keep on good terms with the enemies of
Christ ... that he possibly may have condescended to
bribe his judge, or the like.[8]

James reminds those who might be tempted to retaliate that they
should consider the imminent return of Christ for judgment. In his
words, "The Judge is standing at the door!" Knowing that the Judge
could at any moment step into the middle of their conversations and
evaluate them should have motivated these would-be grumblers to
reassess their conduct. And knowing that even unexpressed things
would be judged should have been a sobering thought. "The sinner is
only one heartbeat away from the Judge. For when death strikes, the
grumbler enters the presence of God, who will judge him for every idle
word he has spoken. Everyone who passes through the portals of death
meets the Judge on the other side."[9]

WE NEED PATIENCE WHEN WE FACE DISAPPROVAL

Now comes encouragement from the Old Testament! There have been those before us who have walked the path of disapproval and difficulty. As an example of suffering and patience, James suggests a look at the prophets who spoke in the name of the Lord:

> Moses had to struggle for many years with a stiff-necked
> and rebellious people; David was hunted by Saul "like
> a partridge on the mountains." And in advanced life he
> had again to become a fugitive, through the rebellion of
> the son he loved most dearly; Elijah's life was sought by
> the wicked rulers of Israel with vengeful fury; Jeremiah's
> life was one of continued persecution ... and so were the
> experiences of all the men of old.[10]

There are at least eleven passages in the New Testament that refer to the persecution of the prophets. Here are three examples:

> Blessed are you when they revile and persecute you,
> and say all kinds of evil against you falsely for My sake.
> Rejoice and be exceedingly glad, for great is your reward
> in heaven, for so they persecuted the prophets who were
> before you. (Matt. 5:11–12)

> O Jerusalem, Jerusalem, the one who kills the prophets
> and stones those who are sent to her! How often I wanted
> to gather your children together, as a hen gathers her
> chicks under her wings, but you were not willing!
> (Matt. 23:37)

> [Stephen speaking] Which of the prophets did your
> fathers not persecute? And they killed those who foretold
> the coming of the Just One. (Acts 7:52)

James' point is that the prophets suffered not because they did anything wrong, but because they were doing right! They spoke in the name of the Lord! They were disapproved by their contemporaries and persecuted for their testimony. And James knew what he was talking about. Four times in these verses he calls the recipients of this letter "brethren." He identifies himself with them in all that he is saying. According to secular historians, James met with a violent death because he would not denounce the messiahship of Jesus. He was thrown down from the pinnacle of the temple by the order of Annas the high priest. Throughout his entire life, he knew what it was like to suffer, and he speaks here to his friends as a fellow sufferer. These prophets to whom James refers were suffering affliction with patience.

Blessed are you poor, for yours is the kingdom of God.
Blessed are you who hunger now, for you shall be filled.
Blessed are you who weep now, for you shall laugh.
Blessed are you when men hate you, and when they exclude you, and revile you, and cast out your name as evil, for the Son of Man's sake. Rejoice in that day and leap for joy! For indeed your reward is great in heaven, for in like manner their fathers did to the prophets.
(Luke 6:20–23)

WE NEED PATIENCE WHEN WE FACE DISASTER

There is a word shift in the text here. James leaves the word *makrothumia*, and the idea of nonretaliation, and installs the word *hupomeno*, which means "steadfast endurance." Long-suffering (*makrothumia*) usually describes the attitude that a person has when he is pressured by other people. Patience (*hupomeno*) usually denotes the response to circumstances.

James is the only New Testament writer who mentions the name of Job. The story of Job actually begins in heaven where Satan is accusing him before God. When God mentions Job as a sterling example of righteousness, Satan replies that Job is godly only because he has everything going for him. He says, "God, if You take away the props, Job will curse You to Your face." So God allows Satan to do just that. In four swift strokes, Job is decimated.

- A messenger arrives and tells Job that the Sabeans have taken all his oxen and donkeys and killed his servants (1:15).
- A second messenger comes in and tells Job that fire from heaven has consumed all of his sheep and the servants who were watching them (1:16).
- Another servant arrives and tells Job that the Chaldeans have taken all of his camels and executed his servants who were watching them (1:17).
- Finally, a fourth servant shows up and tells Job that all of his children are dead; they were killed when the house they were in fell on them (1:18–19).

Job lost ten children: seven sons and three daughters. He was covered with boils from the crown of his head to the soles of his feet. He sat in an ash heap on a dunghill in misery and agony. His wife told him to curse God and commit suicide. Three comforters came to see Job and among other things told him that his suffering was due to his terrible sin. He lost his entire fortune, but he did not give in to the pressure:

> Satan has cast him on a dung heap, but he made the dung heap a throne in the presence of the great God. Satan afflicted him with sores and boils, but Job made them signets of honor. They were citations and medals all over him and Job made Satan eat his words. He made Satan confess that he was a liar, and God was in it all.... God purposed to give Job a double of everything he had, including His grace and His love. And to do that Job had to suffer, for grace and love do not come in any other way than through great trial and great suffering.[11]

The purpose that God had in mind was realized as Job responded to this time of trouble. As you read through these words from Job's journal, you will easily identify the purifying effect of these trials on the ancient patriarch:

> For I know that my Redeemer lives, and He shall stand
> at last on the earth; and after my skin is destroyed, this I
> know, that in my flesh I shall see God, whom I shall see for
> myself, and my eyes shall behold, and not another. How
> my heart yearns within me! (Job 19:25–27)

> [Job speaking] I have heard of You by the hearing of the
> ear, but now my eye sees You. Therefore I abhor myself,
> and repent in dust and ashes. (Job 42:5–6)

> And the Lord restored Job's losses when he prayed for
> his friends. Indeed the Lord gave Job twice as much as he
> had before. (Job 42:10)

> Now the Lord blessed the latter days of Job more than
> his beginning; for he had fourteen thousand sheep, six
> thousand camels, one thousand yoke of oxen, and one
> thousand female donkeys. He also had seven sons and
> three daughters. (Job 42:12–13)

When it was all over, God remembered Job. He was not a perfect man, but his patience was such that today when we see someone going through difficulty and handling it rather well, we often say that the person has "the patience of Job." Job wasn't perfect, just patient:

> Job complained a great deal. He even wished that he
> had never been born. Yet his imperfections and human
> weaknesses are scarcely remembered. Only his patience
> is spoken of. This is very characteristic of God's long-
> suffering toward his saints. How terrible it would be if
> all that God could remember us for were our failings and

weaknesses.... People tend to remember the bad things
about us, but God remembers the good things.[12]

WE NEED PATIENCE WHEN WE FACE DISHONESTY

The last verse in this section has been cut off from the first eleven
verses by many biblical writers. But the connective at the beginning
of the verse is a definite bridge between this final instruction and that
which has gone before. There is a relationship between James' pro-
hibition against oaths and the theme of patience: "But above all, my
brethren, do not swear, either by heaven or by earth or with any other
oath. But let your 'Yes' be 'Yes,' and your 'No,' 'No,' lest you fall into
judgment" (5:12). These words of James are an echo of something
Jesus said:

> Again you have heard that it was said to those of old, "You
> shall not swear falsely, but shall perform your oaths to
> the Lord." But I say to you, do not swear at all: neither
> by heaven, for it is God's throne; nor by the earth, for it
> is His footstool; nor by Jerusalem, for it is the city of the
> great King. Nor shall you swear by your head, because you
> cannot make one hair white or black. But let your "Yes"
> be "Yes," and your "No," "No." For whatever is more than
> these is from the evil one. (Matt. 5:33–37)

Oath taking was very much abused in James' day. It was practiced
as a form of profanity and also used in the clever schemes of the rabbis
to exert control over their followers. But James is talking about the
practice of indiscriminate oath taking during times of hostile confron-
tation. "In times of oppression or persecution, one may be tempted to
deny his guilt by reinforcing his statement with an oath.... An oath
calls upon God as a witness to one's statement and implicates Him to
punish the swearer if falsehood is spoken."[13]

Many have taken the words of James and Jesus to teach that taking an oath in a court of law is forbidden for Christians. However, there are several occasions in the Bible where God (Gen. 22:16–17; 26:3; Heb. 6:18), Paul (Rom. 1:9; 2 Cor. 1:23), and others used oaths without sin:

> What did the Lord and James mean by their absolutes, "Swear not at all," (Matt. 5:34) and "Swear not"? … They forbade the use of those extra meaningless words which were so commonly used then and are used today in order to induce others to believe what we say.… It must have been the custom then to preface every sentence with swearing, perhaps as a sheer matter of habit, just as today we have some standard words or expressions which may not be considered bad in themselves.… It is against such phraseology that James is speaking, and certainly he could speak very loudly to many of us today. Too much affirmation of truth arouses suspicion. It is good to beware of the person who always reminds you that he is telling the truth and nothing but the truth. Such a person may be trying to pull the wool over your eyes.[14]

Helmut Thielicke put it like this:

> Whenever I utter the formula "I swear by God," I am really saying, "Now I'm going to mark off an area of absolute truth and put walls around it to cut it off from the muddy floods of untruthfulness and irresponsibility that ordinarily overruns my speech." In fact, I am saying even more than this. I am saying that people are expecting me to lie from the start. And just because they are counting on my lying I have to bring up these big guns of oaths and words of honor.[15]

Whenever an ancient scribe copied the sacred manuscripts, he would stop before writing the name of God; bathe himself all over; then return to his writing table with a new, hitherto unused, pen; and then proceed to write the name of God in whatever form it appeared. It was always in holy awe and reverence that a scribe even read any of the names of God. Dare we by our flippant oaths invoking God's name show less respect for His name than they?

The patience we have read about in this chapter is easily understood by any who have tried long-distance running. Marathon runners come to a point where they can hardly put one foot in front of another. But if they keep at it, their energy seems to be replenished. In *The Complete Book of Running* we read,

> Over the years there has been a lot of argument about whether there really is such a thing as second wind. There is! Dr. Roy Shepard reports that when researchers questioned twenty students at one minute intervals during a hard twenty-minute workout, eighteen said their breathing improved after a while and fourteen said that their legs felt better.[16]

What the second wind is to the marathon runner, patience is to the believer!

WHAT TO DO WHEN PAIN LEADS TO PRAYER

(JAMES 5:13–20)

The effective, fervent prayer of a righteous man avails much.

If ever a man was qualified to address the subject of prayer, it was James. He is portrayed by an ancient writer as a Nazarite whose times of prayer for his nation were frequent and prolonged:

> He used to enter alone into the temple and be found
> kneeling and praying for forgiveness for the people, so that
> his knees grew hard like a camel's because of his constant
> worship of God, kneeling and asking forgiveness for the
> people. So often did he pray that he was referred to as
> "Old Camel Knees," because he developed knots on his
> knees from his long seasons of prayer. From his excessive
> righteousness he was called the Just.[1]

Most of us find it very hard to identify with a man like James. Who do we know who prays so much that he develops knots on his knees? Perhaps the better question might be, "Who do we know who prays, really prays?" That's not an unfair question, nor is it calculated to instill guilt. It reflects the surveys that have been taken by both Christian and secular researchers. People today are too busy to pray! Author and pastor Bill Hybels has turned that excuse around in the title of his book *Too Busy Not to Pray*. His analysis of our prayerlessness is on target:

> Prayer is an unnatural activity. From birth we have been
> learning the rules of self-reliance as we strain and struggle
> to achieve self-sufficiency. Prayer flies in the face of those
> deep-seated values. It is an assault on human autonomy,
> an indictment of independent living. To people in the fast
> lane, determined to make it on their own, prayer is an
> embarrassing interruption. Prayer is alien to our proud
> human nature.[2]

One of the strongest passages on prayer in the New Testament is now before us as James closes this letter to his scattered Jewish friends. In James 5:7–12, the word *patience* is used seven times. In this passage, the word *prayer* appears seven times. When situations arise where patience is required, prayer is the key. Ralph Martin points out, "By concluding his work with an exhortation to prayer ... James follows a pattern that is common in the New Testament epistles (Rom. 15:30–32; Eph. 6:18–20; Phil. 4:6ff; Col. 4:2–4, 12; 1 Thess. 5:16–18, 25; 2 Thess. 3:1ff; Philem. 22; Heb. 13:18ff; Jude v. 20)."[3]

IT IS IMPORTANT TO PRAY FOR EMOTIONAL REASONS

Three times in these eight verses, James uses the introductory question, "Is any among you" (5:13–14, 19). The first of the three asks, "Is any among you suffering?" The word for *suffering* here should not be confused with the word for *sick* in verse 14. The word translated *suffering* means "hardships and distresses." The New International Version translates this question, "Is any one of you in trouble?" This trouble could involve mental or emotional suffering or a combination of both. The fact that this is not a reference to physical illness is well accepted by most scholars:

> It may be questioned whether the word *kakopatheo* ever
> means "to suffer from disease." With its derivatives
> and compounds it is found about six times in the N.T.
> According to Thayer it means "to suffer (endure) evils

(hardships, troubles); to be afflicted." According to Liddell and Scott, "to suffer ill, to be distressed." And Rotherham translates, "In distress is any among you?" Moreover, the means to be used for the relief of such distress is quite in keeping with the nature of the case: "Let him pray." No promise is added, but abundant experience proves the efficacy of this means of grace and many a child of God has been able to sing,

> In seasons of distress and grief,
> My soul has often found relief,
> And oft escaped the tempter's snare,
> By thy return, sweet hour of prayer![4]

Connecting this with the verse that goes before it, we can see that there are two approaches to unexpected difficulty in life. Verse 12 warns against taking oaths or swearing when difficulty comes. Verse 13 instructs the believer to pray. When facing stresses, the answer is not to swear but to go to prayer. When we fail to follow this advice, we cut ourselves off from God's power, and that compounds our problem by becoming the cause of even greater distress:

> It is hard for God to release His power in your life when you put your hands in your pockets and say, "I can handle it on my own." If you do that, don't be surprised if one day you get the nagging feeling that the tide of battle has shifted against you and that you're fairly powerless to do anything about it.
>
> Prayerless people cut themselves off from God's prevailing power, and the frequent result is the familiar feeling of being overwhelmed, overrun, beaten down, pushed around, defeated. Surprising numbers of people are willing to settle for lives like that. Don't be one of them. Nobody has to live like that. Prayer is the key to unlocking God's prevailing power in your life.[5]

James immediately suggests another kind of emotional response when he asks, "Is anyone cheerful." The word *cheerful* is found in one other place in the New Testament. In Acts 27:22, it is used of Paul's efforts to cheer up his companions before their shipwreck on Malta.

"If one is cheerful" says James, "let him sing psalms." In other words, praising God is viewed in the same measure of seriousness as praying to God. The word *praise* is found 550 times in the Bible. The word here for sing is *psallo,* which describes singing, usually accompanied by the harp or what we would call the guitar. Praising God in song is a form of prayer, and Paul links this with the fullness of the Spirit (Eph. 5:18–19). In 1 Corinthians 14:15, he puts prayer and singing in the same order that James does here. It is proper to sing praises to God when we are filled with joy. I love this summary by William Barclay:

> Always the church has been a singing church. When Pliny, governor of Bithynia, wrote to Trajan, the Roman Emperor, in AD 111 to tell him of this new sect of Christians, he said that his information was that "they are in the habit of meeting on a certain fixed day before it is light, when they sing in alternate verses a hymn to Christ as God." In the orthodox Jewish synagogue, since the Fall of Jerusalem in AD 70, there has been no music, for, when they worship, they remember a tragedy; but for the Christian Church, from the beginning until now, there has been the music of praise, for the Christian remembers an infinite love and enjoys a present glory.[6]

By his instruction in this verse, James reminds us that we have a God for all seasons:

> Both in periods of suffering and trouble, and in times of joy, prayer and praise alike acknowledge that He is sufficient. To pray to Him is to acknowledge His sovereign power in appointing our circumstances. Whether as the

source of supply in need, or the source of gladness of our
joy, God is our sufficiency.[7]

It Is Important to Pray for Physical Reasons

While this is considered to be the key passage in the New Testament on
the subject of healing, the ideas about its meaning are as varied as the
many opinions about faith healing:

> Some say God wants to heal *all* sickness; others come
> close to conceding that God's purposes may *sometimes* be
> fulfilled in our infirmities. Some equate sickness with sin;
> others stop short of that but still find it hard to explain
> why spiritually strong people get sick. Some blame the
> devil. Some claim to have *gifts of healing;* others say
> they have no unusual healing ability—they simply are
> used of God to show people the way of faith. Some use
> a physical touch or anointing oil; others claim they can
> "speak forth" healings or simply pray for healing and get
> results.[8]

The word translated "sick" in verse 14 is the Greek word *asthenia*;
it means "'to be without strength,' and depicts the debilitating effect of
sickness, incapacitating one for work."[9] As it is found in other passages
in the New Testament:

> It described a royal officer's son who is about to die (John
> 4:46–47). It was used of Lazarus who shortly did die (John
> 11:1–3, 6); of Dorcas, who also died shortly after (Acts
> 9:37); and of Epaphroditus, whose sickness brought him
> close to death (Phil. 2:26–27).[10]

As James uses the word here, it is an obvious reference to a serious
physical illness. The statement "raise him up" would certainly imply
that, and the reference to the elders praying over him would support

that meaning. When a person in the assembly is gravely ill, James says that three things are to be done:

The Sick Person Is to Summon the Elders of the Church

If anyone is seriously ill, according to James, "let him call for the elders." Please note that the sick person is to take the initiative and call for the elders. They are not to be scouting around trying to find the sick. They are to be ready to respond, however, when they are summoned. All of the healing activity is to take place in the home of the infirm. There is no evidence that anointing services ever took place at the front of the church. When James refers to the elders, he has a specific group of men in mind:

> The New Testament records the expression *elder* (presbyter) soon after the founding of the church at Pentecost. In the Jerusalem church, the elders were the representatives of the believers (Acts 11:30; 21:18). They were the men who exercised leadership in pastoral oversight of the congregation they represented (Acts 20:28;1 Peter 5:1–4). On his first missionary journey, Paul and Barnabas appointed elders in each church (Acts 14:23) and Paul instructed Titus to appoint elders in every town in Crete (Titus 1:5).[11]

The Elders Are to Come and Pray Over the Sick Person

The instrument for raising up the sick person is not his own prayer but that of the elders, not his faith but the faith of the elders. The power that raises him up is not the elders' power or faith; it is the Lord's direct intervention. This passage shuts the mouths of those who want to place the blame for continued sickness on the faithless heart of the sick. Because this is one of the stress points of this chapter, I want to cite two illustrations that demonstrate the damaging effect of misapplying James' instruction.

The first comes from a book written by medical doctor, William

Nolen. *Healing: A Doctor in Search of a Miracle* documents his research into the healing ministry of Kathryn Kuhlman. Here is his firsthand report of one of her healing services:

> Finally it was over. There were still long lines of people waiting to get onto the stage and claim their cures, but at five o'clock, with a hymn and final blessing, the show ended. Miss Kuhlman left the stage and the audience left the auditorium.
>
> Before going back to talk to Miss Kuhlman I spent a few minutes watching the wheelchair patients leave. All the desperately ill patients who had been in wheelchairs were still in wheelchairs. In fact, the man with the kidney cancer in his spine and hip, the man whom I had helped to the auditorium and who had his borrowed wheelchair brought to the stage and shown to the audience when he had claimed a cure was now back in the wheelchair. His "cure," even if only a hysterical one, had been extremely short-lived.
>
> As I stood in the corridor watching the hopeless cases leave, seeing the tears of the parents as they pushed their crippled children to the elevators, I wished Miss Kuhlman had been with me. She had complained a couple of times during the service of "the responsibility, the enormous responsibility," and of how her "heart aches for those that weren't cured," but I wondered how often she had really looked at them. I wondered whether she sincerely felt that the joy of those "cured" of bursitis and arthritis compensated for the anguish of those left with their withered legs, their imbecilic children, their cancers of the liver. I wondered if she really knew what damage she was doing. I couldn't believe that she did.[12]

The second vignette is from the pen of former United States Surgeon General Dr. C. Everett Koop. He recalls this incident from his days as the president of the Evangelical Foundation:

We hired an investigative reporter to look into some of the cults and into faith healers specifically. Our investigator traveled to a Southwestern city where a healing campaign had been advertised some weeks in advance. Adjacent to the huge tent into which thousands would pour for the services was a smaller tent. For the whole week prior to the services, those who had physical infirmities came to this smaller tent in order to be screened by associates of the healer.... Among those who applied for healing was an elderly Christian gentleman who lived out on the prairie. His vision was becoming dim, and he most likely was developing cataracts. The only lighting in the little cabin where he lived was a kerosene lamp. He was a devout Christian, read his Bible daily—or tried to—and had all the faith necessary for healing, if faith does secure healing. His major complaint was that his sight had deteriorated to the point where he could no longer read his Bible.

On the night of his appearance before the healer, the old man was brought up in the atmosphere of a sideshow. The faith healer said, "Well, Pop, you can't see anymore. You've gotten old, you can't even see with your glasses. Your vision is failing." Then he reached over and took off the man's spectacles, threw them on the platform, stamped on them, and broke them. He then handed the elderly gentleman a large-print Bible, which, under the lights necessary for television in those days, enabled the gentleman to read John 3:16 out loud, to the astonishment and applause of the audience.

The elderly gentleman praised God, the healer praised God, the audience praised God, and the old man went back to his dimly lit cabin and could not find his Bible, because his glasses were destroyed. The man went back to the healer but was told the most discouraging thing a godly man like that could possibly hear: "You didn't have enough faith, or the healing would have stuck."[13]

I don't think J. I. Packer's words are too strong in appraising these tragic experiences:

> To be told that longed-for healing was denied you because
> of some defect in your faith when you had labored and
> strained every way you knew to devote yourself to God and
> to "believe for blessing," is to be pitchforked into distress,
> despair, and a sense of abandonment by God. That is as
> bitter a feeling as any this side of hell—particularly if,
> like most invalids, your sensitivity is already up and your
> spirits down.[14]

The Elders Are to Anoint the Sick Person with Oil in the Name of the Lord

The third thing mentioned concerning the prayer for the sick is the anointing with oil. Oil was widely believed to have medicinal value in biblical times:

> But wounds and bruises and putrefying sores; they have
> not been closed or bound up, or soothed with ointment.
> (Isa. 1:6)

> [The Good Samaritan] went to him and bandaged his
> wounds, pouring on oil and wine. (Luke 10:34)

There is only one other reference in the New Testament that mentions the anointing with oil in connection with healing (Mark 6:13). Jesus is never said to have used oil in any of His healings. However, in spite of the scarcity of biblical information about this early church practice, it grew in popularity until it became "The Sacrament of the Sick" within the Roman church:

> By the third century AD it had become the custom for
> oil used in anointing the sick to be "consecrated" by the

bishop of the area in which it was to be used. By the tenth
century, it was increasingly the practice to insist that the
anointing be carried out by a "priest." By the twelfth century, the terms "extreme unction" and "sacrament of the
dying" are found and the anointing is restricted to those
whose imminent death seems certain. In the thirteenth
century, the ceremony of anointing was declared to be one
of the "seven sacraments" instituted by Christ Himself.[15]

One does not have to be a great theologian to sort this out! The
practice of "extreme unction" was for the purpose of preparing someone for death. The purpose of anointing with oil according to James
was to restore a sick person to health!

Before we move on, I want to make sure there is no misunderstanding about God's ability to heal the sick. It is proper for the believer to
ask for healing from the Lord. God still heals! Sometimes He does it
directly without any visible means, and often He employs means in the
process. Our text is stating that the prayer of faith will heal and that
medical means are to be used. Here are some other instances where
"means" were employed in healing:

> Now Isaiah had said, "Let them take a lump of figs, and
> apply it as a poultice on the boil, and he shall recover."
> (Isa. 38:21)

> So they went out and preached that people should
> repent. And they cast out many demons, and anointed
> with oil many who were sick, and healed them.
> (Mark 6:12–13)

> No longer drink only water, but use a little wine for your
> stomach's sake and your frequent infirmities. (1 Tim. 5:23)

One excellent illustration of the activity of God in regard to sickness
occurs in Acts 28, when Paul and Luke the physician are shipwrecked

in Malta. The father of Publius was very ill, and Paul "went in to him and prayed, and he laid his hands on him and healed him" (v. 8). The Greek word used here to describe the miraculous healing by Paul is *iaomai*. The others on the island who were sick were also brought to be healed (v. 9). The Greek word used to describe their healing is from *therapeuo* and clearly indicates that medicine was practiced on them by Luke. God does heal with and without means. In fact, if there is healing, God did it. Here again are the words of C. Everett Koop:

> I don't know how many operations I actually performed in my surgical career. I know I performed 17,000 of one particular type, 7,000 of another. I practiced surgery for thirty-nine years, so perhaps I performed at least 50,000 operations. I was successful and I had a reputation for success. Patients were coming to me from all over the world, and one of the things that endeared me to the parents of my patients was the way my incisions healed.
>
> Now, no one likes a big scar, but they are especially upsetting to mothers when they appear on their children. So I set out early on to make my scars small, as short and as thin as possible. These "invisible" scars became my trademark. But was I the healer?
>
> The secret of thin scars is to make the incision precise— no feathered edges—and in closing, get the edges of the skin in exact apposition. I would do this by sewing the stitches inside the skin but not through it, and the knots were tied on the bottom. All you have to figure out is how I crawled out after doing that.
>
> I was the one who put the edges together, but it was God who coagulated the serum. It was God who sent the fiberblasts out across the skin edges. It was God who had the fiberblasts make collagen, and there were probably about fifty other complicated processes involved about which you and I will never know. But did God come down and instruct the fiberblasts to behave that way?

In a sense He did. But He did it through His natural laws,
just the way He makes the grass grow, the rain fall, the
earth quake. The question, then, is not, Does God heal?
Of course He heals! We are concerned with this question:
Granted that God heals, is it normally according to natural
laws or an interruption of those laws ... i.e., a miracle?[16]

As another writer points out:

When the aspirin works, it is the Lord who has made it work;
when the surgeon sets the broken limb and the bone knits, it
is the Lord who has made it knit.... There is always a spiritual
dimension in healing.... On no occasion should a Christian
approach the doctor without also approaching God.[17]

IT IS IMPORTANT TO PRAY FOR SPIRITUAL REASONS

Although sin is not always the cause of sickness in our lives, it is mentioned in verses 15–16 and 19–20 as a possible cause:

Physical illness may result from sin, and experience
provides numerous examples. Venereal diseases, alcohol-
ism, and narcotics addiction are a few of the obvious ones.
The Bible also teaches that God may bring sickness as a
discipline for sin (1 Cor. 11:29–30). Nevertheless, this is by
no means always the case. Jesus taught the disciples that
it was neither the sin of the victim nor that of his parents
that caused the case of blindness (John 9:2–3).... The
possibility should be considered and opportunity given for
confession, but it must not be assumed as true in every
case.[18]

"If he has committed sins" is a complex clause: "It carries the
idea of persistence. If someone has openly, knowingly, recklessly, and

rebelliously persisted in sin, those sins will be forgiven him, which implies the sins have been confessed and forgiveness of sin has been asked of the Father."[19]

This section of James is a suggested procedure to follow in cases where sin is suspected to be at the heart of the problem. Counselor Jay Adams makes a valid point when he writes:

> The New Testament teaches that sickness may stem from sin, and James therefore urged the need for ... confrontation by the elders of the church. Pastors always ought to be aware of their obligation in this matter when visiting the sick. It would seem that as a regular practice pastors should inquire into the possibility of sin as the root of the sickness. The need to distinguish between sin-engendered sickness and disease-engendered sickness has been emphasized so strongly in our time that modern conservative pastors rarely raise the issue with the sick. Of course, it also takes courage to do so. One wonders how many illnesses (or at least complications of illnesses) might have been cured by careful attention to and application of James' words. Counselors must learn to take James seriously.[20]

Dick Mayhue has summarized the meaning of the text with this paraphrased explanation:

> The point of the passage then is this: a believer has wandered off into sin, remained in sin, and God has chastised him by bringing sickness into his life to bring him back to Himself. When the believer recognizes that God has brought a very untimely and severe illness to incapacitate him, he is to call for the elders of the church. The elders are to come; he is to confess his sin; and they are to anoint him with oil and pray over him. If sin is the cause of sickness, then God will raise him up. If sin is

cared for through confession, there will be no further need for chastisement. God takes away the chastisement and the believer is restored to physical health.[21]

One of the purposes of confession is the isolation of the offense. Until the sin is isolated and confessed, it cannot be forgiven. I read recently about a college freshman who went to the dorm laundry room with his dirty clothes bundled into an old sweatshirt. But he was so embarrassed by how dirty his clothes were that he never opened the bundle. He merely pushed it into a washing machine and when the machine stopped pushed the bundle into a dryer and finally took the still unopened bundle back to his room. He discovered, of course, that the clothes had gotten wet and then dry, but not clean. God says, "Don't keep your sins in a safe little bundle."

An additional spiritual reason for prayer in the body of Christ is the common experience of backsliding believers. James refers to this in the closing words of his epistle: "Brethren, if anyone among you wanders from the truth, and someone turns him back, let him know that he who turns a sinner from the error of his way will save a soul from death and cover a multitude of sins" (5:19–20).

While prayer is not mentioned specifically in either of these verses, it is certainly legitimate to assume its place in the restoration of a fallen Christian. James puts the responsibility for the wandering brother or sister on the shoulders of the church body. In doing so he is preaching the message of urgency that the writer of the epistle to the Hebrews seeks to convey: "Beware, brethren, lest there be in any of you an evil heart of unbelief in departing from the living God; but exhort one another daily, while it is called 'Today,' lest any of you be hardened through the deceitfulness of sin" (3:12–13).

When James refers to the saving of the sick person's soul, he is not talking about his salvation. The word for *soul* is frequently used to describe the life of a person—the whole human being. The redeemed sinner's life will be "saved" from physical death. While he may suffer chastisement, he will not die!

When Christian brothers restore one who has fallen along the wayside, not only is that fallen brother's soul saved from death, but, James also promises, a multitude of sins is covered. As you can well imagine, this statement has been the subject of much discussion and misunderstanding. Peter has a similar statement in his first letter: "Above all, keep fervent in your love for one another, because love covers a multitude of sins" (4:8 NASB). In this passage, Peter is reminding his readers that when they love someone, they forgive him and refuse to expose his sins.

Both James and Peter may have been reflecting words from Proverbs: "Hatred stirs up strife, but love covers all sins" (10:12).

When we restore a stumbling believer, we don't get our own sins forgiven; what we get is the joy of knowing that the pattern of sin in our brother's life has been stopped!

It Is Important to Pray for National Reasons

For the fourth time, James refers to an Old Testament character to illustrate his point (vv. 17–18). He has already cited Abraham (2:21–24), Rahab (2:25), Job (5:11), and now he appeals to Elijah. His selection of Elijah was calculated to produce an immediate response, since Elijah was one of the most honored men in Jewish history. He is mentioned by New Testament writers more often than any other Old Testament prophet. His name occurs nine times in Matthew, nine times in Mark, eight times in Luke, twice in John's gospel, and once each in Romans and James. His prominence was especially stimulated by the prophetic announcement in Malachi 4:5 connecting his reappearance with the coming of the Messiah.

Two incidents in the New Testament illustrate the important place Elijah occupied in the thinking of the early believers. His appearance on the Mount of Transfiguration does not seem to have startled the disciples. They were "sore afraid" but not apparently surprised. On the contrary, Peter immediately proposes to erect a tent for the prophet whose arrival they had been so long expecting (Matt. 17:1–13 KJV).

The cry of our Lord from the cross (*Eli, Eli*), contained only a slight resemblance to the name of Elijah, yet immediately Elijah came to the minds of the bystanders: "Some of those who stood there, when they heard that, said, 'This Man is calling for Elijah!' ... The rest said, 'Let Him alone; let us see if Elijah will come to save Him'" (Matt. 27:47–49).

But this revered figure, according to James, was a "man with a nature like ours" (5:17). The word that is translated "nature" is the Greek *homoiopathes*:

> It ... denotes that Elijah was subject to the same human emotion and liable to the same weaknesses that we all have. The word was used by Barnabas and Paul when the mob at Lystra assumed them to be gods: "We are also men of the same nature as you" (Acts 14:15 NASB). Though the great Elijah at times allowed his feelings to sway him and depression to overwhelm him (1 Kings 19:4, 10, 14), God answered his prayers.[22]

Through the prayers of this average man, God did a miraculous thing in Israel: "[Elijah] prayed earnestly that it would not rain; and it did not rain on the land for three years and six months. And he prayed again, and the heaven gave rain, and the earth produced its fruit" (James 5:17–18).

When Elijah prayed the first time, rain was prevented. When he prayed the second time, rain was provided. Herman Hoyt summarizes the power in Elijah's praying:

> So powerful were these prayers that nature moved at the word of this prophet of God, and an evil king and a whole nation bowed down to recognize that Jehovah is God. But the power of these prayers was not in Elijah but the God who wrought within Elijah. Remembering that Elijah was of like passions with us, and that it is God working in believers that produces powerful prayer, Christians should take heart and pray for the sick that they might be healed.[23]

During their agonizing imprisonment at the Nazi death camp of Ravensbruck, Corrie ten Boom and her sister Betsie suffered from ill treatment and lack of medical care. They were treated worse than common criminals, though their only "crime" had been sheltering Jews who were seeking to escape the murderous tyranny of Nazism:

The prison they were confined in was overcrowded, and the living conditions in the barracks were atrocious. Disease and malnutrition were rampant, and they feared that they, like so many of the prisoners around them, would soon be languishing in death.

In their misery, they often were forced to depend wholly on God. And God heard and answered their prayers, sometimes demonstrating His miraculous protection in the times of their deepest need.

When Betsie was desperately ill on one occasion, Corrie realized that the tiny bottle of Davitamon was down to the very last drops. "My instinct," she wrote, "was always to hoard—Betsie was growing so very weak! But others were ill as well. It was hard to say no to eyes that burned with fever, hands that shook with chill. I tried to save it for the very weakest—but even these soon numbered fifteen, twenty, twenty-five ... " Corrie's heart went out to them, but she desperately feared that sharing those precious drops with all the others would rob Betsie of the only chance she had for survival.

Betsie recognized her need for the medication, but she reminded Corrie of the account of the widow of Zarephath who shared with Elijah and whose handful of meal and small amount of oil lasted as long as there was a need. Betsie was convinced that God could perform a similar miracle for them. Corrie initially belittled the idea of such a miracle in modern times, but she soon was a believer: "Every time I tilted the little bottle, a drop appeared at the top of the glass stopper. It just couldn't be! I held it up to the light, trying to see how much was left, but the dark brown glass was too thick to see through."

Each day she continued to dispense what she thought was the very last drop, until one day when a female guard who had shown kindness to the prisoners before, smuggled a small quantity of vitamins into the barracks for the prisoners. Corrie was thrilled, but she determined to first finish the drops in the bottle. "But that night, no matter how long I held it upside down, or how hard I shook it, not another drop appeared."[24]

James' final message to his scattered believing friends is this: God still answers prayer. Whether our praying is in the emotional, physical, spiritual, or national realm, God is ready to hear and willing to answer. "The effective, fervent prayer of a righteous man avails much."

READERS' GUIDE

FOR PERSONAL REFLECTION AND GROUP STUDY

READERS' GUIDE

For Personal Reflection

Settle into your favorite chair with your Bible, a pen or pencil, and this book. Read a chapter, marking portions that seem significant to you. Write in the margins. Note where you agree, disagree, or question the author. Look up endnotes and relevant Scripture passages. Then turn to the questions listed in this study guide. If you want to trace your progress with a written record, use a notebook to record your answers, thoughts, feelings, and further questions. Refer to the text and to the Scriptures as you allow the questions to enlarge your thinking. And pray. Ask God to give you a discerning mind for truth, an active concern for others, and a greater love for Him.

For Group Study

Plan ahead. Before meeting with your group, read and mark the chapter as if you were preparing for personal study. Glance through the questions, making mental notes of how you might contribute to your group's discussion. Bring a Bible and the text to your meeting.

Arrange an environment that promotes discussion. Comfortable chairs arranged in a casual circle invite people to talk with each other. They say, "We are here to listen and respond to each other—and to learn together." If you are the leader, simply be sure to sit where you can have eye contact with each person.

Promptness counts. Time is as valuable to many people as money. If the group runs late (because of a late start), these people will feel as robbed as if you had picked their pockets. So, unless you have mutual agreement, begin and end on time.

Involve everyone. Group learning works best if everyone participates more or less equally. If you are a natural talker, pause before you enter the conversation. Then ask a quiet person what he or she thinks. If you are a natural listener, don't hesitate to jump into the discussion. Others will benefit from your thoughts—but only if you speak them. If you are the leader, be careful not to dominate the session. Of course, you will have thought about the study ahead of time, but don't assume that people are present just to hear you—as flattering as that may feel. Instead, help group members to make their own discoveries. Ask the questions, but insert your own ideas only as they are needed to fill gaps.

Pace the study. The questions for each session are designed to last about one hour. Early questions form the framework for later discussion, so don't rush by so quickly that you miss valuable foundation. Later questions, however, often speak of the here and now. So don't dawdle so long at the beginning that you leave no time to "get personal." While the leader must take responsibility for timing the flow of questions, it is the job of each person in the group to assist in keeping the study moving at an even pace.

Pray for each other—together or alone. Then watch God's hand at work in all of your lives.

Notice that each session includes the following features:

> **Session Topic**—a brief statement summarizing the session.
>
> **Community Builder**—an activity to get acquainted with the session topic and/ or with each other.
>
> **Discovery Questions**—a list of questions to encourage individual or group discovery and application.
>
> **Prayer Focus**—suggestions for turning one's learning into prayer.
>
> **Optional Activities**—supplemental ideas that will enhance the study.
>
> **Assignment**—activities or preparation to complete prior to the next session.

1 WHAT TO DO WHEN THE HEAT'S TURNED UP
JAMES 1:1–12

Session Topic
Trials and temptations will come. The question is, how will we respond?

Community Builder (Choose One)

1. Describe an experience when you were significantly refined by a difficult situation. What did you learn then about yourself? About life? About God?

2. Name the "wisest" person you know. Give an illustration, if you can, of that person's wisdom.

Discovery Questions

1. Read aloud James 1:1–12. What all do you see in this passage that is contrary to current secular thought?

2. Do you think James is saying that we have to be happy when bad or difficult things happen to us? Explain.

3. James says that "testing" produces patience. Do you think that this happens automatically? If not, what do you think you can do during a time of testing that would lead toward patience?

4. Why can believers rejoice in times of suffering—other than because they will learn endurance?

5. When something terrible happens to us, it is easy to wonder what we did to deserve it. Job's friends assumed that God was punishing him; they told him to confess his hidden sin. Do we need an explanation for our trials before we can trust God? Explain.

6. What all do you find in James 1:1–12 that would help you endure suffering— even if you never discovered its reason? (Check each verse.)

7. What connections can you draw between suffering and wisdom? (Consider several verses from the James text as well as your own observations of life.)

8. Movies, television, magazines, and even some media preachers tell us we should try to escape from difficulty and pain. What influence do you think these forces have on you?

9. Having faith in Christ doesn't guarantee that we will be happy, financially secure, or have perfect marriages. What, according to James, does persevering faith guarantee? Of what value is that promise to you?

10. Suffering can create opportunities to know God. What has God shown you about Himself because of your own periods of grief or hardship? (Be specific.)

11. James says that God can use suffering to bring us wisdom and patience. What practical advice would you offer a suffering friend who wanted to allow God to grow him or her in that way?

Prayer Focus

- Jesus said that His followers would face persecution because of their belief in Him. But Jesus suffered on the cross so that our suffering would not be in vain. Thank Jesus for the gift to you of His own suffering.
- Read aloud 1 Peter 4:12–16. Take some time now to pray about those situations in your life where you see God allowing you to suffer for His sake.

- Thank God for the opportunities He gives you to grow as His child. Ask Him to provide you with the grace to be His witness even during periods of hardship.

Optional Activities

1. Meditate on the teaching of Peter in 1 Peter 2:20–25. Take time to ponder the suffering that Christ endured on your behalf so that you might live free from the power of your sins. How does the awareness of Christ's sacrifice cause you to respond to Him?

2. How do you define "fulfillment"? What does it look like to you? Record your thoughts, so you can review them later.

Assignment

1. If you do not already keep a journal, begin one this week. Start keeping a record of your insights concerning the book of James. Each week focus on the particular passage you have studied. Make journaling a regular part of your devotional time. What have you learned about trials this week?
2. Read chapter 2 in *Turning Toward Integrity*.
3. Memorize James 1:2–4.

2 WHAT TO DO WHEN WRONG SEEMS RIGHT
JAMES 1:13–18

Session Topic

Temptation—It's what we do with it that matters.

Community Builder (Choose One)

1. Think of a time when you were tempted by something but overcame the impulse to give in. What was so attractive about the temptation? What helped you to resist it?

2. Name a song or movie that talks about temptation. What message about temptation does that song or movie convey? Do you agree with its message?

Discovery Questions

1. Read aloud James 1:13–18. If you were to create a painting for each of these two paragraphs, what would you include in each painting? (Consider color, lines, objects, brushstrokes, how you would want the observer to feel.)

2. If you were to autograph each painting with the name of the proper artist (according to James), whose name would you write at the bottom of each painting?

3. Put into your own words the process of sin that James describes in vv. 14–15. What are the "stages" of sin? (Keep in mind your own experiences with temptation and also refer to pp. 37–40 in the book.)

4. According to Hebrews 4:15, Jesus was tempted, but He did not sin. What are some practical steps that you can take to keep temptation from turning into sin?

5. The Bible says that God disciplines us because He loves us (Heb. 12:6). Sometimes that means God puts us in places where we have to make tough choices. What is the difference between saying, "God is tempting me" and "God is disciplining me"?

6. James 1:16 begins with the words "Do not be deceived." Why is it easy to be deceived about the source of good in our lives?

7. What "good" and "perfect" gifts are you thankful to God for? Take time, right now, to thank Him for one of those gifts.

8. Why might God's gifts, as described in James 1:16–18, make it easier for you to resist temptation?

9. Think of a situation when you gave in to temptation. In retracing your steps, at what point could you have turned back from sinning? What could you have done, at that point, to stop the downward spiral?

10. Martin Luther said, "You cannot stop birds flying about your head, but you can prevent them from building a nest in your hair." What did he mean?

11. James 1:18 says, "Of His own will He brought us forth by the word of truth." Think of a temptation that is "routine" in your life. How can you express God's gift of new birth, this week, when you encounter that temptation?

Prayer Focus

- The "good news" is that God knows we would always be defeated by sin, if it were not for Him. But Jesus Christ has borne our temptations and been victorious over sin! Thank Him for that.
- Read aloud Hebrews 2:14–18. Praise God that He has shown you mercy, not left you to your sin, but has made a way for you to live a life that pleases Him.
- Ask God to make you sensitive to the "process" of temptation, that you would be more faithful to turn away and not sin against Him.

Optional Activities

1. In what area of your life are you most tempted to sin against God? Form a reasonable plan to help you "resist the devil" (James 4:7). Tell a friend to ask you regularly how well you are honoring God in this area.

2. Write a letter to Jesus. Express to Him how you appreciate His sacrifice so that you would not have to be defeated by sin. Tell Him how much you need Him, every day, to grow you in wisdom, character, and love. Ask Jesus to make you worthy of being called His disciple. (Remember: The time is

coming soon when you will see Jesus face-to-face. Then you won't need to write to Him; you will be able to tell Him how much you love Him!)

Assignment

1. Record your insights on temptation in your prayer journal.
2. Read chapter 3 in *Turning Toward Integrity*.
3. Memorize Hebrews 2:18.

3   WHAT TO DO WHEN THE MIRROR DOESN'T LIE
JAMES 1:19–27

Session Topic

True faith is demonstrated in our actions.

Community Builder (Choose One)

1. David Jeremiah cites the statistic that only 11 percent of Americans read the Bible daily (p. 48). What do you think people are reading (or doing) instead? What long-term effect do you think this will have?

2. Are you more of a "thinker" or a "doer"? Give an example.

Discovery Questions

1. Read aloud James 1:19–27. What opposites do you see in this passage? (Example: "lay aside all filthiness," "receive … the implanted word.") In view of these opposites, what choices do Christians have to make?

2. What do you think James means by "be swift to hear, slow to speak, slow to wrath"? What is hard (for you) about obeying that command?

3. How might anger hinder the righteousness that James speaks of in verse 20?

4. Look more carefully at verses 21–25. According to James, what effects should God's Word have on us?

5. James says that we cannot separate what we believe from what we do. But Howard Hendricks says that many Christians don't do what the Bible says, because they're "functionally illiterate Christians" (p. 55). What problems can occur when Christians try to live their faith but don't know much about the Bible?

6. Study verses 26–27. What does James mean when he says that the one who claims to be a Christian but can't control what he or she says "deceives his own heart" and has a "useless" religion?

7. Notice the examples of "pure and undefiled religion" that James cites in verse 27. If you were to act on that description, what activities would you have to add to your schedule? What would you have to take out?

8. What are you already doing that expresses your faith in ways similar to what James describes?

9. David Jeremiah outlines six steps toward becoming both a hearer and a doer of the Word: preparation, examination, application, meditation, memorization, and demonstration. Which steps need strengthening in your life, and what can you do about it?

10. Mortimer Adler (*How to Read a Book*) notes how much more thoroughly we read a love letter than other types of writing. Yet the Bible is God's love letter to us, an invitation to know Him. How can God's love impact the way you feel about biblical do's and don'ts?

11. Taking time to think about what you read in Scripture is the first step toward becoming a "doer" of the Word. When is your best time of day to read and think on Scripture? How are you spending that time now? How can you make it a richer time with God?

Prayer Focus
- God desires that we be different from the world in our thoughts and actions. Read aloud Galatians 5:19–25. Allow these words to search your own behavior.
- Take two to three minutes for individual silent confession of any sinful thoughts and actions.
- Ask God to grant you grace to know His truth. Ask that this knowledge of truth would prompt a desire to please Him in all that you think and do.

Optional Activities
1. Think of two people in your life: one whom you would like to disciple you into becoming a more mature follower of Christ and one whom you would like to encourage in faith. Pray for an opportunity to suggest the idea to them. Then follow through on that opportunity.

2. Is there someone you know who is in need—an "orphan" or "widow"? Find ways to care for that person and so give expression to your faith.

Assignment
1. Journal your insights on being both a hearer and a doer of the Word.
2. Read chapter 4 in *Turning Toward Integrity*.
3. Memorize James 1:22.

4 WHAT TO DO WHEN JUSTICE ISN'T BLIND
JAMES 2:1–13

Session Topic
Since God does not discriminate against us, we ought not to show partiality toward one another.

Community Builder (Choose One)

1. Lewis Smedes says that we can sometimes identify our areas of favoritism by taking a look at what we first want to know about a person we've just met. What are you likely to wonder first about a new acquaintance—even if you'd never ask the question?

2. When have you worshipped with a group of people very unlike yourself? What was your reaction to that experience?

Discovery Questions

1. Read aloud James 2:1–13. What does this passage reveal about the biases of the people to whom James wrote his letter? What prejudices were they themselves subjected to?

2. What reasons does James give for not favoring one person over another? (Find answers in almost every verse.)

3. What kinds of people do you see as "the poor of this world"?

4. Liberation theology says that the poor are always closer to God than other people. What problems do you see with this view?

5. David Jeremiah notes several categories in which we tend to discriminate: appearance, ancestry, age, achievement, affluence. In your community, what values do people show greater respect for? Do you see these values at work in your church? Explain.

6. Why do you think God chose "the poor of this world to be rich in faith" (2:5)? What does he mean by poor? Think of the makeup of your church. Do you see people from different social and ethnic backgrounds represented in the congregation and the leadership? (While diversity in itself isn't "better," the lack of it may indicate a bias toward certain people.) What conclusions do you draw from your observations?

7. James says that the showing of partiality is sin just like murder and adultery (2:9–11) and that God will severely judge His people for it (v. 13). Why, according to James, is favoritism such a serious sin in God's eyes?

8. In your church, are there ways in which believers are demonstrating the grace of God toward all people? Give examples. Where do you see room for improvement? How can you be an instigator for greater faithfulness to Christ in this area?

9. James summarizes God's law about human relationships with a statement he calls the "royal law": "Love your neighbor as yourself" (v. 8). What relationship do you see between this law and the teachings of James about favoritism?

10. What temptations do you encounter to play favorites? (Consider your family, your work, your friends, your church.) What steps can you take to better obey Christ in this area?

11. This section of James ends with the statement, "Mercy triumphs over judgment." Name some ways that God has shown you mercy. What are some practical ways that you can allow this awareness of God's mercy to shape the way you treat others?

Prayer Focus
- The cross demonstrates our common need for God. No matter who we are or what we have, none of us deserves God's mercy. Take a few moments to meditate on the mercy of God.
- Read 1 Corinthians 1:18–31. Confess silently how you have valued the power and status of some people instead of their position in Christ.
- Ask God to remind you of His mercy toward you and to help you be generous toward all people, regardless of their status.

Optional Activities
1. Take time this week to look at some examples in the Scripture where God taught His people not to show favoritism: Moses in Deuteronomy 1:1–17, Peter in Acts 10:1–35 and also in 1 Peter 1:14–19, and Paul in Romans 1:18—2:16. Write your findings in your journal.

2. Take a personal survey of who you may be discriminating against. What are some ways this week that you can demonstrate the mercy God has shown you to those people? Determine ways to obey Christ in this area.

Assignment
1. Record your insights on favoritism in your prayer journal.
2. Read chapter 5 in *Turning Toward Integrity*.
3. Memorize James 2:1.

5 WHAT TO DO WHEN FAITH DOESN'T WORK
JAMES 2:14–26

Session Topic
Faith that does not change the way we act is no faith at all.

Community Builder (Choose One)
1. Name a person you know who demonstrates faith by actions. Give an example of the way that person expresses his or her faith.

2. What attempts have you made to put your own faith into action? What successes have you seen? What failures?

Discovery Questions

1. Read aloud James 2:14–26. Suppose a Christian said, "Jesus forgives all of my sins: past, present, and future. What I do or don't do makes no difference at all." What would James say to that person? (Use information from the entire passage.)

2. What situations can you imagine where a person might not have opportunity to demonstrate faith but would still genuinely believe in Christ?

3. Put in your own words James' statement that "faith without works is dead."

4. Read the satirical piece found on pp. 86–87. In which of these areas has your church demonstrated a faith that works? Where do you think your church could improve its practical expressions of faith?

5. Read the list on pp. 86–87 once more. This time, mentally insert your own name in place of the word *you*. Where, on the list, would you have say, "Guilty, as charged"? Explain.

6. Take a moment of silence to confess your failure to God. Ask Him to bring to your mind a particular person who needs your help and particular ways that you can help that person. Then mention one way, with God's help, that you hope to express your faith by action.

7. The many needy people in our world can overwhelm our desire to help. Read Dietrich Bonhoeffer's statements on p. 87 concerning meeting the needs of others. What guidelines would you suggest for deciding the needs you can respond to and those you must ignore?

8. Read Romans 3:21–30 and James 2:20–24. Martin Luther was not able to reconcile these two descriptions of faith—so he rejected the entire book of James. What ideas could you offer that might help people accept both Paul and James?

9. David Jeremiah says that many people today define faith not in biblical terms but as a "positive mental attitude." Where have you seen evidence of this kind of thinking? How has the PMA view of faith affected you?

10. If we follow Christ, our actions will set us apart from those around us. What do you hope that unbelievers will think of Christ as they observe the way you live out your faith?

Prayer Focus

- Christ has given us the supreme example of faith in action. Read aloud 1 John 3:16–18. Thank God for this gift and its invitation to you.
- Confess to God opportunities to act out your faith that you chose to ignore.
- Thank God for His forgiveness. Ask Him to help you live up to your title: a "child of God."

Optional Activities

1. Study some of the people in the Bible who demonstrated true faith: Abraham and Isaac (Gen. 22:1–19); Rahab (Josh. 2); and Shadrach, Meshach, and Abed-Nego (Dan. 3). Record in your journal ways that these people demonstrated their faith with action.

2. Choose two or three people (either believers or unbelievers) who know you well and will give you honest feedback. Ask them to tell you what your actions say about what you really believe. Take these answers to God in prayer.

Assignment

1. Try to construct a definition of faith that agrees with both Paul and James. Record your definition in your prayer journal.
2. Read chapter 6 in *Turning Toward Integrity*.
3. Memorize James 2:17.

6 WHAT TO DO WHEN YOUR TONGUE ISN'T TIED
JAMES 3:1–12

Session Topic

We must control our tongues; what we say has the power either to hurt or to heal.

Community Builder (Choose One)

1. Describe a time when someone encouraged you by his or her words.

2. When have you been on the receiving end of someone's verbal "deadly poison"?

Discovery Questions

1. Read aloud James 3:1–12. What is the gist of this passage?

2. James begins this section on the tongue by saying that not many of us should be teachers. In view of his main topic, why do you think he begins with this kind of warning?

3. James uses a variety of word pictures in this text to illustrate the tongue. What does a ship's rudder, a fire, and a spring of water suggest about the tongue? (Consider each separately.)

4. James says in verse 8 that no one can tame the tongue. Why then do you think James gives these instructions?

5. David Jeremiah says that gossip and flattery are two types of verbal poison. Sometimes it is hard to know when a conversation turns from merely giving "information" about someone to indulging in gossip. How can you tell the difference?

6. What ways would you suggest to keep normal "sharing of information" from turning into gossip? How would you keep "giving encouragement" from turning into flattery?

7. Read Proverbs 18:21. In view of this proverb, how can you cultivate a healthy fear of the power of your words?

8. David Jeremiah points out that the word "perfect" in James 3:2 means "mature" (see James 1:4), meaning that the ability to control one's speech is the mark of a mature believer. In what ways are you more "mature" in speech than you were ten years ago?

9. In what situation are you still tempted to speak without control? What steps have you seen leading up to that temptation?

10. What can you do in one of the early steps toward sinful speech to keep yourself from hurting people and offending God?

11. James says in verse 9 that we may use our tongues to praise God. What are some of your favorite ways to praise God? How can you use the teachings of this passage to praise God wholeheartedly?

Prayer Focus

- God takes us seriously—sometimes more seriously than we wish. Knowing that God holds us responsible for our words should sober us.
- Read aloud Matthew 12:36–37. Ask God to forgive you for any careless or hurtful words you have spoken. Confess your need for the Holy Spirit to convict you and to help you be more self-controlled.
- Thank God that He allows you to use the gift of speech for good: to praise Him and to be His instrument of healing for others.
- Praise God for qualities in His character that you appreciate.

Optional Activities

1. Is there someone you have hurt by speaking thoughtlessly or unkindly? You may have spoken directly to that person—or about that person to someone else. Determine to remedy the situation either by apologizing directly to that individual or by confessing your wrong to the person you spoke to about him or her.

2. The author gives several examples of people in the Bible who struggled to control what they said: Moses in Psalm 106:32–33, Isaiah in Isaiah 6:5–7, Job in Job 40:4, and Peter in Matthew 26:69–75. Meditate on Proverbs 10:19; 12:22; 13:3; and 15:1. Record your insights from all of these passages in your journal.

Assignment

1. Make note of your insights on the power of your words in your prayer journal.
2. Read chapter 7 in *Turning Toward Integrity*.
3. Memorize Proverbs 18:21.

7 WHAT TO DO WHEN WISDOM IS FOOLISH
JAMES 3:13-18

Session Topic
Godly wisdom is the ability to make right choices in life.

Community Builder (Choose One)

1. Read the closing quotation of David Jeremiah's chapter about man's ultimate destiny (p. 132). What do you think of this statement?

2. When have you experienced the limitations of your own wisdom? What was the situation? How does God's wisdom differ from yours?

Discovery Questions

1. Read aloud James 3:13-18. How would you describe the basic difference between earthly wisdom and heavenly wisdom? What are the origins of both?

2. According to James, what are the general characteristics of heavenly wisdom? Of earthly wisdom?

3. Give three or four examples of earthly wisdom? Why do you think that these forms of wisdom gather followers?

4. What are the assumptions behind these forms of earthly wisdom? (For example, some believe that education is the answer to all of our problems. They assume that we humans, if given enough information, are able to be better people.) What is wrong with these assumptions? Discuss several forms of earthly wisdom.

5. James says in verse 13 that true wisdom leads to meekness. Why do you think that a truly wise person is also humble?

6. Name one of your favorite examples of this kind of person. What have you learned from that person? (Consider actions as well as teachings.)

7. Since it is true that Christians have the truth of Christ within, why does Paul warn us to be on guard not to follow the wisdom of the world (Col. 2:8)?

8. Os Guinness observes the impact that Freud and Jung have had on the American psyche, saying: "The couch has become as American as the baseball diamond and the golden arches" (p. 115). What are some of the benefits and some of the dangers of this form of wisdom?

9. Television has become a universal and powerful transmitter of worldly wisdom to passive viewers. Take a moment to quickly calculate the number of hours you watched TV in the past week. In view of James' teachings on wisdom, are you satisfied with the number? Explain.

10. Read aloud John 2:23–25. Jesus had a healthy distrust of human opinion. Do you find yourself accepting the messages of this world, or do you try to challenge popular thinking? Give an example.

11. Where do you typically turn for wisdom? Do these sources compete with God? Or would you say that the sources you normally seek for wisdom come from God?

12. What are some practical steps you can take to grow in God's wisdom and guard yourself against early philosophies? (Remember that you are called to be an instrument of change in your world, so your steps should involve you with both believers and unbelievers.)

Prayer Focus

- God knows that this world continually competes for your devotion, and He is jealous for your full attention.
- Read aloud 1 John 2:15–17. Confess any tendency you have to follow after the wisdom of this world instead of seeking God's wisdom.
- Thank God that though this world and its philosophies are passing away, God is creating in you an eternal work by the power of the Holy Spirit.

Optional Activities

1. Do a word study on "wisdom," both earthly and heavenly. What characteristics do you find for both? Record your insights in your journal.

2. Jesus tells us to ask, seek, and knock—He wants us to actively seek after Him. What are some specific ways you can more diligently pursue the wisdom of God in your relationships, your work, your Bible study?

Assignment

1. Record your insights on earthly and heavenly wisdom in your prayer journal.
2. Read chapter 8 in *Turning Toward Integrity*.
3. Memorize James 3:13.

8 WHAT TO DO WHEN WORSHIP TURNS TO WAR
JAMES 4:1–12

Session Topic

God is on the side of the humble in heart.

Community Builder (Choose One)

1. Dissension in the church is obviously not pleasing to God. What are some ways the problems in the Tazewell church could have been addressed to prevent the fight that occurred in this church service and the fire in the sanctuary?

2. What are some peaceful avenues you have seen churches take to resolve personal differences?

Discovery Questions

1. Read aloud James 4:1–12. James asks in verse 1, "Where do wars and fights come from among you?" Answer his question using material from throughout the rest of the passage.

2. What, according to James, are we to do about these internal disputes? (Draw information from almost every verse.)

3. What differences in heart attitude do you see in the text between those who war with each other and those who make peace?

4. In verse 4, James calls Christians who war with each other, "adulterers and adulteresses." Why? Who have they been unfaithful to, and who is receiving their love? What does this term suggest about the kind of relationship God wants with His people?

5. David Jeremiah says it is hard to overestimate the power sin can have over us (p. 136). Read Ecclesiastes 4:4. What is the power of envy according to this verse? What part does envy play in disputes between believers?

6. Read again James 4:6. How might humility (as opposed to envy) enable a person to obey the commands in verses 7–12?

7. When have you seen one person with a humble attitude bring peace to a volatile situation?

8. How might the information in James 4:12 keep you humble during a disagreement with another Christian?

9. Compare James 4:3 with James 1:6. Do you think that God waits until your motives are totally pure before He will answer your prayers? Explain.

10. What are some ways that you can check your motives when you ask God for something in prayer? At what point, in your normal praying, could you place that check?

11. Bring to mind a situation you are facing where you could be the first to humble yourself in order to bring about a resolution. What is one way that you could demonstrate the grace of God as you try to bring about peace?

Prayer Focus

- God desires that His church be a testimony to the world of His grace.
- Read aloud 1 Peter 2:9–12.

- Ask God to purify your motives so that your relationships and prayers will glorify Him.

Optional Activities

1. Take time this week to examine some of your motivations behind the "good" you do. Are your motives pure; or are they filled with worldly desires to look good in front of others, or to outdo someone in the church, or to get ahead? Take your observations to God, and ask Him to cleanse your motives for serving Him so that you may produce fruit that pleases Him.

2. Where do you see rifts between brothers and sisters in your church? Commit to praying that God's grace will be manifested in those situations so that the witness of the church will demonstrate the power of God over sin.

Assignment

1. Record your insights about motives in your prayer journal.
2. Read chapter 9 in *Turning Toward Integrity*.
3. Memorize James 4:7.

9 WHAT TO DO WHEN YOUR GOALS ARE NOT GOD'S
JAMES 4:13–17

Session Topic

We must trust in God, not in ourselves, for the future.

Community Builder (Choose One)

1. Describe a time when your plans fell through. What did you learn about yourself at that time? About God?

2. What is difficult about giving up control of your life to anyone—even to God?

Discovery Questions

1. Read aloud James 4:13–17. Suppose James was writing a short booklet titled *Planning Guide for Christians*. Based on this paragraph, what all do you think he would put in that booklet?

2. What is the difference between making responsible plans for your future and boasting about your future?

3. James says that our lives are a vapor. What does he mean?

4. What are some ways our modern, technological society gives us the illusion that we are in control of our lives and our futures? Be specific.

5. How should the mistlike quality of life affect the way you make plans?

6. What circumstances have helped you to live in the way that James describes here?

7. Some people take the words of verse 15 quite literally. They write or speak the words "God willing" after every statement about the future. How could you express a similar attitude about the future, even if you do not say those exact words?

8. James warns us that failure to do "good" is a sin (4:17). How might the view of life, as it is presented in this text, encourage you to do (promptly) the good you ought to do?

9. What "good" do you think you ought to be doing?

10. David Jeremiah notes that one mistake we often make is presuming that we know the future. How do you see yourself presuming knowledge of the future in the decisions you make?

11. What is one of your most persistent worries about the future?

12. James says that we are to do the good that we know to do. What "good" ought you to be doing in the area that you mentioned above?

13. If you are not yet doing what you ought, ask God's help in meeting the tasks ahead. If you are already doing all that you should in this area that worries you, take time now to name this worry to your loving Lord and place it in His powerful hands.

Prayer Focus
- Take a minute to silently reflect on how God has provided for you in unexpected ways in the past. Thank Him for that.
- In light of your study of James, read aloud and meditate on the words of Jeremiah 9:23–24.

Thus says the Lord:
"Let not the wise man
glory in his wisdom,
Let not the mighty man
glory in his might,
Nor let the rich man
glory in his riches;
But let him who glories glory in this,
That he understand and knows Me,
That I am the Lord, exercising
lovingkindness, judgment, and
righteousness in the earth.
For in these I delight," says the Lord.

- Close with a time of confessing trust in God for your future. Thank God that He promises never to leave us to face difficulties alone.

Optional Activities

1. Meditate on the strong teaching in 2 Peter 2:21 and Luke 12:47–48. Make a list of four or five things you know God wants you to do, but, for whatever reason, you have not done. Commit yourself to addressing these items over the course of the next month.

2. Reread Jeremiah 9:23–24. Ask a family member or good friend to rate you (honestly) on how well you demonstrate that you "glory" in knowing God and not in your own abilities. Spend time in prayer reflecting on their feedback, confessing areas of your life where you are trusting in your own strength instead of in God.

Assignment

1. Record your insights on depending on God in your prayer journal.
2. Read chapter 10 in *Turning Toward Integrity*.
3. Memorize Psalm 37:3–4.

10 WHAT TO DO WHEN YOUR NET WORTH IS WORTHLESS
JAMES 5:1–6

Session Topic

God will severely judge those who gain wealth through exploitation.

Community Builder (Choose One)

1. Are you more comfortable with people who are richer than you? Poorer than you? About the same economic level as you? Why?

2. Imagine that you live in a village composed of representative families from each country of the world. What would you enjoy about your neighbors? What difficulties, other than language, do you think you would have in relating to them? Where would you likely fall on the economic scale of your village?

Discovery Questions

1. Read aloud James 5:1–6. James begins this chapter by saying that rich people ought to weep and howl. Why? (Use the whole text.)

2. What all had these wealthy people done wrong?

3. Why are these kinds of sins particularly tempting to the wealthy?

4. In view of the accusations of this text, what responsibilities seem to come with wealth?

5. Read Proverbs 11:28. What does it mean to "trust in riches," and why is this so tempting? Why is trusting in riches dangerous?

6. How would you describe the function and purpose of money? Where does its value come from?

7. What are some ways Christians who have great financial resources can serve the purposes of God? (Be creative.) What are some of the potential dangers to be wary of?

8. Are there ways in which the church has allowed prosperity to wrongly affect its teaching and witness? What are some examples?

9. Paul said that he had learned the secret of being content regardless of circumstances (Phil. 4:10–13). What are some of the valuable lessons you can learn from being in need?

10. Look again at the village described in point two under "Community Builder." If you lived your current lifestyle in that village, do you think that some of the accusations of James 5 might be made against you? Explain.

11. If you lived in that village, what adjustments would you probably make in your lifestyle?

12. Think about how you spend your money: the portion that you spend to meet your own needs and responsibilities and the portion that you give to those who have less than you. What are some specific ways you can better use your income to meet the needs of others around the world?

Prayer Focus

- God desires to meet our needs as well as to work through us to meet the needs of others. With our heavenly Father there is no need to fear for our future. Commit your future, and your fears about your future, to Him.
- Read aloud Proverbs 30:7–9:

Two things I request of You

(Deprive me not before I die):

Remove falsehood and lies far from me;

Give me neither poverty nor riches—

Feed me with the food allotted to me;

Lest I be full and deny You,

And say, "Who is the LORD?"

Or lest I be poor and steal,

And profane the name of my God.

- Ask God to make you sensitive to the needs of others and to show you ways to be generous toward them.

Optional Activities

1. If you are not already involved at some level with feeding the hungry, clothing the naked, or visiting the sick and imprisoned (these groups represent people who must depend on the mercy of those who have more than they), find an outreach program and begin to volunteer some of your time and resources toward being Christ to people in need.

2. Examine your finances to see where your money is being spent. Are there ways you can live more simply and give more away? What can you do without altogether? What are you willing to sacrifice, for Christ's sake, so that someone else might benefit? Determine where you will make changes, and don't let anyone else know. Secret blessings sometimes come from honoring God in private.

Assignment

1. Record your insights on riches in your prayer journal.
2. Read chapter 11 in *Turning Toward Integrity*.
3. Memorize Matthew 6:19–21.

11 WHAT TO DO WHEN YOU'RE IN A HURRY AND GOD ISN'T
JAMES 5:7–12

Session Topic

Prepare yourself to faithfully endure persecution, knowing that Christ is coming back soon.

Community Builder (Choose One)

1. Think of a time when you suffered for doing the right thing. Did you (1) try to "get even," (2) tell a bunch of people how much you were suffering, or (3) pray to be able to love and forgive the person?

2. Tell about a time in your life when you were required to be patient beyond your own ability? What were the circumstances, and how did the experience shape you?

Discovery Questions

1. Read aloud James 5:7–12. James begins this section with the words, "Be patient." What examples of patience can you find in this text?

2. What harm could come from a lack of patience in each of the settings mentioned in these verses?

3. Verse 7 speaks of Christ's return. What effect does the promise of Christ's return have on your own attempts at patience?

4. Until Christ returns we are promised that evil will be a reality of life. What does the example of the farmer (vv. 7–8) mean in this context? Why must the farmer wait with patience?

5. Review James 5:9–11. James says that God is "compassionate and merciful." Why do you think James described God in this way when he had just described the suffering God allowed to Job and the prophets?

6. Read aloud 1 Peter 2:21–23. David Jeremiah reminds us that Jesus Christ Himself is our best example of one who endured suffering without retaliating. What are some ways Christ's example can encourage you in your own periods of suffering?

7. What is one of your greatest obstacles to patiently enduring suffering? What steps can you take to overcome that obstacle?

8. Read Revelation 21:4–5. Why do you think Christians today spend so little time reflecting on heaven? How can you allow the reality and expectation of heaven to encourage you during difficult times?

9. If you knew Christ was coming back next year, what would you begin to change or to do in order to prepare? Even though we don't know when Christ will return, how can your answer help you today?

10. James says that our patience must also extend to one another in the body of Christ (v. 9). Are there relationships in your fellowship where you are complaining rather than working to lovingly reconcile the situation? What can you do differently?

11. What are some of your feelings when you see another believer suffering? In view of your study of James, how can you help a suffering Christian to know God in the midst of trial?

Prayer Focus

- Read aloud Hebrews 12:1–3. Take a minute or two to silently think about the people or circumstances that are testing the limits of your faith.
- Confess to the Lord those times when you have not honored Him with your response to trials: your own trials and the trials of others.
- Ask God to help you throw off every sin that hinders you and to focus on Jesus, who ran the race before you so that you might win the joyous prize of eternal life.

Optional Activities

1. Who do you know who is suffering for doing what is right? What can you do as their brother or sister in Christ to encourage them to respond in a way that honors Christ?

2. Job 42:10 says that God restored Job when he prayed for his friends (these friends had only added to his suffering with their worldly counsel). Bring to mind a person who has hurt you that you could be praying for instead of holding a grudge. Commit that person to the Lord, and trust that God will be the Judge.

Assignment

1. Record your insights on patience in your prayer journal.
2. Read chapter 12 in *Turning Toward Integrity*.
3. Memorize James 5:8.

12 WHAT TO DO WHEN PAIN LEADS TO PRAYER
JAMES 5:13–20

Session Topic

God says that we are to pray in all circumstances because He answers our prayers.

Community Builder (Choose One)

1. What has been your experience with praying for healing, either your own or someone else's?

2. C. Everett Koop, the former surgeon general, raises the question of whether God heals through natural processes or through miracles (read pp. 209–210). What do you think? Is it an either/or situation? What has been your experience?

Discovery Questions

1. Read aloud James 5:13–20. According to James, what kinds of situations ought to draw us to prayer?

2. If you were listening in on each of the situations James describes, how do you think the prayers would differ? (Consider mood, tone, content, people present.)

3. Many people feel that they do not pray often enough or well enough. What are some of the reasons behind your own failures in prayer?

4. James 5:13 says we are to thank God for our times of joy. Why do we often take our happiness for granted and only pray for our needs?

5. What, according to James 5:13–16, is the responsibility of the person who is ill? What all is the church to do for that person? (Cite details in each verse.)

6. To what extent does your church provide the kind of ministry to the sick described in James 5? What steps could your church take to better meet these kinds of responsibilities to the sick?

7. The Bible teaches several explanations for illness or suffering. (First Corinthians 11:29–30 mentions personal sin, but John 9:1–13 speaks of

displaying the work of God.) How should knowing that there is no single explanation for physical suffering affect your prayers for healing?

8. God often chooses to heal people through the prayers of others. Why do you think God does this? Should you feel responsible if the person you pray for is not healed? Explain.

9. David Jeremiah cites several stories of irresponsible healing ministries (pp. 204–206). What appropriate ministry could churches provide to people who are attracted to faith healers?

10. James says that Elijah was just like us (5:17), and yet when he prayed, it didn't rain for three and a half years. Why don't we see things like that happening today—or do we? How might Elijah's example affect your praying for global, national, and local concerns?

11. Look more carefully at the way James ends his book with verses 19–20. What could these verses contribute to your practical actions? To your prayers?

12. Describe what your prayer life is like now. Where would you make changes in light of this study? What are some practical ways you can make these changes happen?

Prayer Focus
- God has chosen to work through the prayers of His children, though He is not limited to them. Focus on this knowledge as you pray.
- Read aloud Ephesians 3:20–21.
- Ask God to raise your sights to see His glory and power: to heal, to save, to work throughout all of His creation, so that when you pray you are mindful of who it is who receives your prayers.

Optional Activities
1. Have you knowingly or unintentionally hurt people you prayed for by your approach? Go to them and ask their forgiveness for being insensitive to their pain. If it seems appropriate, share with them some of the new things you have learned in this study about healing.

2. If you are not already meeting with other Christians for prayer, seek out some people who desire to be people of prayer, and begin to get together on a regular basis. Keep the format simple—pray as the Holy Spirit leads you.

Assignment
1. Record your insights on prayer in your journal.
2. Read back over your journal entries from the previous studies. Give God thanks for this opportunity to know and obey Him more faithfully.
3. Memorize Ephesians 3:20–21.

NOTES

INTRODUCTION

1. Stephen R. Covey, *The 7 Habits of Highly Effective People* (New York: Simon & Schuster, Inc., 1989), 148.
2. Lewis Smedes, *A Pretty Good Person: What It Takes to Live with Courage, Gratitude and Integrity* (San Francisco: Harper, 1990), 57.
3. Alexander Whyte, *Bible Characters: The New Testament* (Grand Rapids: Zondervan, 1964), 142–43.
4. Josephus, *Antiquities of the Jews*, 20.9 (197–203) trans. Louis H. Feldman, The Loeb Classical Library (Cambridge: Harvard Univ. Press, 1965), 495–96.
5. Os Guinness & John Seel, eds., *No God but God: Breaking with the Idols of Our Age* (Chicago: Moody Press, 1992), 12.

CHAPTER 1

1. Tom Burgess, "Navy's SEALs Go Through Hell," San Diego *Union*, 18 January 1987.
2. Homer A. Kent Jr., *Faith That Works: Studies in the Epistle of James* (Grand Rapids: Baker, 1986), 34–35.
3. Philip Yancey, *Where Is God When It Hurts?* (Grand Rapids: Zondervan, 1977), 13–14.
4. Burgess, "Navy's SEALs."
5. Spiros Zodhiates, *The Behavior of Belief* (Grand Rapids: Eerdmans, 1959), 21.
6. Yancey, *Where Is God*, 87–88.
7. Michael P. Green, ed., *Illustrations for Biblical Preaching* (Grand Rapids: Baker, 1989), 349–50.
8. John White, *The Fight* (Downers Grove, IL: InterVarsity, 1976), 106–7.
9. William Barclay, *The Letters of James and Peter*, trans. William Barclay (London: Westminster Press, 1961), 51.
10. George W. Sweeting, in *How to Solve Conflicts* (Chicago: Moody Press, 1973), 21.
11. David Jeremiah, *The Wisdom of God* (Milford, MI: Mott Media, 1985), 2.
12. Dorothy L. Sayers, *Christian Letters to a Post-Christian World* (Grand Rapids: Eerdmans, 1969), 14.
13. Guy King, *A Belief That Behaves* (London: Marshall, Morgan & Scott, LTD, 1941), 13.
14. Green, *Illustrations for Biblical Preaching*, 386.
15. Ibid., 388.
16. Burgess, "Navy's SEALs."

CHAPTER 2

1. John Fischer, *Real Christians Don't Dance* (Minneapolis: Bethany House, 1988), 31–32.

2. Tom L. Eisenman, *Temptations Men Face* (Downers Grove, IL: InterVarsity, 1990), 16–17.

3. Michael P. Green, *Illustrations for Biblical Preaching* (Grand Rapids: Baker, 1989), 372–73.

4. John White, *The Fight* (Downers Grove, IL: InterVarsity, 1976), 78.

5. Charles Caldwell Ryrie, *Balancing the Christian Life* (Chicago: Moody Press, 1969), 135.

6. Oswald Chambers, *My Utmost for His Highest*, ed. James Reimann (Grand Rapids: Discovery House, 1992).

7. Erwin Lutzer, *How to Say No to a Stubborn Habit* (Wheaton, IL: Victor Books, 1979), 26.

8. Robert Johnstone, in *Lectures Exegetical and Practical on the Epistle of James* (Minneapolis: Klock & Klock, 1978), 104.

9. Spiros Zodhiates, *The Behavior of Belief* (Grand Rapids: Eerdmans, 1959), 71.

10. Roy Roberts, in *Life in the Pressure Cooker: Studies in James* (Winona Lake, IN: BMH Books, 1977), 22.

11. Johnstone, *Lectures Exegetical and Practical*, 100.

12. Lois Mowday, *The Snare* (Colorado Springs: NavPress, 1988), 84.

13. Eisenman, *Temptations Men Face*, 228.

14. White, *The Fight*, 79.

15. Homer A. Kent Jr., *Faith That Works: Studies in the Epistle of James* (Grand Rapids: Baker, 1986), 50–51.

16. Simon J. Kistemaker, *New Testament Commentary: Exposition of the Epistle of James and the Epistles of John* (Grand Rapids: Baker, 1986), 52–53.

17. Mark McMinn, *Dealing with Desires You Can't Control* (Colorado Springs: NavPress, 1990), 4–5.

18. William Barclay, *The Letters of James and Peter*, trans. William Barclay (London: Westminster Press, 1961), 61.

19. Eisenman, *Temptations Men Face*, 28.

20. Frank Houghton, *Amy Carmichael of Dohnavur* (London: Society for the Propagation of Christian Knowledge, 1954), 62.

CHAPTER 3

1. Howard G. Hendricks and William D. Hendricks, in *Living by the Book* (Chicago: Moody Press, 1991), 10.

2. *USA Today*, 1 February 1990.

3. Donald S. Whitney, in *Spiritual Disciplines for the Christian Life* (Colorado Springs: NavPress, 1991), 34.

4. Spiros Zodhiates, *The Work of Faith* (Grand Rapids: Zondervan, 1977), 105.

5. Simon J. Kistemaker, *New Testament Commentary: Exposition of the Epistle of James and the Epistles of John* (Grand Rapids: Baker, 1986), 58.

6. Mortimer J. Adler, *How to Read a Book* (New York: Simon & Schuster, 1966).

7. Robert A. Traina, *Methodical Bible Study: A New Approach to Hermeneutics* (Wilmore, KY: Robert A. Traina, 1952), 97–98.

8. Hendricks and Hendricks, *Living by the Book*, 11.

9. George Sweeting, *How to Solve Conflicts* (Chicago: Moody Press, 1973), 47.

10. Zodhiates, *The Work of Faith*, 110.

11. Geoffrey Thomas, *Reading the Bible* (Edinburgh, Scotland: The Banner of Truth Trust, 1980) 22, cited by Donald S. Whitney, *Spiritual Disciplines for the Christian Life* (Colorado Springs: NavPress, 1991), 34.

12. Whitney, *Spiritual Disciplines*, 43.

13. Lorne Sanny, "Five Reasons Why I Memorize Scripture," *Discipleship Journal* 32, (1986): 10.

14. Kistemaker, *New Testament Commentary*, 64.

15. Zodhiates, *The Work of Faith*, 144.

16. Richard Wolff, in *Contemporary Commentaries—James and Jude* (Wheaton, IL: Tyndale House, 1969), 36.

17. V. C. Grounds, *The Reason for Our Hope* (Chicago: Moody Press, 1945), 88–89.

CHAPTER 4

1. *Westways*, May 1992.

2. Rick Warren, "How to Treat People Right" (message, Saddleback Community Church, Mission Viejo, California, 26 October 1986).

3. Lewis Smedes, *A Pretty Good Person* (San Francisco: Harper Collins, 1990), 135.

4. Carl Franke, *Defrost Your Frozen Assets* (Waco, TX: Word, 1969), 47.

5. J. B. Phillips, *The New Testament in Modern English* (New York: Macmillan, 1958), 495.

6. Tom L. Eisenman, *Temptations Men Face* (Downers Grove, IL: InterVarsity, 1990), 113–14.

7. Vernon Doerksen, *James, Everyman's Bible Commentary* (Chicago: Moody Press, 1983), 56.

8. Homer A. Kent Jr., *Faith That Works: Studies in the Epistle of James* (Grand Rapids: Baker, 1986), 82.

9. Lehman Strauss, *James, Your Brother: Studies in the Epistle of James* (Neptune, NJ: Loizeaux Brothers, 1956), 95.

10. Doerksen, *James*, 60.

11. Franke, *Defrost Your Frozen Assets*, 53.

12. Kent, *Faith That Works*, 85.

13. Stephen R. Covey, *The 7 Habits of Highly Effective People* (New York: Simon & Schuster, 1989), 30–31.

CHAPTER 5

1. James Patterson and Peter Kim, *The Day America Told the Truth* (New York: Prentice Hall, 1991), 199–200.

2. Charles Colson, *The Body* (Dallas: Word, 1992), 42–43.

3. John MacArthur, *The Gospel According to Jesus* (Grand Rapids: Zondervan, 1988), 218.

4. Peter H. Davids, *The Epistle of James, New International Greek Testament Commentary* (Grand Rapids: Eerdmans, 1982), 121.

5. A. T. Robertson, *Word Pictures in the New Testament* (Nashville: Broadman, 1933), 34.

6. MacArthur, *The Gospel According to Jesus*, 170.

7. Homer A. Kent Jr., *Faith That Works: Studies in the Epistle of James* (Grand Rapids: Baker, 1986), 88.

8. Carl W. Franke, *Defrost Your Frozen Assets* (Waco, Texas: Word, 1969), 22.

9. Kent, *Faith That Works*, 89.

10. Alexander Maclaren, *Hebrews, Chaps. VII to End, Epistle of James in Expositions of Holy Scripture* (Grand Rapids: Eerdmans, 1944), 416.

11. From *The Churchman*, Diocese of Dallas, quoted in Charles Allen, *You Are Never Alone* (Old Tappan, NJ: Revell, 1978), 143–44.

12. Dietrich Bonhoeffer, *Ethics* (New York: Macmillan, 1965), 137.

13. James B. Adamson, *The Epistle of James, The New International Commentary on the New Testament* (Grand Rapids: Eerdmans, 1976), 124.

14. Rudolf Stier, in *The Epistle of St. James* (Minneapolis: Klock & Klock Christian Publishers, 1982), 351–52.

15. R. V. G. Tasker, *The General Epistle of James: An Introduction and Commentary*, Tyndale New Testament Commentaries (Grand Rapids: Eerdmans, 1957), 66.

16. Adamson, *The Epistle of James*, 125.

17. D. Edmond Hiebert, *The Epistle of James* (Chicago: Moody Press, 1992), 168.

18. William Barclay, *The Letters of James and Peter* (Philadelphia: Westminster, 1976), 73.

19. William Barclay, *The Letters to the Corinthians* (Philadelphia: Westminster, 1969), 289.

20. Manfred George Gutzke, *Plain Talk on James* (Grand Rapids: Zondervan, 1969), 81.

21. Simon J. Kistemaker, *New Testament Commentary: Exposition of the Epistle of James and the Epistles of John* (Grand Rapids: Baker, 1986), 96.

22. Note in *The Believer's Study Bible* (Nashville: Thomas Nelson, 1991), 1760.

23. Hiebert, *The Epistle of James*, 158.

24. Alexander Ross, *The Epistles of James and John, The New International Commentary on the New Testament* (Grand Rapids: Eerdmans, 1986), 53.

25. Herbert F. Stevenson, *James Speaks for Today* (Westwood, NJ: Revell, 1966), 58.

26. Kistemaker, *New Testament Commentary*, 99.

27. John Calvin, *Commentaries on the Catholic Epistles—The Epistle of James*, ed. and trans. John Owen (Grand Rapids: Eerdmans), 316.

28. Hiebert, *The Epistle of James*, 179.

29. Frank Gaebelein, *The Practical Epistle of James* (Great Neck, NY: Doniger & Raughley, 1955), 73.

30. *A National Study of Protestant Congregations*, Search Institute, March 1990.

31. C. H. Spurgeon, "Serving the Lord with Gladness," *Metropolitan Tabernacle Pulpit* (London: Passmore and Alabaster; repr. 1868, Pasadena, TX: Pilgrim Publications, 1989), vol. 13, 495–96.

32. Os Guinness, *Of Two Minds* (Downers Grove, IL: InterVarsity, 1976), 128.

CHAPTER 6

1. W. A. Criswell, *Expository Sermons on the Epistle of James* (Grand Rapids: Zondervan, 1975), 63.

2. Curtis Vaughan, *James: A Study Guide* (Grand Rapids: Zondervan, 1969), 69.

3. Richard Wolff, in *Contemporary Commentaries: General Epistles of James & Jude* (Wheaton, IL: Tyndale House, 1969), 57.

4. Roxane S. Lulofs, "The Hit-and-Run Mouth," *Christian Herald*, July/August 1986, 34.

5. William Barclay, *The Letters of James and Peter* (Philadelphia: Westminster, 1976), 81.

6. Spiros Zodhiates, *The Behavior of Belief* (Grand Rapids: Eerdmans, 1959), 81–82.

7. Roy Roberts, in *Life in the Pressure Cooker* (Winona Lake, IN: BMH Books, 1977), 77.

8. Simon J. Kistemaker, *New Testament Commentary: Exposition of the Epistle of James and the Epistles of John* (Grand Rapids: Baker, 1986), 110.

9. Vernon Doerksen, *James, Everyman's Bible Commentary* (Chicago: Moody Press, 1983), 81.

10. Zodhiates, *The Behavior of Belief*, 112–13.

11. Kistemaker, *New Testament Commentary*, 112.

12. George Sweeting, in *How to Solve Conflicts* (Chicago: Moody Press, 1973), 77.

13. Michael P. Green, *Illustrations for Biblical Preaching* (Grand Rapids: Baker, 1989), 174–75.

14. John Blanchard, *Truth for Life* (West Sussex, England: H. E. Walter Ltd., 1982), 108.

15. Robert Brow, "The Taming of the Tongue," *His Magazine*, June 1985, 16.

16. Ibid., 16.

17. Doerksen, *James*, 83.

18. Dietrich Bonhoeffer, *The Cost of Discipleship* (New York: The Macmillan Co., 1948), 11.

CHAPTER 7

1. Os Guinness, "America's Last Men and Their Magnificent Talking Cure," *No God but God*, eds. Os Guinness and John Seel (Chicago: Moody Press, 1992), 111, 116.

2. Lloyd John Ogilvie, *Discovering God's Will in Your Life* (Eugene, OR: Harvest House, 1982), 119.

3. Roy R. Roberts, *Life in the Pressure Cooker* (Winona Lake, IN: BMH Books, 1977), 93.

4. William Barclay, *The Letters of James and Peter* (Philadelphia: Westminster, 1977), 94.

5. Barclay, *Letters of James and Peter*, 93.

6. Guy King, *A Belief That Behaves* (Fort Washington: Christian Literature Crusade, 1963), 73.

7. Vernon Doerksen, *James, Everyman's Bible Commentary* (Chicago: Moody Press, 1983), 90.

8. John White, "God's Perfect Peace," *Moody Monthly*, December 1962, 24.

9. Homer A. Kent Jr., *Faith That Works: Studies in the Epistle of James* (Grand Rapids: Baker, 1986), 135.

10. R. W. Dale, in *The Epistle of James* (London: Hodder and Stoughton, 1895), 113.

11. Ibid., 118.

12. Alan Walker, "Beyond Science—What?" *Pulpit Digest*, September 1967, 24.

CHAPTER 8

1. "Tenn. Church Destroyed by Fire after Members Come to Blows at Meeting," an Associated Press story in the *Chicago Tribune*, October 8, 2009, at http://www.chicagotribune.com/news/nationworld/sns-ap-us-odd-church-fight,0,3984318.story. Accessed October 9, 2009.

2. Author unknown.

3. Vernon Doerksen, *James, Everyman's Bible Commentary* (Chicago: Moody Press, 1983), 94.

4. D. Edmond Hiebert, *The Epistle of James* (Chicago: Moody Press, 1992), 223.

5. Herbert F. Stevenson, *James Speaks for Today* (Westwood, NJ: Revell, 1966), 69–70.

6. Doerksen, *James*, 95.

7. W. A. Criswell, *Expository Sermons on the Epistle of James* (Grand Rapids: Zondervan, 1975), 78.

8. Doerksen, *James*, 96.

9. William Barclay, *The Letters of James and Peter* (Philadelphia: Westminster, 1976), 100.

10. R. Kent Hughes, *James: Faith That Works* (Wheaton, IL: Crossway, 1991), 169–70.

11. Criswell, *Expository Sermons*, 76–77.

12. Simon J. Kistemaker, *New Testament Commentary: Exposition of the Epistle of James and the Epistles of John* (Grand Rapids: Baker, 1986), 133.

13. Richard Wolff, *General Epistle of James & Jude* (Wheaton, IL: Tyndale House, 1969), 68.

14. "Here's Joni!" *Today's Christian Woman*, January/February 1990, 24–25.

15. Annie Johnson Flint, "He Giveth More Grace," *The Hymnal for Worship and Celebration* (Waco, Texas: Word Music, 1986), 415.

16. Homer A. Kent Jr., *Faith That Works: Studies in the Epistle of James* (Grand Rapids: Baker, 1986), 148.

17. Stevenson, *James Speaks for Today*, 76.

18. John Calvin, *Commentaries on the Catholic Epistles: The Epistle of James*, ed. and trans. John Owen (Grand Rapids: Eerdmans, 1948), 334.

19. Kistemaker, *New Testament Commentary: James and John*, 141.

20. Mark Littleton, "Putting Out the Fire of Gossip," *Discipleship Journal* 31 (1985).

21. Colson, *The Body*, 92, 94, 97.

CHAPTER 9

1. William M. Alnor, *Soothsayers of the Second Advent* (Old Tappan, NJ: Revell, 1989), 9.

2. *Bible Prophecy News* 17 (January, February, March, 1988): 11.

3. Spiros Zodhiates, *The Behavior of Belief*, Pt. 3 (Grand Rapids: Eerdmans, 1959), 18.

4. W. A. Criswell, *Expository Sermons on the Epistle of James* (Grand Rapids: Zondervan, 1975), 83.

5. Simon J. Kistemaker, *New Testament Commentary: Exposition of the Epistle of James and the Epistles of John* (Grand Rapids: Baker, 1986), 146.

6. Robert Johnstone, *Lectures Exegetical and Practical on the Epistle of James* (Grand Rapids: Baker, 1954), 340.

7. William Barclay, *The Letters of James and Peter* (Philadelphia: Westminster, 1976), 113.

8. Zodhiates, *The Behavior of Belief*, 15.

9. Homer A. Kent Jr., *Faith That Works: Studies in the Epistle of James* (Grand Rapids: Baker, 1986), 161.

10. Johnstone, *Lectures Exegetical and Practical*, 344.

11. Richard A. Swenson, MD, *Margin* (Colorado Springs: NavPress, 1992), 147–48.

12. James B. Adamson, *The Epistle of James, The New International Commentary on the New Testament* (Grand Rapids: Eerdmans, 1979), 179.

13. Zodhiates, *The Behavior of Belief*, 24.

14. Kistemaker, *New Testament Commentary: James and John*, 151.

15. Alec Motyer, *The Message of James* (Downers Grove, IL: InterVarsity, 1985), 162.

16. Lewis B. Smedes, *Shame and Grace* (Grand Rapids: Zondervan, 1993), 149.

17. Kent, *Faith That Works*, 163.

18. Michael P. Green, ed., *Illustrations for Biblical Preaching* (Grand Rapids: Baker, 1989), 288.

CHAPTER 10

1. Randy Alcorn, *Money, Possessions and Eternity* (Wheaton, IL: Tyndale House, 1989), 54–55.

2. Richard A. Swenson, *Margin* (Colorado Springs: NavPress, 1992), 164.

3. R. Kent Hughes, in *James: Faith That Works* (Wheaton, IL: Crossway, 1991), 211.

4. R. V. G. Tasker, *The General Epistle of James*, The Tyndale New Testament Commentaries, ed. R. V. G. Tasker (Grand Rapids: Eerdmans, 1980), 109–110.

5. D. Edmond Hiebert, *The Epistle of James* (Chicago: Moody Press, 1992), 259–60.

6. John Calvin, *Commentaries on the Catholic Epistles: The Epistle of James*, ed. and trans. John Owen (Grand Rapids: Eerdmans, 1948), 343.

7. Swenson, *Margin*, 179.

8. Hiebert, *The Epistle of James*, 262–63.

9. Peter H. Davids, *Commentary on James, The New International Greek Testament Commentary* (Grand Rapids: Eerdmans, 1982), 177.

10. Homer A. Kent Jr., *Faith That Works: Studies in the Epistle of James* (Grand Rapids: Baker, 1986), 171.

11. Adolf Deissmann, *Light from the Ancient East* (Grand Rapids: Baker, 1965), 248.

12. James B. Adamson, *The Epistle of James, The New International Commentary on the New Testament* (Grand Rapids: Eerdmans, 1976), 186.

13. C. Leslie Mitton, *The Epistle of James* (Grand Rapids: Eerdmans, 1966), 180.

14. Alec Motyer, *The Message of James* (Downers Grove, IL: InterVarsity, 1985), 167.

15. Alcorn, *Money, Possessions and Eternity*, 61.

16. Richard Holloway, *Seven to Flee, Seven to Follow* (London: Mowbray, 1986), 33–35.

17. A. W. Tozer, *The Pursuit of God* (Camp Hill, PA: Christian, 1993), 21–22.

18. Manfred George Gutzke, *Plain Talk on James* (Grand Rapids: Zondervan, 1969), 156.

19. Motyer, *The Message of James*, 168.

20. Joshua ben Sira, 34:21–22 RSV.

21. Adamson, *The Epistle of James*, 188.

22. Simon J. Kistemaker, *New Testament Commentary: Exposition of the Epistle of James and the Epistles of John* (Grand Rapids: Baker, 1986), 159.
23. John Piper, *Desiring God* (Portland: Multnomah, 1986), 156.
24. L. S. Stavrianos, in *The Promise of the Coming Dark Age* (San Francisco: W. H. Freeman & Co., 1976), 165.

CHAPTER 11

1. Nancy Gibbs, "How America Has Run Out of Time," *Time*, 24 April 1989, 58.
2. Jerry Bridges, *The Practice of Godliness* (Colorado Springs: NavPress, 1983), 204–5.
3. W. E. Vine, *Vine's Expository Dictionary of Old and New Testament Words—III* (Old Tappan, NJ: Revell, 1981), 12.
4. William Barclay, *A New Testament Workbook* (New York: Harper & Brothers, n.d.), 84.
5. Bridges, *The Practice of Godliness,* 204.
6. Spiros Zodhiates, in *The Behavior of Belief* (Grand Rapids: Eerdmans, 1959), 87.
7. D. Edmond Hiebert, *The Epistle of James* (Chicago: Moody Press, 1979), 272.
8. Robert Johnstone, *The Epistle of James* (Minneapolis: Klock & Klock Christian Publishers, 1871), 377.
9. Simon J. Kistemaker, *New Testament Commentary: Exposition of the Epistle of James and the Epistles of John* (Grand Rapids: Baker, 1986), 166.
10. Johnstone, *The Epistle of James*, 380.
11. W. A. Criswell, *Expository Sermons on the Epistle of James* (Grand Rapids: Zondervan, 1975), 99–100.
12. Zodhiates, *The Behavior of Belief,* 106.
13. Homer A. Kent Jr., *Faith That Works: Studies in the Epistle of James* (Grand Rapids: Baker, 1986), 181.
14. Zodhiates, *The Behavior of Belief,* 111.
15. Helmut Thielicke, *Life Can Begin Again* (Philadelphia: Westminster, 1980), 55.
16. James Fixx, *The Complete Book of Running* (New York: Random House, 1977), 70.

CHAPTER 12

1. Eusebius, in *Ecclesiastical History*, Vol. I, trans. Kirsopp Lake, The Loeb Classical Library (Cambridge, MA: Harvard University Press, 1965), 171 (II 23:3–9).
2. Bill Hybels, *Too Busy Not to Pray* (Downers Grove, IL: InterVarsity, 1988), 7.
3. Ralph P. Martin, *Word Biblical Commentary—Vol 48—James* (Waco, TX: Word, 1988), 205.
4. Carl Armerding, "Is Any Among You Afflicted?" *Bibliotheca Sacra* 95 (1938): 195–201.
5. Hybels, *Too Busy Not to Pray*, 13.
6. William Barclay, *The Letters of James and Peter* (Philadelphia: Westminster, 1976), 1229.
7. Alec Motyer, *The Message of James* (Downers Grove, IL: InterVarsity, 1985), 188.
8. John F. MacArthur Jr., *Charismatic Chaos* (Grand Rapids: Zondervan, 1992), 197.
9. D. Edmond Hiebert, *The Epistle of James* (Chicago: Moody Press, 1992), 294.

10. Homer A. Kent Jr., *Faith That Works: Studies in the Epistle of James* (Grand Rapids: Baker, 1966), 187.
11. Simon J. Kistemaker, *New Testament Commentary: Exposition of the Epistle of James and the Epistles of John* (Grand Rapids: Baker, 1986), 175.
12. William Nolen, *Healing: A Doctor in Search of a Miracle* (New York: Random House, 1974), 60.
13. C. Everett Koop, "Faith Healing and the Sovereignty of God," in *The Agony of Deceit: What Some TV Preachers Are Really Teaching*, ed. Michael Horton (Chicago: Moody Press, 1990), 179–80.
14. James I. Packer, "Poor Health May Be the Best Remedy," *Christianity Today*, 21 May 1982, 15.
15. Motyer, *The Message of James*, 191.
16. Koop, "Faith Healing," 169–70.
17. Motyer, *The Message of James*, 191.
18. Kent, *Faith That Works: Studies in the Epistle of James*, 191.
19. Richard Mayhue, *Divine Healing Today* (Chicago: Moody Press, 1983), 113.
20. Jay Adams, *Competent to Counsel* (Phillipsburg, NJ: P&R, 1970), 109–10.
21. Mayhue, *Divine Healing Today*, 114.
22. Vernon Doerksen, *James, Everyman's Bible Commentary* (Chicago: Moody Press, 1983), 136.
23. Roy Roberts, in *Life in the Pressure Cooker: Studies in James* (Winona Lake, IN: BMH Books, 1977), 162.
24. Corrie ten Boom, *The Hiding Place,* with John Sherrill (Old Tappan, NJ: Revell, 1971), 202–3.

COMMENTARIES

Adamson, James B. *The Epistle of James*. The New International Commentary on the New Testament series. Grand Rapids: Eerdmans, 1976.

Barclay, William. *The Letters of James and Peter*. Rev. ed. Philadelphia: Westminster, 1976.

Calvin, John. "Commentaries on the Epistle of James." *Calvin's Commentaries*. Vol. 22. Grand Rapids: Baker, 1979.

Criswell, W. A. *Expository Sermons on the Epistle of James*. Grand Rapids: Zondervan, 1975.

Davids, Peter H. *The Epistle of James*. The New International Greek Testament Commentary series. Grand Rapids: Eerdmans, 1982.

Doerksen, Vernon. *James*. Everyman's Bible Commentary series. Chicago: Moody Press, 1983.

Fickett, Harold T. *James*. Glendale, CA: Regal, 1972.

Gutzke, Manford George. *Plain Talk on James*. Grand Rapids: Zondervan, 1969.

Hiebert, D. Edmond. *The Epistle of James*. Chicago: Moody Press, 1979.

Hughes, R. Kent. *James: Faith That Works*. Wheaton, IL: Crossway, 1991.

Johnstone, Robert. *Lectures Exegetical and Practical on the Epistle of James*. Grand Rapids: Baker, 1954.

Kent, Homer A., Jr. *Faith That Works: Studies in the Epistle of James*. Grand Rapids: Baker, 1986.

King, Guy H. *A Belief That Behaves*. London: Marshall, Morgan & Scott, LTD., 1956.

Kistemaker, Simon J. *New Testament Commentary: Exposition of the Epistle of James and the Epistles of John*. Grand Rapids: Baker, 1986.

Mayor, Joseph B. *The Epistle of St. James*. Grand Rapids: Zondervan, 1913.

Mitton, C. Leslie. *The Epistle of James*. Grand Rapids: Eerdmans, 1966.

Motyer, Alec. *The Message of James*. Downers Grove, IL: InterVarsity, 1985.

Roberts, Roy R. *Life in the Pressure Cooker: Studies in James*. Winona Lake, IN: BMH Books, 1977.

Stevenson, Herbert F. *James Speaks for Today*. Westwood, NJ: Revell, 1966.

Strauss, Lehman. *James, Your Brother: Studies in the Epistle of James*. Neptune, NJ: Loizeaux Brothers, 1956.

Tasker, R. V. G. *The General Epistle of James*. The Tyndale New Testament Commentaries series. Grand Rapids: Eerdmans, 1956.

Wiersbe, Warren W. *Be Mature*. Wheaton, IL: Victor Books, 1976.

Wolfe, Richard. *General Epistles of James & Jude*. Wheaton, IL: Tyndale House, 1969.

Zodhiates, Spiros. *The Behavior of Belief*. Grand Rapids: Eerdmans, 1959.

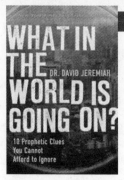
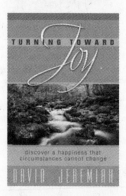
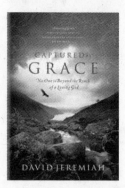

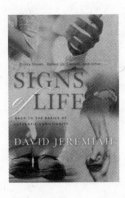

Signs of Life

Signs of Life will lead you on a journey to a fuller understanding of the marks that identify you as a Christian. Personal imprints can impact souls for eternity and help you become a person of influence who radiates relevancy, authenticity, generosity, and compassion every day – just like Jesus did.

When Your World Falls Apart

Drawing from the deep truths of the Psalms, David Jeremiah identifies the tramautic events that inspired this writing and finds his focus changing. Instead of asking "Why?" he began to ask "What, O Lord? What do You have to teach me? What would You have me do?" If you're walking through difficult times, this book may serve as a helpful resource.

P.O. Box 3838
San Diego, CA 92163
(800) 947-1993
WWW.DAVIDJEREMIAH.ORG

STAY CONNECTED

Take advantage of two great ways to let Dr. David Jeremiah give you spiritual direction every day! Both are absolutely FREE!

Turning Points Magazine and Devotional

Receive Dr. David Jeremiah's monthly magazine, *Turning Points* each month:

- Monthly Study Focus
- 48 pages of life-changing reading
- Relevant Articles
- Special Features
- Humor Section
- Family Section
- Daily devotional readings for each day of the month!
- Bible study resource offers!
- Live Event Schedule
- Radio & Television Information

Your Daily Turning Point E-Devotional

Start your day off right! Find words of inspiration and spiritual motivation waiting for you on your computer every morning! You can receive a daily e-devotion communication from David Jeremiah that will strengthen your walk with God and encourage you to live the authentic Christian life.

Sign up for these two free services by visiting us online at www.DavidJeremiah.org and clicking on DEVOTIONALS to sign up for your monthly copy of *Turning Points* and your Daily Turning Point.